W9-BZD-867

SHAYA

SHAYA

An Odyssey of Food, My Journey Back to Israel

ALON SHAYA

with Tina Antolini

Alfred A. Knopf · New York · 2018

This Is a Borzoi Book Published by Alfred A. Knopf

Copyright © 2018 by Alon Shaya

All rights reserved. Published in the United States by Alfred A. Knopf, a division of Penguin Random House LLC, New York, and distributed in Canada by Random House of Canada, a division of Penguin Random House Canada Limited, Toronto.

www.aaknopf.com

Knopf, Borzoi Books, and the colophon are registered trademarks of Penguin Random House LLC.

Library of Congress Cataloging-in-Publication Data
Names: Shaya, Alon, author.
Title: Shaya : An Odyssey of Food, My Journey Back to Israel / Alon Shaya.
Description: First edition. | New York : Alfred A. Knopf, 2018. | "This is a Borzoi book." | Includes index.
Identifiers: LCCN 2017011263 (print) | LCCN 2017010159 (ebook) | ISBN 9780451494160 (hardcover : alk. paper) | ISBN 9780451494177 (ebook)
Subjects: LCSH: Cooking, Israeli. | LCGFT: Cookbooks.
Classification: LCC TX724 .S4835 2018 (ebook) | LCC TX724 (print) | DDC 641.595694—dc23
LC record available at https://lccn.loc.gov/2017011263

Jacket photograph by Denny Culbert
Jacket design by Stephanie Ross
Photographs by Rush Jagoe
Illustrations by Frances Rodriguez
Styling by Emily Shaya
Recipe development by Rémy Robert

Manufactured in China
First Edition

To my mother, Aliza. You have spent your entire life living for mine,
and have always loved, believed, and trusted in me,
even when I gave you reason not to.

CONTENTS

III · FINDING HOME IN THE SOUTH

IV · AN ITALIAN SOJOURN

V · HOMECOMING

VI · ESSENTIALS

PREFACE

It's rarely a straight path to our vocation. Few of us grow up saying, "I want to be a chef" (or a doctor or a lawyer or a ballerina), and pursue that with single-minded purpose. We usually end up doing what we do through a series of twists and turns, of meeting people who make an impression, of opportunities that arise, of doors that open and close. My journey to opening one of the most celebrated new restaurants in the country—an Israeli restaurant in the heart of the American South—is one full of those twists and turns. It starts in Israel and winds through Italy and New Orleans before turning back to Israel. Food is the thread that runs throughout that whole journey. It's guided my personal decisions as well as my professional ones, and punctuated every memory, every turning point in my life.

Even beyond my personal narrative, though, there's something about Israel that draws me. The mixture of cultures and faiths, the richly varied landscape, the tensions that have been deeply woven into the place since its beginning: so much about this country is magnetizing. Religiously, politically—and culinarily. Israeli cuisine is a gumbo, a melding of many food cultures. In only a few decades, the population of a country smaller than the state of New Jersey has gone from just over a million people to eight million. Jewish immigrants brought their family recipe books from Germany, Bulgaria, Yemen, France, Spain, Turkey, Morocco, Greece, and many other countries to a land with an already rich Arab food culture. My Bulgarian grandparents were among those new arrivals. Many migrants arrived on the heels of the Holocaust and had to start their lives over from scratch. Their children married one another; a Polish woman made a family with a Syrian man, a Moroccan woman with a Frenchman. Their children's lunchboxes would reflect these hybrids. Bulgarian borekas would sit side by side on a table with Libyan shakshouka.

Over a few generations, Israeli cuisine has flourished—though, as with so many things in this part of the Middle East, it's also controversial. A photo of knafeh, a syrupy cheese pastry, posted on the Internet can alternately be called "Israeli" or "Palestinian," and will prompt a barrage of comments either way. I am a product of this place, with my Israeli-Bulgarian mother and my Romanian-Israeli father. And my food reflects the weaving together of all these culinary strands, along with those of my own migrations to the American South and to Italy. The recipes of this cookbook reflect both this range—hummus to bolognese, kugel to za'atar-dusted fried chicken—and the core of my Israeli cultural identity, which has persisted, even as I explored the cuisines of other places.

This is not a typical cookbook; it's not a primer on Israeli cuisine or a seasonally organized collection of menus. It's a collection of stories of place, of people, and of the food that connects them. It's the autobiography of my culinary sensibility, which began in Israel and has returned there.

NOTES ON COOKING

HOW TO USE THIS BOOK

The recipes in this book aren't divided into neat boxes—salads, seafood, meat, desserts, and so forth—any more than life is subdivided into holidays, anniversaries, and dinners with friends. Instead, they follow the course of all the flavors I've tried, places I've traveled, things I've experienced, and lessons I've learned. That's the best (and only) way I can imagine writing an authentic personal cookbook.

If I were to cook this book cover to cover, I think the results would taste like my life flashing before my eyes. My hope is that if you were to do the same, you'd capture some of the themes that have stuck with me: things as simple as my grandmother's trick of caramelized tomato paste, as elemental as making dough, as joyful as cooking feasts for a crowd. Maybe the recipes will inspire you to try something you've never dreamed of. But if you've got a stronger idea of what you want to cook—say you need to pick something for dinner tonight—flip to page 399 for an easy, quick reference to every recipe by category.

INGREDIENTS

As a cook, I've learned from Israeli and Italian principles. In both places, when you do the shopping you can find specialists—butchers, fishmongers, cheese makers, spice merchants—who provide the best ingredients, much as you can go to the farmers' market for the best produce. Here in the

United States, you sometimes need to do a little extra research or planning to get comparable quality (although it's increasingly easy to find solid, reliable ingredients on supermarket shelves, just a matter of knowing what to buy). The extra bit of effort is worth it. The more you shop like an Israeli or an Italian, the more you cook like one, which starts with considering each ingredient and how it factors into your food as a whole. If you're shopping for any of these ingredients, here's my advice on what to look for.

Cooking Salt and Finishing Salt

Salt is so common that we forget to discuss it alongside other seasonings. I could never cook without it; it has a way of elevating flavors and making foods taste more like themselves. I use kosher salt, which has wide, flat crystals that you can pinch between your fingers and that melt nicely throughout your food. Across the board, kosher salts are purer in flavor and less adulterated than table salts.

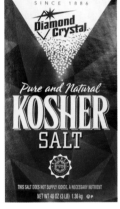

Still, not all salts are created equal. Diamond Crystal kosher salt, the brand you'll find in most restaurant kitchens, weighs about half as much as Morton kosher salt, which is what's in nearly any supermarket. (Look at the crystals next to each other: Diamond Crystal is much thinner and flakier.) This means that 1 teaspoon of Morton adds about the same amount of salt as 2 teaspoons of Diamond Crystal. Rather than risk having you add twice as much salt as you really need, all of these recipes specify Morton. If Diamond Crystal is your salt of choice, you can figure that the salt should be doubled.

Finishing salt—Maldon is a great brand and by far the most common—is a different animal altogether. With very wide, flat, crystal-like flakes that melt on your tongue, it's bad for cooking but great for putting the finishing touches on a dish. My advice: keep both cooking and finishing salts on hand.

Spices and Other Seasonings

We cook with spices to introduce layers of flavor. Anytime you see a spice called for in a recipe, I believe it'll be worth it for you to seek it out and dedicate some space to it in your pantry. But, ultimately, spices are meant to bring you joy, so omit any that don't.

Spice grinders can be found for less than twenty dollars and are worth the investment. Almost all spices are better and taste like their truest selves if you buy them whole and grind them yourself. Grind a little at a time; their scent starts to weaken as soon as they're ground. For the sake of clarity, though, my ingredient lists always call for ground spices wherever they should be ground and whole spices only where you need them whole.

It's impossible to know how long a jar has been sitting on the supermarket shelf, which gives you no control over its potency. That's why I try to buy all my spices from discerning retailers, such as La Boîte, or international markets with knowledgeable staff and wide variety. Other spices are ubiquitous in their dried (shelf-stable) form and far less commonly available fresh. I love fresh bay leaves, and if you've got access to a bay laurel tree, you can always substitute two fresh bay leaves for every one dry. Red-pepper flakes appear in a lot of my recipes, but in the summertime, if you've got a windfall of small fresh red chilies such as Thai bird's eye or cayenne, remove the seeds and use one to replace every ¼ teaspoon of red-pepper flakes. There are also some liquids that I use as seasonings, such as orange blossom water and rose water.

Ultimately, some spices are expensive or hard to come by, and you may prefer to spend a limited grocery budget on fresh ingredients rather than a jar of spices you don't know how to use. Build your pantry gradually—start with those that interest and excite you (you may find yourself sneaking them into the rest of your cooking), and buy another every few shopping trips.

Oils and Vinegars

Good olive oil is as much a cooking fat as it is a seasoning, with a distinct richness that isn't desired in all cooking (there's a reason you never see it at Chinese restaurants). Because of this, it's worth spending as much as you can comfortably afford on an oil whose flavor you'll be excited to feature and revisit. If there are limited options where you live, you can order it online. When you find one you love, buy large canisters to stock your kitchen and keep costs down.

Other oils—canola, grapeseed, vegetable—are more neutral, giving you more control over the flavor of the finished dish.

They're also cheaper, making them ideal for deep-frying. Sometimes I combine olive oil with something mellower to keep the olive flavor from being dominant; in terms of the quantity you need in a given recipe, though, they're interchangeable, so use what suits you.

Vinegars, like olive oil, are dynamic, and you'll taste the difference when you use good ones. Apple-cider vinegar tastes fruity and bright with a little funk; balsamic is warm, round, and deep; wine vinegars (both red and white) should be crisp and bright, with traces of the wines that made them. To sample them, pour a spoonful, dip a sugar cube in it, and suck the vinegar out of the sugar. It neutralizes the acidity so you can taste the vinegar's true essence.

More Staples for Your Kitchen

These are as important to my food as any oils and spices, so I always keep my pantry stocked with them.

- **Tahini:** This single ingredient, known as tehina in Israel, is the basis of so many recipes throughout this book. It should contain just one ingredient—sesame seeds—with a warm, nutty flavor and a thick consistency that doesn't separate, good enough to eat by the spoonful. Like a good party guest, it hits it off with anyone in the room, from hummus (page 114) to halvah iced latte (page 378). My favorite brand is Soom.

- **Canned tomatoes:** Not only for long-cooked Italian sauces, these can take the place of an unripe fresh tomato when you're making things like tomato soup (page 15) or stuffed cabbage (page 171), and they're great because they have that concentrated sweetness and acidity. You can find them whole, diced, crushed, or puréed. I always get whole canned tomatoes, which are the best quality, and have fun crushing them myself.

- **Tomato paste:** I'll let you in on a little secret that'll make you do a double take at the cans collecting dust in your pantry or fridge: this is a powerhouse ingredient that wants to be treated like anchovies or garlic, a solid foundation on which you can build any number of other flavors. When you caramelize it, as my grandmother so often did, it goes from Clark Kent to Superman.

- **Dried pasta:** Not all pasta is created equal. My favorite brands of dried pasta are Rustichella d'Abruzzo and Benedetto Cavalieri. You can find them both online.

- **Chicken and/or vegetable stock:** It's great to have a store-bought version that you know you like and can keep on hand. Even if it doesn't taste as rich or full-flavored as your homemade versions, using it will still lead to far better results than you'd get with water. I keep 1 or 2 quarts on hand. Look for brands with short lists of recognizable ingredients.

- **Molasses:** You're probably familiar with cane molasses, which pops up in gingerbread and other American baking. Blackstrap molasses is the sharpest and most intense version. There are so many other kinds, and all are great friends for adding flavor, from the sharp tartness of pomegranate to the chocolaty depth of carob. Once you've welcomed them into your kitchen, experiment.

- **Essentials:** I've grouped some simple recipes for spice blends and sauces in the back of the book for easy access (pages 385–395). Many will cost you only 5 or 10 minutes of active cook time, and with them in your back pocket (or your fridge or pantry), you'll feel better able to dive into many of the recipes that feature them. If you can't make them from scratch, most of these recipes include my best suggestion for a store-bought substitute.

Flours (Wheat and Otherwise)

Most of us think of flour as just flour, a neutral ingredient that you can find anywhere in the world, knowing it'll always be the same. All of these recipes call for your standard all-purpose cake and bread flours. Those are still my standby for the bulk of home cooking; I appreciate that they're so consistent and useful.

But it bears mentioning—and highlighting—that more and more people are milling their own flours from all kinds of grains, wheat being only the first. If you try stone-ground cornmeal for cornbread, polenta, or grits, you know that the difference can be huge. These flours have deeper flavor, richer aroma, and better texture, retaining more of their nutrients and essential oils. You can store them in the freezer to extend their shelf life.

They also give you a lot of room to experiment. Do some research and find farmers or millers in your area; they'll know how to best use their flours, so seek their advice on conversions. (Anson Mills also makes great products that are available online.) Starting out, I'd suggest substituting for a fraction of the all-purpose or bread flour, and going with recipes with which you're already confident. As you get comfortable, broaden your horizons!

Anytime you're measuring flour, first give it a good stir to aerate it, then use a spoon to add it to your measuring cup (rather than scoop the measuring cup in the bag of flour). Once the cup is heaping, use a knife to level it. This is a proper measure, keeping your food from being dense and dry. If you're curious about when to use volume and when to weigh it, flip to page xxii.

Bread (and Breadcrumbs)

Bread is only as good as the flour that makes it, so, as you might be able to guess, I always reach for the best I can find. Whether you're getting a baguette, ciabatta, or a seedy whole-grain loaf, what matters is that a human baked it. It's worth making an extra stop at the local bakery.

Likewise, breadcrumbs are infinitely better when they're made from real bread, to the extent that you could treat them like completely different ingredients from the kind in a can. (If you get stuck, panko is a fine plan B.) For a neutral flavor that complements any recipe, I go for Italian or hoagie rolls. If they're too soft to crumble, split them in half and let them dry at room temperature, or break them into bite-sized pieces and dry them out in a 200°F oven. Depending on how much moisture is in the bread to begin with, this could take 10 minutes, 30 minutes, or somewhere in between, so just keep an eye on them. The easiest way to make the actual crumbs is to blitz the dried bread in a food processor, but you can also tear it apart by hand or try grating it on a box grater. Store any leftovers in the freezer for easy access.

Meat and Fish

A lot of things happen before meat gets to your plate, and every detail, from what the animal eats to how much exercise it gets, can affect the meat's texture and flavor. Buy from a reputable grocery store, butcher shop, or farmers' market, from people who can speak to the quality of the meat. Ask them what's good, what they'd serve if they were having a dinner party. Don't be afraid of fat—most recipes depend on a good, healthy balance of it—and don't worry if the meat is frozen, which is often the case at farmers' markets, to keep the meat fresh. The more control you have over the raw product, the more you'll ultimately have over the dish.

If you buy your meat from the supermarket, strike up a conversation with the person at the counter and ask him or her what's best. Ask, too, about good substitutes if what you need is unavailable. Whatever you do, don't buy meat pre-ground. It can pick up "off" flavors from the packaging and, worse, may not be fresh. The guy at the counter will be happy to ground it for you if you don't own a meat grinder.

You'll see the starkest contrast in quality when you're buying fish, where the good is *amazing* and the bad is practically inedible. Shop for it as critically as you do meat (though it doesn't freeze quite as well); I've been known to cross town in order to get the best available. The best way to judge it is by smell, which should be clean and nonfishy; if you can see the whole fish, gaze into its eyes; you want them to be clear and bright, not cloudy.

Cheese and Butter

Like wine, these ingredients run a spectrum. There's a lot of bad stuff. You don't have to buy the most expensive cheese at the store, but you should buy something that was made by an individual and not in a big factory. If Parmigiano-Reggiano isn't in your budget, for instance, Grana Padano is a good substitute. The powdered stuff you'll find in cans isn't even Parmesan!

For soft cheeses, such as ricotta, burrata, and mozzarella, the only way to make sure they're actually *fresh* (and not loaded down with preservatives that compromise their taste and texture) is to buy them somewhere you trust. In Italy, fresh cheeses are typically eaten on the day they're made, at most the day after.

If your grocery store has a cheese counter, ask the attendant what's available.

Whenever I say "butter" in this book, I mean the real thing—not margarine, not butter spread—and it should be unsalted.

Yogurt and Labneh

Greek yogurt is strained, making it incredibly thick and smooth. Bulgarian yogurt is much thinner and more sour. Both are great ingredients, adding some acidity that's balanced with a great creaminess that you could only get from dairy.

If you strain Bulgarian yogurt, you get labneh (page 38), one of the easiest cheeses to make. It sounds fussier than it is, because you need cheesecloth and must let it sit overnight, but its rewards are greater than the effort it requires, whether you use the labneh as a dip (page 38) or in your baking (cheesecake, page 102, and banana bread, page 244). If you can find a good store-bought labneh (*not* the kind preserved in oil), feel free to use it. In a pinch, you can substitute sour cream or Greek yogurt.

Water

Last but not least. Presumably, you're cooking from this book in a place with potable water, so it's unlikely that you're putting water on your grocery list. But when you treat it right, water is as much an ingredient as anything else. That's why I list specific quantities for boiling pasta or blanching vegetables; this way, it's as seasoned as you need it to be.

TECHNIQUES AND EQUIPMENT

A Well-Equipped Kitchen

All you really *need* are a refrigerator, a stove, and a conventional oven. (If your oven has a convection setting, ignore it for these recipes, or alter the cooking time accordingly.) There are many more tools and gadgets, but only you can know what will actually be useful, depending on what you like to cook. A stand mixer is great if you like making dough and baked goods, and you can find attachments for everything from grinding meat to rolling pasta—mine are basically a part of the family. Food processors are essential for thick purées like hummus, and blenders are a huge help for making sauces, soups, and dressings. Before you rush to buy any of these things, think about what you like or hope to make, and let that guide you.

You're in Control

Unless you cook for a living, you might forget that you're the boss of your food. Consider this a friendly reminder. If a recipe calls for a spice you don't have or a vegetable you dislike, you can decide to ditch it. On the other hand, if a spice or a sauce calls your name, mix and match at will; so many of the flavors in this book—za'atar, tahini, labneh, garlic, duqqa, and so forth—get along well with each other. For most cooking, medium heat is your friend, the sweet spot where you can move things along without letting them get out of hand. And although it's not necessary, an instant-read thermometer is a great tool for providing consistency, in anything from meat to caramel.

When it comes to being in control of your food, there's no better example than dough. It's so interactive, whether you're waiting for yeast to rise, kneading a mess of flour into a smooth and elastic ball, or gently incorporating cold butter for borekas (page 19) or pie crust (page 338). Being decisive and efficient is essential. As the dough comes together, use your senses to judge whether to add flour or liquid, and keep your tools—bench scraper, rolling pin—at the ready to help you shape it. When you roll, do so with even weight and even pressure, keeping your rolling pin clean and your ingredients at the right temperature. Nothing can take the place of muscle memory, which you'll develop each time you make a dough, but don't get caught up in perfectionism. Keep calm and knead on.

Life Is Better with Sharp Knives

Not only are sharp knives safer and more effective in chopping, but they'll also actually improve your cooking. Dull knives bruise delicate herbs and force you to hack away at meat, whereas sharp knives make clean, quick cuts. It's good to own a whetstone (a fine-grained stone used for sharpening knives) if you do a lot of cooking, but there are so many places now that can sharpen your knives while you wait. Word to the wise: honing steels—those long rods that come with many knife sets—don't actually make your knife sharper. Through regular use, your knife's blade very subtly comes out of alignment, and a honing steel works to realign it.

Take Time to Prepare

Also known as *mise en place,* this is rule number 1 in restaurant kitchens but often falls by the wayside when we cook at home. Sometimes that's fine, but if you take some time to gather your ingredients and prepare them before you start, you won't realize halfway through cooking that you need to run to the store or somehow track down a rare ingredient. You'll also ensure that your food doesn't overcook while you prepare something else on the sidelines. Keep a bowl for scraps and other waste in easy reach, so you're not running back and forth from the counter to the trash can or compost pile. These tips go a long way to keeping you organized, on task, and in control. Some recipes may require advance planning (such as an overnight soak for chickpeas, for example); these recipes are indicated with a clock icon (🕐), so you can plan ahead.

When to Weigh

Most kitchens are equipped with measuring cups and spoons. Scales are a lot less common. But there's a handful of recipes in which the precision you get from weighing ingredients is necessary for the success of the dish. In some doughs, the equivalent of a tablespoon of flour can make a difference. If it's humid where you live, or if the flour is old, it may weigh more because it absorbs moisture from the air, so a simple volume measurement can weigh down more delicate doughs. And when I make gnocchi (page 152), I weigh the potatoes as soon as I've peeled them, to take into account how widely they vary in size; it's not as if you can easily add or subtract cooked potatoes after you start making the dough. I'll call for weight only where I truly believe it's necessary, so I recommend getting a scale if those recipes are on your to-cook list.

When to Season

Most of the time, seasoning happens as you go, or you can add it to taste at the end. Pre-seasoning—think marinating, brining, or salting—is a separate beast. This is a huge part of the way I cook, and an effective way of taking your food from good to great. When you're cooking with meat, pre-seasoning condenses all the natural flavors and helps other flavors work their way through. It takes a little extra time and planning, but I think you'll find it's worth it.

Toasting and Charring

Though they're very different, toasting and charring have one thing in common: using heat to transform an ingredient. Char—specifically, the aroma it provides—is practically an ingredient in things like lutenitsa (page 8) and baba ganoush (page 368). And toasting brings out the essence of nuts, spices, and rice before you even use them.

You'll go about these two techniques in almost exactly opposite ways: with charring, you use an aggressive flame, and with toasting, you keep it slow and even. I toast all nuts in a 325°F oven; dry grains and spices go in a skillet over medium heat. You'll know both nuts and spices are toasted as soon as they're fragrant—trust your nose. Charred eggplants, on the other hand, could spend a while over a high flame and be better for it, collapsing with creaminess and thoroughly infused with the scent of smoke.

I

ECHOES
OF
ISRAEL

My Grandmother's Peppers and Eggplants

I can trace all of my food memories back to one moment. I was in first grade, still the new kid in Philadelphia, still trying to learn English and forget Hebrew. After school one day, I opened the front door of my house and was hit by the scent of roasting eggplants and sweet peppers. I knew immediately what that smell meant: my grandparents were visiting from Israel, and my safta, my grand-mother Matilda, was cooking. For the next month, I would get the feeling of family and closeness that, at that point in my life, I didn't otherwise have.

•

WHEN I WAS FIVE, everything in my world shifted, so much that I have very little recollection of what came before that year. I have snapshot memories of our life in Israel: a glimpse of a neighbor who took me under her wing when I was being punished for disobedience; a brief image of my older sister, Anit, going to school. But when I was four, my mother, sister, and I moved from Israel to the United States to join my father, who'd come a couple of years earlier. We flew to Philadelphia on my birthday, December 8. I got in trouble on the plane ride over for stealing sodas—more than half a dozen different cans—from the galley and hiding them under my seat.

My mother, Aliza, didn't want to come to America. Her life, her parents, her world were in Israel. The only consolation was that her sister had moved to Philadelphia before us. But for my father, Alex, this was the fulfillment of a longtime dream, ever

ROASTED PEPPERS AND EGGPLANTS

since his childhood in Romania. That dream propelled him through several hard years at first in Pennsylvania, struggling to piece together odd jobs, not speaking the language. He was able to get more stable work through overhearing some men talking in Hungarian—the language of his youth—at a diner and introducing himself to them. At that moment, he was down to his last few dollars. They owned some kind of machine-repair business and gave him a job. He was able to save enough money to bring the rest of us over.

That first year, living in an apartment building in Northeast Philly, was a rough one. I remember arguments, shouting. A year later, I was told we were moving to a new house in Narberth, a suburb of Philadelphia, just minutes away from where my aunt Debbie, my mom's older sister, and her family lived. It was only when we were getting in the car to leave that I realized my father wasn't coming with us. He was going to a different house.

After that, my life became solitary. My mom was now on her own, trying to support two little kids. We were able to afford the house we'd moved into because Aunt Debbie had bought it for us. My saba, my mother's father, Nissim, had helped organize that from Israel. We were completely alienated from my father. At one point, we got an answering machine, and we weren't allowed to pick up the phone, in case it was my dad calling. My mom got two jobs—one selling tickets at a train station, the other in accounts payable at an oil firm—to try to make ends meet. This meant she was at work all the time. My sister, who's five years older than me, took refuge at friends' houses. I was often alone.

This was why arriving home to the aroma of peppers and eggplants hit me so powerfully. Safta was charring vegetables on little metal grates set over the gas stovetop. Saba would lift me onto his shoulders, and Safta would give me tastes of all the dishes she'd been cooking. There would be a casserole dish of cabbage stuffed with ground beef and rice, stewed in tomato sauce. Next to it would be a tall pot stacked with stuffed grape leaves nestled together. A bowl of chopped cucumbers with yogurt, lime, and dill would be waiting for their drizzle of extra-virgin olive oil before being served. Another bowl, filled with chopped chicken liver, would be mixed with hard-boiled egg and diced red onion. Bulgarian sheep's-milk yogurt would be hanging in a cheesecloth from the faucet over the kitchen sink. Golden oniony leek patties bound together with potato, breadcrumbs, and eggs would sit on paper-towel-lined platters. Sliced eggplant would be piled high on a platter after being breaded, pan-fried until crispy, and painted with a garlicky, caramelized tomato paste. One of my favorite things to do was to grab two pieces of white bread, spread them with Philadelphia cream cheese, and then slide one of those rounds of fried eggplant in between and eat it cold.

I loved to eat these dishes. More than that, though, they meant that for the next few weeks, while my grandparents were in town, we would live a family life. Instead of being carted by taxi from elementary school to day care, I would be picked up by my saba in the car he'd bought for my mom, in which he'd taught her how to drive.

And their visits meant I would cook with my safta. We would spend days together in the kitchen. "Peel these peppers and eggplants," she would say. I sat there and peeled, and felt that life was better. I would fake being sick in order to skip school and spend more time with her in the kitchen. We had old radiators in our house; I'd stick the thermometer into one of them until it read 102 degrees or so. Then I would call down from my bedroom, "I can't go to school! I'm really sick!" My safta would run up and look at the thermometer and say, "Oh my God, you have a fever!" And I would ask, "Can you make tomato soup with rice?" "Right away," she would say, and run downstairs to start cooking. I would come down and sit with her in the kitchen, rewarded for my lie with a big bowl of warm tomato soup that she puréed with cream, having cooked the rice in the soup so that it was almost porridgey.

My safta was a caretaker; she knew how to make people feel

GRINDING KEBAB MEAT

PURÉEING TOMATO SOUP

better. For me it was through food, but for most people she knew, it was through medicine. She was a pharmacist who'd escaped Bulgaria after World War II and made her way to Jaffa in 1948, the year Israel was founded. She was a quiet person, more comfortable making people happy through her actions than through words. I felt warm and peaceful in her presence. In the kitchen, she would give me tastes of whatever she was making. She would guide my actions as I worked the hand-cranked meat grinder attached to our countertop with a C clamp. She would look over my shoulder as I cracked eggs and added allspice, paprika, and cumin to a bowl of raw lamb shoulder to make Bulgarian kebabs. She'd add a touch of baking soda to the meat mixture, which would lend the kebabs an almost bouncy texture. The scent of frying lamb would permeate the whole house for days. As the years went by, each time Safta and Saba would visit, it was always the same in the kitchen, though I kept getting taller and accumulating responsibilities along the way.

LUTENITSA

YIELD: ABOUT 2 CUPS

The aroma of peppers and eggplant charring over an open flame is what made me fall in love with food. Intense but simple, it takes me back to that early feeling of being so nourished by my grandparents' visits. It really doesn't require a lot of skill; patience—in thoroughly charring the vegetables, then peeling them and slowly, gently cooking them into the most concentrated version of themselves—is more important than anything else you could add. Eat this dish with bread or on its own. It's great companions with hummus (page 114) or labneh dip (page 38).

4 red bell peppers
1 large (1-to-1½-pound) eggplant
4 tablespoons extra-virgin olive oil, divided
¼ cup tomato paste
1 clove garlic, minced
1 teaspoon Morton kosher salt
¾ cup canned whole tomatoes with their juice
2 tablespoons lightly packed fresh parsley leaves, chopped

1. Set the peppers on their sides over high heat on a gas stovetop's burners or grill so they're exposed directly to the flame (you may want to line the burners with foil to prevent a mess, and if you've got one, use a small metal grate to keep the peppers from falling into the burner, so they char more evenly). Cook until that side is completely blackened, 3 to 4 minutes, then rotate; they're done when they're charred black all over. Remove from the heat, and set aside to cool.

2. Use a fork to prick the eggplant a few times all over. It gives off a fair amount of liquid as it cooks, so lining your burner with foil as mentioned in step 1 makes for easy cleanup. Lay the eggplant on its side over the burner, as you did with the peppers, and cook over medium-high heat until the bottom is blistered and blackened with bits of papery white char. Rotate and keep cooking until the whole thing is uniformly charred—depending on your stove, this usually takes about 45 minutes. It'll be ugly, and you'll think you overcooked it. You didn't. This is what gives it a ton of flavor and a creamy texture. Remove it from heat, and set aside to cool.

3. When the peppers are cool enough to handle, use wet fingers to rub off all their papery, charred skin. Resist the urge to run them under water in the sink; although that lets you peel them faster, it also rinses away the smoky flavor you just built. Once the skins are removed, pull or cut out the stems, halve the peppers lengthwise, and scrape out all the seeds and any pith. Chop the peppers and set them aside; you should have about 1½ cups' worth.

4. Halve the eggplant lengthwise, and cut off the top. The inside should be creamy all the way to the center, but if it's not, you can finish the job by placing the halved eggplant in a 375°F oven for 5 to 10 minutes. Use a spoon to scoop out the flesh gently, taking care not to bring too much charred skin with it, and set it aside with the peppers; you should have about ¾ cup's worth.

5. Set a large skillet over medium heat, and add 2 tablespoons olive oil. Once it's warm, add the tomato paste, and use a wooden spoon or spatula to break it up as much as you can, to build a toasty flavor.

6. Once the olive oil is orange and the tomato paste doesn't smell so raw, add the garlic and cook just until it starts to soften and smell great. Add the roasted peppers, eggplant, and the salt, and stir to incorporate. Roughly crush the canned tomatoes by hand, or chop them, then add them to the pan with their juice.

7. Reduce the heat to low, and cook, uncovered, for about 1 hour. You want the mixture really to dry out, thicken, and kind of slump into itself. Stir it occasionally to scrape up the brown bits and prevent the bottom of the pan from burning. It's done when it tastes sweet and deeply caramelized. Set it aside, and cool to room temperature. To serve: scatter with parsley and drizzle on the remaining 2 tablespoons olive oil.

WATERMELON AND FETA SALAD WITH HARISSA

This is a great salad for the hottest days of summer, when you barely want to move, let alone cook. Feta and watermelon complement each other perfectly: salty and sweet, creamy and crisp, briny and fresh. You might've seen that before. The harissa is really what makes this special, bringing out the best of both and adding a whole new dimension, a darker, ruddier flavor, to the mix. If you've already made the harissa, you can assemble this dish in 5 minutes, but even if you make it specifically for this dish, it's the only thing that'll take any of your attention, and the rest is quick. (And if you're using a store-bought harissa, it'll likely be a more concentrated paste, so use only 2 to 3 tablespoons, according to taste, and add an extra tablespoon of olive oil.)

1. Use a sharp knife to cut the watermelon into 1-to-2-inch slices, then trim off the rind and gently scrape away any seeds before cutting it into chunks; you want to have about 3 quarts total. Stick the chopped melon in a colander to drain while you prepare the rest.

2. In a large salad bowl, combine the harissa with the olive oil and white-wine vinegar. Finely chop ¼ cup walnuts and add them, too; stir it all to combine.

3. Add the watermelon to the salad bowl. Roughly chop the remaining cup of walnuts and the parsley; scatter it with the feta all over the watermelon, using your hands to toss gently. Serve this right away—when it's allowed to sit, the watermelon gives off a lot of juices that dilute all the great flavors in the dressing.

About 4 pounds watermelon, skin on
¼ cup harissa (page 389)
3 tablespoons extra-virgin olive oil
1 tablespoon white-wine vinegar
1¼ cups walnut pieces, toasted, divided
3 tablespoons lightly packed fresh parsley leaves
1½ cups crumbled sheep's-milk feta, preferably Bulgarian

FRIED EGGPLANT WITH CARAMELIZED TOMATO AND GOAT CHEESE

Like the best eggplant Parmesan, this is all about the textures: soft whipped cheese to mimic the eggplant's creamy center and balance its crisp crust. Don't stress about finding the perfect mix of herbs—as long as they're fresh and you have about 1 tablespoon chopped, you can use any kind or combination that you like. The result is similar to Boursin, which would be a great substitute; you could also use 4 ounces of only cream cheese or only goat cheese if you don't have both.

The tomato sauce is this recipe's secret weapon. Look in your fridge or pantry: I bet there's a can or tube of tomato paste hiding behind all the other jars. Safta taught me about transforming this humble staple into a higher version of itself by making it an herb-infused pesto of sorts—call it paste-o! Once you try it and get initiated to that inimitably savory, caramelized, concentrated tomato flavor, you'll be looking for every chance to use it. Don't stop here; toss it with pasta or whip it into soup. Both the herbed cheese and the paste-o can be made a couple hours ahead and left at room temperature until it's time to eat.

- 3 sprigs fresh thyme
- 1 small sprig fresh rosemary
- 2 fresh sage leaves
- ¼ cup (2 ounces) cream cheese, softened
- ¼ cup (2 ounces) goat cheese, softened
- 1¼ teaspoons Morton kosher salt, divided
- 3 tablespoons extra-virgin olive oil
- 1 clove garlic, minced
- 2 tablespoons lightly packed fresh parsley leaves, chopped, plus more for garnish
- ½ cup tomato paste
- ½ cup all-purpose flour
- 3 eggs
- 3 tablespoons water
- 1½ cups fresh breadcrumbs or panko
- 1 medium (about ¾-pound) eggplant
- 1 cup canola oil

1. Pull the leaves from the thyme and rosemary, mince them with the sage, then mash them into the cheeses with ¼ teaspoon salt and set aside.

2. To make the "paste-o": Put the olive oil, garlic, and parsley in a nonstick skillet, then turn the heat to low and bring it up nice and slow, which will keep the garlic from getting too brown and bitter. It's ready when it smells like garlic bread; the parsley will be a deep, dark green.

3. Add the tomato paste and ½ teaspoon salt, and break it up with your spoon as best you can; at first it won't want to cooperate, but gradually it will start to melt. Continue to cook over low heat, stirring occasionally, for 5 or 6 minutes, until it's broken down and smells nicely caramelized. Set it aside.

4. Combine the flour with the last ½ teaspoon salt, and put the mixture in a shallow bowl. Beat the eggs with the water, and put them in another shallow bowl. Put the breadcrumbs in a third shallow bowl. *(recipe continues)*

TOMATO "PASTE-O"!

5. Trim the ends from the eggplant, and cut it into roughly
   ¾-inch slices. Line a plate with paper towels, and put the
   canola oil in a large skillet over medium heat. Test the
   oil by dropping in a couple breadcrumbs: it's ready when
   they sizzle as soon as they hit the pan, but too hot if they
   immediately brown.

6. Working in batches of four or five slices, dredge the eggplant
   first in the flour, patting off any excess; then in the eggs; and
   finally in the breadcrumbs, gently patting them into an even
   crust that clings to each piece.

7. Add the slices to the pan in batches, making sure they're not
   too crowded. Fry, flipping occasionally, until both sides get
   crispy and brown and the eggplant is creamy at the center,
   5 or 6 minutes total. Move to the lined plate to drain any
   excess oil, and continue with the remaining slices of eggplant
   until you've cooked them all.

8. When the fried eggplant has cooled slightly, smear each slice
   with a thin layer of tomato "paste-o," then dollop the herbed
   cheese on top. Sprinkle generously with parsley before
   serving, and eat the eggplant while it's warm.

TOMATO SOUP WITH RICE

People call chicken soup with rice "the Jewish grandmother's prescription," a cure for whatever ails you (or whatever you're pretending ails you). This vegetarian version may be even more so; it just makes you feel good. A word of advice: if your child tries to stay home from school and sucker you into making it, verify his or her internal temperature before proceeding. This is a real celebration of good tomatoes, and if you have a surplus in the summer, you can purée and stockpile them in the freezer until there's enough for a batch. You can also substitute two 28-ounce cans of whole tomatoes.

4 pounds very ripe tomatoes
½ cup extra-virgin olive oil, plus more for serving
1 large yellow onion, thinly sliced
1 clove garlic, thinly sliced
1 tablespoon Morton kosher salt
1 dried bay leaf
1 star anise pod
1 teaspoon Aleppo pepper
1 tablespoon sweet paprika
¼ cup tomato paste
2 cups water
⅓ cup jasmine rice

1. Use a paring knife to cut the cores out of the tomatoes. Roughly chop the tomatoes and purée them in a blender or food processor, in batches if necessary.
2. Put the olive oil in a large, heavy-bottomed pot over medium heat. Once it's warm, add the onion, garlic, and

(recipe continues)

salt. Stir occasionally so the onion slices sweat and soften, but don't let them build any color.

3. When the vegetables are translucent and soft, add the bay leaf, star anise, Aleppo, and sweet paprika. Give everything a good stir, and toast the spices for a minute or two, until they're super-fragrant. Add the tomato paste, and stir to combine, letting it toast and build flavor for another couple of minutes.

4. Add the puréed tomatoes and water, and increase the heat to high. Bring everything up to a boil, skim off any foam (being careful not to strain out the spices), and decrease the heat to medium-low. Cook for 10 minutes, until it's just starting to thicken.

5. Meanwhile, rinse the rice in a sieve until the water runs clear. Be thorough here, or the starch can gum up the soup. Once the soup has thickened a bit, add the rice to the pot and let it simmer away, stirring occasionally, until the rice is cooked, 20 to 30 minutes.

6. Before you serve the soup, fish out the spices (or make it a game and see who finds them in the bowls). Finish each bowl with a drizzle of olive oil.

BULGARIAN LAMB KEBABS

YIELD: 4 TO 6 SERVINGS

A little like meatballs, a little like burgers, a little like dumplings, these kebabs have the best qualities of each. Unlike Greek kebabs, which have large chunks of meat on a skewer, these are made of tender ground meat. My favorite part—the most special thing about them—is their impossibly soft, almost springy texture in the center, not dry and crumbly the way so many meatballs are. A few things contribute to this: the bread and fatty meat for moisture, the tiniest pinch of baking soda for lift, and powdered milk, which retains forty times its weight in liquid and essentially traps every drop of the meat's juices. With texture this good, the flavors of the spices shine through; I remember the smell of cumin and paprika permeating the entire house as my safta fried them up.

You typically see these cooked over coals, or "al ha'esh," in the Bulgarian neighborhoods of Israel. That's how I do it now, but there are also directions for making them on the stovetop as Safta does—you'll have excellent kebabs either way. If you have trouble finding lamb or are worried its flavor will be too strong, a good, fatty beef brisket would work just as well. Grinding it yourself is the best way to make sure it tastes great and fresh, but you can ask most butchers to grind it for you at the counter.

1. Cut the bread into ½-inch pieces and toss it with the buttermilk in a large bowl until each piece is moistened. Add the lamb, onion, salt, spices, and baking soda; chop ½ cup parsley leaves, and add them as well. Sift the powdered milk evenly over the mixture, and combine it all with your hands, a potato masher, or a spatula, mixing it thoroughly but taking care not to manhandle the mixture.

2. Scoop the mixture into ½-cup mounds and shape it into logs that are 4 or 5 inches long (you'll have eight to ten kebabs). Place them on a plate, cover loosely in plastic, and refrigerate for at least 30 minutes; this gives the fat in the lamb a chance to firm up before it cooks, so it keeps its integrity.

3. If you're grilling the kebabs, heat the grill until the fire has burned out but the coals are white-hot. (The fire needs to die down before you cook, or else the fat from the kebabs could melt and make it flare up.) Place each kebab directly on the grill, and cook for 3 to 4 minutes, until they're deeply golden with a nice crust, then turn and cook for another 2 to 3 minutes. Cut into one; it should be cooked through but still very juicy.

4. If you're not grilling the kebabs, heat your oven to 400°F, and add the canola oil to a large ovenproof skillet over high heat. Put the flour in a wide, shallow bowl, and set it aside. Test the oil by dropping a pinch of flour into the pan; you're ready to cook when it sizzles right away but doesn't immediately turn brown.

5. Lightly dredge the kebabs in flour, one at a time, so all sides are coated, patting them gently between your hands to reshape them and shake off any excess flour. Lay them side by side in the pan and decrease the heat to medium. Cook these in batches if you need to; it's important that the pan doesn't get overcrowded.

6. Let the kebabs cook, undisturbed, for 5 to 6 minutes, or until the bottoms are a deep golden-brown. Flip them, and immediately transfer the skillet to the oven. Bake for 7 to 8 minutes, until they're no longer pink in the middle.

7. Move the kebabs to a serving platter, and drizzle the tahini and olive oil over them. Chop the cilantro and remaining 2 tablespoons parsley, and scatter them over the tops.

---

3 slices soft white or whole-wheat bread

½ cup buttermilk

1½ pounds ground lamb

½ yellow onion, finely chopped

1½ teaspoons Morton kosher salt

1 tablespoon smoked paprika

1 tablespoon ground cumin

1 teaspoon freshly ground black pepper

⅛ teaspoon baking soda

½ cup plus 2 tablespoons lightly packed fresh parsley leaves, divided

½ cup milk powder

½ cup canola oil (for stovetop option only)

½ cup all-purpose flour (for stovetop option only)

¼ cup prepared tahini (page 392)

2 tablespoons extra-virgin olive oil

2 tablespoons lightly packed fresh cilantro leaves

2

✦✦✦

Show-and-Tell Borekas

The hardest part of going to school was my name. "Alon" means "oak tree" in Hebrew. My mom, my aunt and uncle, my sister—they all pronounced my name the way we had in Israel: "Ah-LUN." But when I started school in the United States, I'd tell people my name and they'd call me "Alone." No one could get it right, and it made me really self-conscious. So I changed the pronunciation to "Ah-LAWN," and that stuck. It took me a while to speak English well. My English-language skills were learned from watching Elmo talk about the alphabet. As a child, I had Cookie Monster's accent.

I was bullied in school, starting when I was five. A kid who lived down the street from me was my archenemy, following me off the school bus and pushing me into the snow. That kept up until around second grade, when I began hitting back. I was brazen; I wasn't afraid to pick up a huge stick and whack some kid over the head with it, or even pull a knife on somebody. There were a few times in grade school when the police showed up at our house after I'd beaten the crap out of someone. I didn't know how to express myself. We were a poor family, living on the edge of one of the wealthiest communities in the country. I would go to school with millionaires' kids while my mom struggled to keep us fed and clothed.

I kept hoping, though, that people would see beyond that and get a glimpse of who I really was. One day in second grade, we were given an assignment to bring something into class for show-and-tell that would demonstrate who we were, tell our story. I decided to make borekas, so that everyone would realize that being Israeli is *cool*.

Borekas were one of my favorite foods. They were a dish my family had always cooked: warm, flaky pastries stuffed with feta cheese, black pepper, and occasionally spinach, then brushed with golden egg yolk and sesame seeds. I'd make them with my mother and grandmother, carefully rolling out the dough, spreading it with butter, folding it again, chilling it, and repeating that process. Each fold produced more tender, buttery layers. Finally, we'd fold the pastry into a triangle, stuff it with the salty feta and black pepper, and seal the edges with the back of a fork to ensure that none of the cheese would leak out. The assignment came during one of my safta's visits to Philadelphia, and I asked her to set me up to make the borekas for show-and-tell.

The next morning, I grabbed the bag she'd prepared from the fridge and headed straight to school. It was only when I arrived and began laying out my ingredients that I realized it would be a disaster. I had no feta cheese, no spinach, only puff pastry and eggs. There wasn't even an oven in which to bake them! I was doomed. When my turn came, I stood there in front of all the other students, fumbling with my story of why I loved this dish that no one could taste. I didn't even have pre-made borekas to pass around. Sitting back down, I internally berated myself. *How will anyone ever understand me now?*

As I think back on it today, I don't know whether I simply missed other bags of ingredients my safta had prepared, or if she was trying to teach me a lesson. But whether she intended it or not, one message stuck from that first, failed cooking demonstration: Get your shit together. Take responsibility for your assignments. It was a lesson I'd have to keep learning for years to come.

TOP TO BOTTOM: EVERYTHING BOREKAS, POTATO AND EGG BOREKA TART, SWEET TAHINI BOREKAS

BOREKA DOUGH

Borekas—stuffed puff pastry—were something that I adored as a child and still love today. They were always just sitting on the table, ready to snack on. This "rough puff" method cuts out some of the steps that you'll see in making traditional puff-pastry dough but yields comparable results. Laminate doughs can be intimidating if you've never made them, but as long as you've got patience, it's hard to screw them up. Here's what's nonnegotiable: the dough needs to be kept cold (to prevent the butter from melting), and you need to keep the ends square (so the layers puff up evenly). It helps to keep *everything* cold, including your mixing bowl with the measured flour and salt. Beyond that, the timeline is actually really flexible; the dough can be prepared in the course of one day of downtime at home, or stop and go, throughout a busy weekend. It also freezes flawlessly, so, if you're feeling motivated, make some now and save it for a rainy day.

20 ounces (5 sticks) unsalted butter, cold
5¼ cups (630 grams) all-purpose flour, plus more for dusting
1½ teaspoons Morton kosher salt
4 teaspoons canola oil
4 teaspoons distilled white vinegar
1¼ cups club soda, cold, plus more as needed

1. Cut the butter into slices ¼ to ½ inch thick. Spread them in a layer on a plate or baking sheet, and refrigerate until they're very firm, at least 1 hour.

2. Meanwhile, combine the flour and salt in a large mixing bowl (preferably the bowl of your stand mixer) and keep it in the freezer. Gradually stir the butter into the flour mixture, with the paddle attachment on low speed, or with a pastry cutter, until the smallest chunks are pea-sized and the larger pieces have broken down a bit.

3. Pour in the canola oil and vinegar, then gradually add the club soda and continue to mix until a rough dough forms; make sure you scrape the sides of the bowl periodically to moisten the flour at the bottom. There will still be distinct pieces of butter and dry bits of flour, so gauge whether it's ready by pinching pieces between your hands; it's done when it starts to clump together. If it's still too dry, add more club soda 1 tablespoon at a time, but be careful that the dough doesn't get too wet.

4. Spread a piece of parchment at least 18 inches long on your work surface, then dust it with flour. Empty the dough onto it and, using a light touch and the heels of your hands, shape it into a rectangle about 2 inches thick. Be careful not to

let the butter start melting on you: a decisive touch will get the job done faster, so don't linger with it. Fold the sides of the parchment around it to seal, then wrap the whole thing tightly in plastic, and refrigerate for at least 2 hours, until it's very cold throughout. You can store it like this for as long as a couple days before proceeding.

5. On a floured surface, roll the chilled dough into a rectangle about 12 by 18 inches; use the sides of your hands or a bench scraper to square off the edges so they stay neat and even, and dust with more flour as needed to keep the dough from getting sticky. Fold it in thirds, as you would a letter (a bench scraper is helpful here, to help you lift and manipulate the dough), then glide your rolling pin lengthwise along the dough once or twice, just to smooth out any air pockets. Fold it in half crosswise, wrap it in plastic, and refrigerate for at least 1 hour.

6. This process—rolling, folding, and chilling—constitutes one "turn" in the process of making laminated dough. Do it two more times, then cut the dough in half and wrap each piece tightly in plastic. Allow the dough to chill in the refrigerator for at least 4 hours, until it's thoroughly cold throughout, before you use it in a recipe. If you prefer, you can store it in the freezer until you're ready to use it, then let it thaw completely in the fridge.

Feta and kashkaval make these creamy and mild with just the right amount of salt. Sesame seeds or poppy seeds alone will give you the same great, subtle crunch if you don't want to mix up the topping, and if you can't track down kashkaval, any good-quality sharp provolone does the trick.

1 cup crumbled sheep's-milk feta, preferably Bulgarian
¾ cup grated kashkaval or provolone cheese
1 egg
½ teaspoon freshly ground black pepper
All-purpose flour, for dusting
1½ pounds boreka dough (preceding recipe) or store-bought puff pastry
Water, for sealing
1 tablespoon sesame seeds
1 tablespoon poppy seeds
1½ teaspoons dried onion flakes
1½ teaspoons dried garlic flakes
1½ teaspoons Maldon or other flaky sea salt
1 egg yolk
2 teaspoons milk

1. To make the filling: Stir together the cheeses, egg, and black pepper, mashing them with your spoon or spatula just until they're incorporated. Set the mixture aside until you're ready to fill the dough.

2. Line a baking sheet with parchment paper. Generously dust flour over a work surface, your rolling pin, and the dough; if it's so cold that it's impossible to work with, let the dough sit at room temperature for 5 or 10 minutes. Roll it into a rectangle a little bigger than 12 by 16 inches, about ¼ inch thick; dust with flour as needed, flipping the dough occasionally so it doesn't stick, and keep the edges neat. Trim away any uneven edges.

3. Dust off any excess flour, and brush a little water over the dough. Cut it in thirds lengthwise, then make four even cuts crosswise, to get twelve 4-inch squares. Spoon 1 heaping tablespoon of filling into the center of each one, wrap the dough around the filling to make a triangle, and firmly pinch the edges to seal. Arrange the borekas on the lined baking sheet, and refrigerate for at least 30 minutes.

4. When you're ready to bake, heat the oven to 450°F with a rack in the center of the oven. Make the everything-bagel topping by combining the sesame seeds, poppy seeds, dried onion flakes, dried garlic flakes, and flaky sea salt. In a separate bowl, beat together the egg yolk and milk.

5. With the tines of a fork, crimp the chilled borekas' edges well, so they're completely sealed. Brush the egg wash all over their tops, and sprinkle each one with about ½ teaspoon of the bagel seasoning. Bake for 10 minutes, then decrease the heat to 400°F, rotate the pan, and bake for another 15 or 20 minutes, until they're deeply golden all over. Serve warm, or cool to room temperature and store in an airtight container for a day or two. These reheat beautifully in a 400°F oven for 5 minutes.

POTATO AND EGG BOREKA TART

This is my take on one of my favorite snacks in the Jerusalem market. It's got essentially the same ingredients, but I've transitioned it from the market to the breakfast table: it looks beautiful as the centerpiece of a big spread. If you haven't yet had a breakfast party, this will be a reason to start. You can make and fill the whole thing the night before, so it comes together quickly in the morning; it reheats beautifully at 400°F in 5 to 8 minutes. Feel free to add as many or few of the toppings as you like—it's so good that it can stand on its own as a simple and unadorned potato boreka. Prepared tahini and harissa, if you've got them on hand or don't mind making them, are the traditional accompaniments and will transport you right to Israel.

- ½ pound Yukon Gold potato (about 1 medium)
- 2 quarts water, plus more for boiling the eggs
- ¼ cup plus 1 tablespoon milk, divided
- 2 tablespoons unsalted butter
- ½ teaspoon Morton kosher salt
  All-purpose flour, for dusting
- 1½ pounds boreka dough (page 22) or store-bought puff pastry
  Ice water for an ice bath
- 3 eggs
- 1 egg yolk
- ¼ red onion
- 8 cornichons
- 2 teaspoons lightly packed fresh parsley leaves
- ⅓ cup prepared tahini (page 392), optional
- 1 tablespoon harissa (page 389), optional

1. Peel the potato, cut it into 1-to-2-inch chunks, and add them to a large saucepan with 2 quarts water. Bring to a boil over high heat, then reduce the heat to medium and simmer until the potato pieces are tender and almost crumble when pierced with a fork, 10 to 12 minutes.

2. While the potato cooks, heat ¼ cup milk with the butter and salt in the microwave, or in another saucepan over very low heat until the butter melts and the milk is warm.

3. Drain the potato well, combine the chunks with the warm milk and butter, and use a potato masher or fork to mash them until they're very smooth. (If you have a food mill or potato ricer, you can instead pass the potato through that before adding the milk mixture.) The potato will be looser than you're used to, which is important, so you can spread it on the pastry without tearing the dough. Let it cool completely at room temperature.

4. Line a baking sheet with parchment paper, and generously dust a work surface, your rolling pin, and the dough with flour. If it's too cold to work with, let it soften slightly, just for around 10 minutes, at room temperature. Cut it in half, and roll each piece into a 10-by-14-inch rectangle of ¼-inch thickness, as evenly sized as possible; to keep the dough from softening or sticking to the counter, loosen its edges with a bench scraper or thin spatula as you work, occasionally flip it, and sprinkle flour as needed. *(recipe continues)*

5. Wipe away any excess flour, and lift one piece of dough onto the lined baking sheet for assembly. Leaving a 1-inch border, spread the mashed potato over it. Place the other half over the top, and use the tines of a fork to crimp the edges and seal it. Trim away any jagged edges and refrigerate it for at least 1 hour.

6. Meanwhile, fill a pot with water and bring it to a boil; fill a separate bowl with ice water for an ice bath. Boil the eggs in their shells for 9 minutes, then plunge them into the ice bath to cool completely.

7. Heat the oven to 425°F. Beat the remaining tablespoon of milk with the egg yolk. Brush this all over the top of the pastry, and prick it a few times with a fork. Bake for 15 minutes before decreasing the heat to 375°F and rotating the pan. Continue to bake for another 10 to 15 minutes, until it's deeply golden and puffed up.

8. Peel the eggs, and quarter them lengthwise; thinly slice the onion, halve the cornichons lengthwise, and chop the parsley. With the tart still warm, scatter these ingredients on top of the tart with dollops of the tahini and harissa if you're using them. Serve warm. You can make the tart a day in advance, store it in the refrigerator, then bring it to room temperature before reheating in a 400°F oven and then adding the toppings.

SWEET TAHINI BOREKAS

YIELD: 16 BOREKAS

One of my favorite bakeries in Jerusalem is an Israeli institution called Marzipan. They make a sweet boreka that inspired this version, which has a subdued nutty richness, like halvah. Note that you need cream of coconut, which comes sweetened and isn't the same thing as coconut cream—it's the key to the filling's fudgy consistency, which balances the crisp pastry so well. You'll sometimes find it with the cocktail mixers. The dulce de leche is available at many Latin American markets.

1. Line a baking sheet with parchment. Whisk together the tahini, dulce de leche, and cream of coconut until the mixture is thick and tacky; then transfer the mixture to a pastry bag or sturdy ziplock bag. Set it aside.

2. Generously dust a work surface, your rolling pin, and the dough with flour. If the dough is very cold and impossible to roll, let it soften slightly at room temperature, just 10 minutes or so. Roll it into a 16-to-18-inch square, about ¼ inch thick. As you work, flip it occasionally, loosening the edges with a bench scraper or thin spatula, to make sure it doesn't soften or stick; sprinkle with more flour as you need it to keep the dough from getting sticky. Use a knife or pizza cutter to trim away any jagged edges.

3. Wipe away any excess flour, then cut the dough into approximately 4-inch squares and brush a thin layer of water all over the tops. Snip the corner of the pastry bag so you have a ½-inch opening, and pipe about 1 tablespoon of filling in a thick line along one side of each square, leaving a 1-inch border from the edge. Pull that edge of the dough over the filling, gently pressing it all around to seal, then continue to roll it around itself until you have a tight cigar. Gently pinch the seams shut with your fingers.

4. Arrange the borekas on the lined baking sheet, snuggled closely side by side, seam side down. Unlike most baked goods, these should touch each other a little as they cook— that helps the sides stay tender while the tops brown more deeply. Refrigerate for at least 30 minutes.

5. Heat the oven to 425°F, and beat together the egg yolk and milk. Brush this evenly over the borekas, and sprinkle about ½ teaspoon of sesame seeds on top of each one. Bake for 15 to 20 minutes, rotating the pan halfway through; you're looking for the tops to be crisped up and deeply golden. Meanwhile, combine the sugar and water in a saucepan over low heat or in the microwave, stirring just until the sugar dissolves.

6. As soon as the borekas are out of the oven, paint the sugar syrup over their tops; they might hiss a little. Serve warm or at room temperature.

½ cup raw tahini
¼ cup dulce de leche
¼ cup cream of coconut
   All-purpose flour, for dusting
1½ pounds boreka dough (page 22) or store-bought puff pastry
   Water, for sealing
1 egg yolk
1 tablespoon milk
3 tablespoons sesame seeds, toasted
¼ cup sugar
¼ cup water

3

✦✦✦

Solo Hamantashen

The first dish I ever cooked by myself was hamantashen. The small triangle-shaped fruit-filled cookies are for Purim, a Jewish holiday of joyous celebration. I was nine years old. My life, by then, had settled into a lonely routine. My dad was still estranged from us after my parents' divorce, and my mom was still juggling two jobs. My older sister, Anit, had convinced my aunt and uncle to let her move in with them, eager for a chance to live in a more structured household. I spent long hours after school alone, with television as my only company. One day, I decided to give myself a project: I would make hamantashen.

I knew the basics of the legend around the cookie, which mimics the triangular shape of the evil Haman's hat. The story revolves around Queen Esther, who successfully defended her people, the Jews, against Haman's desire to have them killed on a massive scale. I'd made hamantashen for Purim with my mother. I called her at work to ask her where she'd put the recipe.

My mother, Aliza, always did the best she could. So much of her life, she'd had to make do, persist under challenging circumstances. She was born with cerebral palsy in her right arm, a condition that curled her hand shut and meant she could use only her left arm and hand. She could use her right arm to carry grocery bags or hold something steady, but not to hold a rolling pin, say, when we were baking together. This stopped her from serving in the Israeli army and, I'm sure, has shaped her life in countless other ways. She's always been eager to please, willingly sacrificing herself in favor of others, almost to the point where she couldn't tell you what *she* actually wanted. In light of that, it's amazing to me that she mustered the courage to leave my father and establish a home for us away from him, on her own.

She'd been managing that for a few years when I called her about the hamantashen recipe. She was reluctant to give it. Her nine-year-old son wanted to bake cookies—use the oven—by himself? There was so much that could go wrong, but she could tell I was serious. She gave me the recipe, and I set to work, mixing the dough, rolling it out, and cutting it into circles with a water glass. She called me every 30 minutes or so, and asked me questions: "Is the house on fire?" "What's the oven like right now?" By the third call, I asked her not to bother me while I was working. We had a can of cherry-pie filling that I used along with some of the traditional poppy-seed mixture to stuff the cookies. When they were done baking, I laid them out on the table, waiting for her to come home.

I'd never seen my mom more excited. She proclaimed them the best hamantashen ever: "Even better than mine!" She brought them to synagogue and passed them out to her friends. I still remember being complimented on the cookies. This was one of the rare moments in my childhood when I got positive feedback from adults; usually, I was in trouble.

The hamantashen gave me a sense of independence that started me on a new after-school routine. I'd come home, watch television, and then cook. My mom often didn't have time to

make complicated dishes for dinner; there were a lot of repeat meals. Lots of baked chicken and mashed potatoes, and always an Israeli salad on the table—diced cucumbers, tomatoes, and onions tossed with lemon, za'atar, olive oil, and some chopped parsley. I loved topping hot mashed potatoes with the bright, cool crunch of Israeli salad. After I'd proved myself with the hamantashen, I often assumed the responsibility of making dinner for my mom and myself, though not because she ever asked me to. I'd make simple things—salad, scrambled eggs, potatoes with cheese melted over the top—whatever combinations I could make from what was in the fridge.

When I was in second grade, I ran into one of my teachers at the grocery store. "Where's your mom?" she asked. "She's at work," I said. "I'm buying groceries for dinner and have lots of prep to do," I said, rolling my eyes when I saw how impressed she was. These days, I think a teacher might be concerned for the welfare of a kid who was so much on his own. But the next day at school, she called me out in front of the class, admiring how self-sufficient I was, going grocery shopping by myself. I felt a swell of pride in that.

PEACH AND MASCARPONE HAMANTASHEN

YIELD: 10 TO 12 COOKIES

The hamantashen I made as a child were filled with apricot jam or cherry-pie filling out of a can, sometimes poppy seeds and prunes. Now when I think of hamantashen, luscious fresh fruit comes to mind. I've always had a secret crush on cheese Danish, so I brought the two together for this recipe with a lightly sweet, tangy filling. Peaches, unfortunately, aren't in season during Purim, so, if you're making these for the holiday, you can substitute strawberries (you'll need only three or four for this recipe)—they'll be sweeter at that time of year. However, if you're like me and resist strict rules, you can make these in July with peaches!

I've had a lot of dry and crumbly hamantashen in my life. These have a much softer, more tender dough, so don't freak out when they spread a little as they cook. I also think they look cute this way.

1. Combine 1 cup sugar and the orange zest in a mixing bowl, rubbing the mixture between your fingers to release all the fragrant citrus oils. Add the butter, and, with an electric mixer or the paddle attachment of your stand mixer, cream the mixture on medium speed until smooth and soft.

2. Separate 1 egg, adding the white to the mixing bowl and reserving its yolk for the filling. Beat in the other egg along with 1 teaspoon vanilla and the orange blossom water, and mix until incorporated. Add 3 cups flour and the salt; beat on medium-low speed just until the dough forms a cohesive mass that starts to pull away from the bowl.

3. Dust a work surface with flour, and scrape the dough onto it. Pat it into a disc about 1 inch thick, wrap it in plastic, and refrigerate for at least 1 hour or overnight. (This dough can be made ahead, frozen, then thawed overnight in the fridge when you're ready to use it.)

4. While the dough chills, make the filling: To the egg yolk that you reserved when you made the dough, add the mascarpone and the remaining ¼ cup sugar, 2 tablespoons flour, and ½ teaspoon vanilla. Beat or whisk them all together, then cover and refrigerate.

5. If the dough chilled awhile, let it sit at room temperature for 10 or 15 minutes, so it's easier to work with. Line two large baking sheets with parchment paper, and make an egg wash by beating together the egg yolk, milk, and 1 tablespoon honey. Pit the peach, and cut it into ¾-to-1-inch cubes.

6. Flour a work surface and a rolling pin. Roll the dough into a 16-to-18-inch circle, turning and flipping it as you work to keep it at an even thickness; if the edges start to crack, gently reinforce them by pinching them back together, and dust with more flour if it starts to stick.

7. Cut the dough into 4½-to-5-inch circles (if you don't have a cookie cutter that large, the lid of a plastic pint container makes a good stencil), then patch together any excess dough and reroll it, flouring as needed, to cut a few more. Don't reroll it more than once, *maybe* twice, so that it stays tender.

8. Brush the egg wash in a thin, even layer over each circle, add a heaping tablespoon of filling to the center of each cookie, and top with 1 cube of peach. Gently lift the edges of each circle around the filling (use a butter knife or bench scraper to loosen them without tearing), and pinch the corners together to make a triangle. Brush a little more egg

1¼ cups sugar, divided
Grated zest of 1 orange
12 tablespoons (1½ sticks) unsalted butter, softened
2 eggs, divided
1½ teaspoons vanilla extract, divided
½ teaspoon orange blossom water
3 cups plus 2 tablespoons all-purpose flour, divided, plus more for rolling
½ teaspoon Morton kosher salt
1 cup mascarpone
1 egg yolk
1 tablespoon milk
3 tablespoons honey, divided
1 large peach

wash on the cookies' outsides, and set them on the prepared baking sheets with an inch or two between them. Cover with plastic, and chill for at least another 30 minutes.

9. Heat the oven to 375°F. Bake the cookies, straight from the fridge, for 30 to 35 minutes, rotating the sheets after 15 minutes. Look for the tops to become a light but even gold, and don't worry if the dough cracks a bit. Meanwhile, warm the remaining 2 tablespoons honey in the microwave or in a saucepan over low heat, just until it's thin and easily pourable.

10. When the cookies are still warm from the oven, paint them all over with the honey. Cool completely on the baking sheets before eating.

ISRAELI SALAD

My mother always had Israeli salad on our dinner table. When I was a kid, I'd make a well in my mashed potatoes and scoop this inside—I loved the contrast of hot, creamy potatoes with the cool crunch of the salad. This salad is also, for most people, one of the most distinct and evocative flavor combinations of Israeli food. As the vegetables meld together, their juices mingle with the herbs, lemon, and olive oil in the vinaigrette.

2 pints cherry tomatoes
1 large cucumber, preferably seedless
½ red onion
¼ cup lightly packed fresh parsley leaves
1 tablespoon lightly packed fresh mint leaves
1 teaspoon Morton kosher salt
2 teaspoons za'atar, plus more to finish
Grated zest of 1 lemon
¼ cup preserved lemon vinaigrette (page 393)

1. Quarter the tomatoes. If the cucumber has seeds, cut it lengthwise so that you can scoop them out with a spoon. Cut it and the onion into small dice (you should have about 2 cups and ½ cup, respectively). Finely chop the parsley and mint.

2. Add everything to a salad bowl with the salt, za'atar, and lemon zest, then toss with the dressing. Sprinkle more za'atar over the top just before serving.

SCHMALTZY POTATOES

Welcome to your new favorite way to eat potatoes. Nothing soaks up chicken fat the way potatoes do; they crisp up all golden on the bottom like latkes or French fries but have rich, creamy centers like mashed potatoes.

Herb salt perks them up, but if you don't have any on hand, use regular salt and rain some minced fresh herbs—rosemary and sage would be good choices—directly on the warm potatoes. You can find schmaltz in the kosher section of some grocery stores, but making it yourself gives you the perfect excuse to also make gribenes, those mouthwatering chicken-skin "cracklin's" (page 394) that are sometimes referred to as "Jewish bacon." If you can't track down any schmaltz, ghee is a fine substitute.

1. If the potatoes are unevenly sized, cut them all into large chunks of the same size. Add them to a pot and cover them with cold water so they're submerged by about 1 inch. Bring to a boil over high heat, then reduce the heat to medium-low and continue to simmer just until the potatoes are tender and can be pierced with a fork, 12 to 15 minutes.

2. Meanwhile, heat the oven to 500°F with a rack in the upper-middle portion. When the potatoes are ready, drain, and put them in a large bowl. Spoon the schmaltz over them—it will melt immediately—and toss to coat with the herb salt.

3. Spread the potatoes on a rimmed baking sheet. With the back of a fork, gently smash them down just until they're flat (not so much that they crumble), leaving space between them so steam can escape, for maximum crispy goodness.

4. Roast the potatoes for 20 to 25 minutes, rotating the pan about halfway through, until they've got browned edges all around and the bottoms are a deep brown. Serve right away.

3 pounds fingerling potatoes
Water, for boiling
⅓ cup schmaltz (page 394) or ghee
4 teaspoons herb salt (page 391)

MOM'S LEEK PATTIES

YIELD: ABOUT 12

We ate a lot of potato dishes when I was growing up—they were affordable and filling—and my mom learned to make this one, a Bulgarian classic, from my grandmother. The potatoes add body, the leeks give color and crunch, and the lemon zest really sets them both off. The patties are delicate, and they're supposed to be. Here's an idea: throw them into a burger bun with mayo, lettuce, and tomato, and you'll have yourself a fine vegetarian (if a little carb-loaded!) sandwich.

1. Combine 1 gallon water with 2 tablespoons salt, and bring to a boil over high heat. Trim away and discard the tough green ends of the leeks, and halve the white and light-green parts lengthwise, then cut them into ¼-inch slices and rinse them thoroughly—a couple changes of water is a good idea—to remove any grit. Boil them for 1 to 2 minutes, until they're tender with plenty of vivid color. Drain, and set them aside.

2. Peel the potatoes, and cut them into 1-inch pieces. Add them to your pot, cover them with a couple inches of cold water,

1 gallon water, plus plenty for the potatoes
2 tablespoons plus 2 teaspoons Morton kosher salt, divided
4 leeks, white and light-green parts only
1 pound Yukon Gold potatoes (about 3 medium or 4 small)
3 eggs
½ teaspoon freshly ground black pepper
¼ teaspoon finely grated nutmeg
Grated zest of 1 lemon
2 tablespoons cornstarch
1 tablespoon lemon juice
1 cup fresh breadcrumbs
¼ cup extra-virgin olive oil

(recipe continues)

and bring to a boil over high heat. As soon as the water boils, decrease the heat to medium, and keep cooking until the potatoes are very tender, about 12 minutes; then drain, and immediately mash them with a fork or potato masher until no big chunks remain. Stir in the leeks, and let them cool for 10 minutes or so, just until they're not so hot they'll scramble the eggs.

3. In a large mixing bowl, lightly beat the eggs with the pepper, nutmeg, lemon zest, and remaining 2 teaspoons salt. Separately, combine the cornstarch and lemon juice, and whisk this into the bowl with the eggs, followed by the breadcrumbs. Gently mix in the potatoes by hand or with a wooden spoon; no need for the mixture to be perfectly smooth.

4. Heat the olive oil in a nonstick skillet over medium heat, and line a large plate with paper towels. As soon as the oil is hot but before it starts to smoke, scoop the batter into roughly ¼-cup patties, and drop them into the pan, making sure to space them at least 1 inch apart so they aren't overcrowded. Flip after 3 to 4 minutes, when the bottoms have a nice golden crust that goes all the way to the edges, then cook for another 2 to 3 minutes.

5. Move the patties to the lined plate as they finish cooking, and continue with the rest of the batter until they're done. Serve warm.

CLOCKWISE FROM TOP LEFT:
YEMENITE STEWED CHICKEN,
ISRAELI SALAD,
MOM'S LEEK PATTIES,
SCHMALTZY POTATOES, AND
LABNEH DIP WITH PEPPERS AND RADISHES

LABNEH DIP WITH PEPPERS AND RADISHES

Thick, rich, and creamy with a little bit of tartness—like the best of cream cheese, goat cheese, and yogurt combined—labneh is a lesson in how simple it can be to make your own cheese. It may even be so rewarding that you'll go on to try bigger projects! If you haven't planned in advance and have access to a good store-bought version, substitute 2 cups of that for the Bulgarian yogurt and skip steps 1 to 3 altogether, jumping straight ahead to the vegetable prep for this delicious and simple dip. Without those additions, labneh is also an amazing ingredient in baking, the heart of my cheesecake (page 102) and a secret ingredient in my banana bread (page 244); its by-product, the whey, makes a fantastic marinade for chicken (recipe follows).

1. Fold a 30-inch square of cheesecloth into eight layers, and place it in a large sieve set over a deep nonreactive bowl. (Or, for serious Bulgarian street cred, tie the ends of the cheesecloth around the handle of a spoon after you've added the yogurt, and set it over the rim of a large glass jar so it can drip freely.)

2. Combine the yogurt with 1½ teaspoons kosher salt. Pour it into the cheesecloth, cover the top loosely with plastic, and let it sit at room temperature overnight, giving the yogurt plenty of time to release all its excess water. (It's super-acidic and cultured, so it won't go bad, but if this makes you squeamish, the whole thing can be done in the fridge; just allow twice as long for it to drain.)

3. After 12 to 15 hours, you should have 2 to 3 cups of thick, very creamy labneh remaining in the cheesecloth, and at least 5 cups of whey in the bowl. Use a spatula to scrape the labneh into a container, then keep it at room temperature if you're about to serve it; otherwise, cover and refrigerate.

4. Combine the water, 1 tablespoon kosher salt, and baking soda, and bring it to a boil.

5. Cut the pepper lengthwise, remove the seeds and white pith, and finely chop it. Cook in the boiling water for 30 seconds or so, just enough to take off the raw edge. Drain, and rinse with cool water so it cools completely.

8 cups Bulgarian yogurt
1½ teaspoons plus 1 tablespoon Morton kosher salt, divided
2 quarts water
½ teaspoon baking soda
1 small or ½ large mild green pepper, such as Anaheim or bell
⅓ cup extra-virgin olive oil
4 radishes, thinly sliced
½ teaspoon Maldon or other flaky sea salt
Pita (page 302) or crusty bread, for dipping

6. Spread the labneh on a serving platter or in a wide, shallow bowl, making a wide well in the center, so the cheese comes up the sides of the bowl a bit. Add the pepper, olive oil, and radishes to the middle; finish with a generous pinch of flaky sea salt. Serve with plenty of bread for dipping.

YEMENITE STEWED CHICKEN

YIELD: 6 TO 8 SERVINGS

My mom often made chicken with vegetables for dinner; it was a filling dish that she could throw into a single pot and leave bubbling on the stove without too much hands-on time. I loved the way the potatoes would soak up all the chicken fat, becoming nuggets of flavor in the stew. My mom also taught me how to pick a chicken fully clean of its meat, taking the time to excavate every juicy morsel clinging to the bones or hiding in the joints around the backbone. Make sure you do the same.

Whey, which you get when you make labneh (preceding recipe), is far from a throwaway ingredient. To me, it's just as valuable as the thick, velvety labneh; it's got this unmatchable light flavor with an acidic punch that makes it a no-brainer as a marinade. If you don't have the whey on hand, buttermilk is a great substitute.

1. Combine the whey, 1 tablespoon salt, and the sugar in a saucepan over low heat, and stir just until everything's dissolved. Set it aside until it's no longer hot.

2. If you're using a whole chicken, break it down to get two breasts, two wings, two thighs, and two drumsticks (see page 220 for a step-by-step guide); you can use or freeze the spine for stock. Cut the breasts in half, slicing through the rib bones, and combine all the chicken with the brine in a large ziplock bag. Seal, and refrigerate it for at least 4 hours or overnight.

3. When you're ready to cook, let the chicken come to room temperature. Combine the hawaij with the remaining 1½ teaspoons salt. Arrange all the pieces of chicken, skin side up, in a single layer on a plate (discard the brine). Sprinkle

(recipe continues)

4 cups whey (preceding recipe) or buttermilk
1 tablespoon plus 1½ teaspoons Morton kosher salt, divided
1 tablespoon sugar
1 whole chicken (4 to 5 pounds), or 2 breast halves, 2 wings, and 4 leg quarters
1 tablespoon hawaij (page 390)
¼ cup extra-virgin olive oil
2 cloves garlic, minced
1½-inch knob fresh ginger, peeled and minced
¼ teaspoon red-pepper flakes
1 yellow onion, chopped
2 large carrots, peeled and cut into 1-inch chunks
1 pound waxy yellow potatoes, such as Yukon Gold or fingerling, cut into 1-inch chunks
1 sprig fresh rosemary
1 orange, quartered, seeds removed
1 cup chicken stock
3 tablespoons lightly packed fresh parsley leaves
3 tablespoons lightly packed fresh mint leaves
½ cup plain yogurt, preferably full-fat

the hawaij mixture evenly over the chicken pieces, patting it in so it sticks.

4. Heat the olive oil in a Dutch oven or other heavy pot over medium heat. Add the chicken, skin side down, and leave it alone for 4 or 5 minutes so it becomes golden; you'll want to do this in two batches to avoid crowding the pot. Don't be afraid to decrease the heat if the spices in the pan seem to be getting too dark. Flip the chicken, and cook the other side for about 3 minutes, until it builds a little color; then remove it and set it aside.

5. Decrease the heat to medium-low. Combine the garlic, ginger, and red-pepper flakes in the same pot, and cook for 30 seconds or so, until they're fragrant. Add the onion, carrots, potatoes, and sprig of rosemary and continue to cook, stirring occasionally.

6. When you start seeing some color around the edges of the onions, squeeze in the juice from the orange to deglaze the pan, scraping up any brown bits with your spoon. Drop in the orange pieces, and add the chicken along with the stock. Bring it to a simmer, then reduce the heat to low. Cover the pot, and let it cook with lazy bubbles for about 1 hour, maybe longer, until the leg meat pulls easily off the bone with no pink juices and the potatoes are tender. Check the pot every 10 minutes or so, and if the bubbles are too rapid, bursting at the surface, move the pot partially off the burner, to ensure that the chicken doesn't dry out. Once it's done, remove and discard the rosemary.

7. To serve: Spoon a piece of chicken and some of the vegetables into a bowl. Chop the parsley and mint together, and pass them around with the yogurt for dolloping on top, along with knives to pull the tender meat off the bone and spoons for polishing off the savory broth.

4

✦✦✦

Fishing with My Father

My father has never left food on his plate. I've always known him to load up on large servings, and then dive in until the very last crumb is gone. There is a sameness to most of the things my father does; I can predict his movements. When he pulls his car into a parking spot, it will take him 15 minutes to leave it. He has to check the radio, turn on the air-conditioning, turn off the air-conditioning. He'll check his turn signals, on and off. He'll tap the side of the car a couple of times in the same spot. He is a man of habits. None of the knickknacks or furniture in his apartment have changed for decades. For years, he kept a small, stuffed Count Dracula doll hanging from the rearview mirror of his 1984 Subaru. He loved that little doll and would show it off to whoever was in the car, even when the count's black cape was faded to bronze by the sun.

My father kept the Dracula doll because he grew up in Oradea, Romania, which is in the Transylvania region, and was part of Hungary before my father was born. My father's father, Gaza Saja (pronounced "Shaya"), died when my father was still a toddler, his death indirectly connected to his defense of Jewish people at the height of World War II. He was Christian, but he'd married a Jewish woman, my grandmother Ilona. He was angered by the rampant anti-Semitism in Romania in 1944 and began to speak out against the Romanian government and its German allies to his friends and co-workers. His boss at the factory in which he worked was a Nazi supporter and told the authorities. As a form of punishment, my grandfather was sent to the front lines to fight against the Russians, whom the Germans (and therefore the Romanians) were battling. Not inclined to sacrifice himself on behalf of an army that wanted to exterminate his wife, he fled into the woods when he got the chance. He was captured by the Red Army and eventually died in a prison camp. It took my grandmother five years to find out what had happened to him.

Now a widow with a little boy, my grandmother got creative about trying to cover her expenses. She would buy a live pig, hire a butcher to slaughter and process the meat, and then sell sausages, bacon, and frozen pork meat from her house for a profit. She'd also buy grain alcohol, mix it with water and rum extract, and put that up for sale as "quality aged rum."

She was scrappy, but she wasn't much of a loving mother. She'd tell my father that he'd ruined her life. When she got a new boyfriend, my father began to move around a lot, living for long stretches with other relatives. When he was at home, his mother's boyfriend would get drunk and beat him. She forced my father to drop out of school at age eleven and get a job delivering firewood on a cargo train, and would punish him for spending money on bus fare to get home. He told me that sometimes he would walk around town at night, when other families were eating dinner and getting ready for bed, and occasionally they would give him food and let him sleep in their houses. At age seventeen, after a confrontation with his mother's boyfriend, my father moved out altogether, taking up residence in the horse barn that belonged to his boss at the firewood company. The next year, he got a job at a large clothing factory, ironing the same part of the same style of pants every day. With that job, he was able to buy clothes for himself, and such items as socks and nice shoes for the first time in his life. He started taking night classes to earn his diploma. He got into sharpshooting, and took lessons in that, too. He learned that he liked to work with machines, and that he was good at it.

Despite that progress, my dad's wandering life continued. He became infatuated with the Israeli general Moshe Dayan and decided he should go to Israel to become a sharpshooter with the Israeli army. Since Romania was a communist country at the time, in order to move, he had to leave everything behind. He arrived in Israel not knowing a word of Hebrew, and met my mother. Less than a year later, she was pregnant. He fought in the 1973 Yom Kippur War, posted with his machine gun on the front lines. A lot of his friends were killed; he used to tell me stories of watching people right beside him get torn up by fighter-jet bullets. My sister was born just after he returned home; my mother told me her name, "Anit," means "answer," because my father's safe return home from war was an answer to my mom's prayers. By then, however, my parents' relationship was already going downhill. I was born in 1978, and, just two years later, my father struck out for America, on the move again without speaking the language of his new home.

After my parents' divorce, there was a long period when I didn't see my father, even though we both lived in or around Philadelphia. Then we started having Saturday visits with him. He was working at a thrift store and brought us the items that no one would purchase. If we didn't like the gifts, he would get upset and spend an hour explaining how all the cool kids were wearing thick red wool sweaters with bright, glittery material woven into them. My sister and I eventually made a pact that we would always fawn over whatever he'd brought: "I always wanted a pair of tight white shorts with the flags of a dozen countries printed on them! How did you know?!" We'd throw the items in the trash as soon as he left.

Most Saturdays, I went bowling with Dad and then to Boston Market. Crappy used toys and clothes, bowling, and roasted chicken: that's how it usually went. Occasionally, though, my dad would take me fishing south of Atlantic City. It was his idea of father-son bonding. Every time, the same ritual would unfold. He'd rent a 12-foot flat-bottomed boat with an engine no more powerful than a trolling motor. He'd pack a lunch of turkey-and-cheese sandwiches on white bread that would slosh around all day long in a cooler with a bunch of ice and sodas. By the time we removed the ziplock bag from the cooler, it would be dripping with water, and the sandwiches would be all squished up. As we cruised over shallow water, the tide would inevitably fall, and we'd get stuck in the marsh and have to wait for it to come back in so we could motor back out.

But—we would catch fish. The part of the day that I loved, which redeemed the horrible sandwiches and the hours of listening to my dad repeat the same stories he'd told me on each outing, was the frying of the fish. It was a moment when I truly looked up to him and felt happy in his presence. We'd take the fish home and scale and gut them in his kitchen sink. My dad would take the tiny fish—bones still intact—and drag them through seasoned flour before adding them to a pan of sizzling butter. Then we would squeeze half a lemon over the fish, sprinkle them with salt, and pull the golden, tender flesh away from the bones, swabbing it in the nutty brown butter, before eating it. The first time my dad taught me to do this, I was blown away. For all the things my dad struggled with, on those fishing trips he was trying to be the best father he knew how to be. Even with the miserable, soggy sandwiches and the long, boring hours on the boat, at the end we were both rewarded with the gift of fried fish.

PAN-FRIED WHOLE FISH WITH BROWN BUTTER

YIELD: 4 SERVINGS

When my father and I went fishing, we'd eat whatever we caught—often perch or bluefish, but, to be honest, whatever was swimming around. Given the choice, though, I prefer speckled trout. As the small fish cook, all the collagen around the bones melts into the meat, giving you a richness that you'd miss if you just cooked a fillet. As a kid, I loved pulling that succulent meat off the bone, tasting the brightness of lemon against the crispy browned skin.

If you're up for a gardening adventure, try planting a laurel tree, which is where bay leaves come from. They're easy to grow and will bring you years of culinary pleasure every time you pluck a leaf for your cooking. For something as delicate as this dish, I love how they give a subtle savory character to the rich brown butter, one that's accented by the funk of the dried Persian lime and the fresh lime zest. They also add a gorgeous deep green color to the finished plate.

- 4 whole small fish, gutted and fully scaled (preferably about 1 pound each)
- 2 teaspoons Morton kosher salt
- 4 teaspoons grated dried Persian lime, divided
- ½ cup all-purpose flour
- ½ pound (2 sticks) unsalted butter, roughly chopped
- 8 small sprigs fresh thyme
- 4 cloves garlic, not peeled, lightly crushed
- 4 fresh bay leaves (or 2 dried)
- 1 large lime
- ¼ cup lightly packed fresh parsley leaves, chopped

1. Pat the fish dry inside and out, then season each one with about ½ teaspoon each of salt and grated dried lime. Let them sit while you get the pan ready.
2. Set the flour in a plate or shallow bowl. Pull out a large skillet, one that's big enough for the fish to fit comfortably with space to move; you'll probably need to cook one or two at a time.
3. Add the butter, thyme, garlic, and bay leaves to the pan over medium heat. Once the butter is completely melted and foamy—a warm, deep gold—dredge the fish all over with flour and shake off any excess. Lay them side by side in the

(recipe continues)

pan, and cook for 5 minutes or so, until the bottoms have browned; every minute or two, tilt the pan and spoon the butter all over the top. As you do this, monitor the color of the butter, which will be a reflection of the heat; if you notice it starting to darken, take the heat down a bit.

4. Use a thin spatula to flip the fish delicately (move it away from you rather than toward you, so the fat doesn't spatter). Cook for another 4 or 5 minutes, then transfer the fish to a serving dish and cook the rest.

5. Spoon about 2 tablespoons of the butter from the pan over the fish. Zest the lime, grate the zest, and sprinkle it all over the tops of the fish, along with the remaining 2 teaspoons grated dried lime and the parsley. Squeeze the fresh lime juice over the fish to finish, and serve immediately.

A GOOD TURKEY SANDWICH

YIELD: 4 SANDWICHES

They say building the perfect sandwich requires a degree in architecture. Each element of this turkey sandwich—which I could only have dreamed of having while fishing with my father—serves a purpose and is equally important to the structure. The baking technique gives you crisped-up bread like you'd find on a grilled cheese while allowing the provolone to melt over the contents (creamy avocado, sweet peppers, salty olives) like a cozy blanket. Make sure you get real turkey breast, sliced from an actual piece of meat, not the processed stuff that's shaped into a round soccer ball at the deli; ask for meat from a single, intact breast. And don't worry if you're going fishing (or anyplace else where it can't be toasted)—you can eat this sandwich cold and it'll still be delicious, without sticking to the roof of your mouth like ours did.

12	Castelvetrano olives, pitted
¼	cup mayonnaise
8	thick slices any crusty whole-grain bread
1	pound turkey breast, thinly sliced
4	ounces provolone cheese, sliced
1	large avocado, sliced
1	roasted red bell pepper, seeded and sliced
1	large tomato, cored and sliced thin
1	teaspoon Morton kosher salt
	Freshly ground black pepper, for sprinkling
2	tablespoons extra-virgin olive oil

1. Heat the oven to 500°F with a rack in the upper-middle position of the oven.

2. Finely chop the olives, and combine them with the mayo; spread this mixture evenly over four slices of bread, all the way to the edges. Layer ¼ pound turkey and 1 ounce provolone on top of each.

3. Divide the avocado among the other four slices of bread,

followed by the red pepper, then the tomato. Sprinkle the salt and some cracked black pepper over the tomatoes.

4. Drizzle the olive oil over a rimmed baking sheet, and set it in the oven for 2 minutes or so, just long enough for the oil to get hot. Carefully pull the sheet from the oven and tile all the bread to fit in the pan, filled sides up. Toast for 3 to 5 minutes, until the cheese is melted over the turkey.

5. With a wide spatula, flip the cheesy bread slices over on top of their buddies. Slice diagonally, and serve right away.

HUNGARIAN PAPRIKASH

My father's childhood was in a part of Romania that's very close to the border with Hungary. I can imagine my father's mother, whom I never got to meet, making sure that her butcher provided her with all the meat trimmings as well as whatever cut she purchased. She wouldn't have let that meat go to waste; she'd have figured out something to do with it to feed her family. Homemade pork sausage in a rich, paprika-stoked curry with dumplings is a meal she might have been able to make without a lot of money on hand. It's a stick-to-your-ribs kind of meal, perfect for a cold winter night, well spiced but not too spicy. The urfa pepper is special—its smoky, almost chocolaty flavor adds so many layers—but if you have trouble finding it, you can up the Aleppo to 1 tablespoon.

For all its depth of flavor, the stew itself comes together relatively quickly. Don't be daunted by the homemade sausage and dumplings: neither requires any unusual equipment beyond a stand mixer, nor will they set you back too much time, and both can easily be made ahead. You should also feel free to substitute store-bought bulk sausage and egg noodles to save time.

8	tablespoons (1 stick) unsalted butter
½	yellow onion, chopped
2	cloves garlic, minced
½	teaspoon minced fresh ginger
1	dried árbol chili pepper
1½	tablespoons smoked paprika
1	tablespoon sweet paprika
2¼	teaspoons Aleppo pepper
1½	teaspoons urfa pepper flakes
¼	teaspoon cayenne pepper
2	teaspoons Morton kosher salt
1½	tablespoons tomato paste
¼	cup all-purpose flour
1	quart chicken stock
	Grated zest of 1 orange
	Grated zest of 1 lemon
½	cup sour cream
1	large head broccoli
1	recipe tarragon dumplings (recipe follows)
1	recipe fennel sausage (page 54)
2	tablespoons extra-virgin olive oil, divided

1. Cut the butter into a few chunks, and melt it in a large pot or Dutch oven over medium-low heat. As soon as it melts, add the onion, garlic, and ginger; cook for 8 to 10 minutes, stirring occasionally, until the onion is soft and translucent, without any color.

2. Stir in the dried chili, spices, and salt, and let them all toast for 2 minutes or so before adding the tomato paste; use a wooden spoon to break it up as it starts to melt and caramelize. After a minute, whisk the flour into the pot to make a roux. Cook for a couple of minutes, just to get rid of the flour's raw flavor.

3. Add the chicken stock and citrus zest, and increase the heat to high. Once the sauce is simmering, take the heat back to medium-low, and let the stew lazily bubble, without much movement above the surface, for 30 minutes or so, until it thickens a bit and the flavors have concentrated.

4. Remove the pot from the heat, and whisk in the sour cream to make a smoky, creamy, velvet-smooth sauce. Resist the

(recipe continues)

urge to skim off any of the fat, since that's what's carrying so much of the flavor.

5. Meanwhile, heat the broiler with a rack 4 or 5 inches from the heating element. Cut the broccoli into small florets, place them on a large rimmed baking sheet, and toss to coat with 1 tablespoon olive oil. Break the sausage into approximately 1-inch pieces and add it to the sheet, spread in a single layer. Broil, rotating every 2 minutes or so, until everything is golden with nice browned edges, 5 to 6 minutes total. Watch closely to make sure the broiler doesn't scorch anything.

6. Scrape the broccoli and sausage directly into the pot of paprikash sauce. Toss the tarragon dumplings with the remaining tablespoon of olive oil, spread them on the same baking sheet, and broil just as you did the sausage and broccoli. They'll take about as long to crisp up.

7. Stir the dumplings into the paprikash. Serve it right away, or keep the stew in the fridge—it makes killer leftovers for a few days.

TARRAGON DUMPLINGS

YIELD: ABOUT 2 POUNDS

Paprikash is classically served with simple flour noodles like spaetzle. Those are great, but I like something a little more substantial, to help soak up all the delicious sauce. These soft, tender dumplings do the trick, with just a hint of tarragon, to keep them bright with lots of flavor of their own. They're just as great with slow-roasted lamb (page 254).

Dumplings are fun to make, even if you're a beginner, since they come together quickly without any equipment. All you need to do is be gentle enough so that they don't toughen up and get chewy. This recipe makes enough for the paprikash, but feel free to double it if you're serving the dumplings on their own; sauce them as you would pasta (they're excellent with fast tomato sauce, page 155).

1. If there is any excess liquid in the ricotta, pour it off or (if it's especially loose) strain the ricotta in a fine-mesh sieve for 15 minutes.

2. Put the water and 2 tablespoons salt in a pot, and bring to a rolling boil.

3. Meanwhile, strip the leaves from the tarragon, mince them, and stir them into the drained ricotta with the egg, lemon zest, baking powder, and remaining 2 teaspoons salt. Gently fold in the flour until just incorporated.

4. Flour a work surface and your hands, then pour out the dough and sprinkle a little more flour on top of it. With a bench scraper or flat spatula, pull it into a messy, slightly tacky mass. Gently knead it, using the heels of your hands to press it flat and fold it over itself just until it forms a smooth dough; you'll need to do this only a few times before it comes together. Flour as needed—it'll likely be a bit sticky— but be sure not to douse it with too much flour or it'll get tough.

5. Cut the dough in quarters with your bench scraper or a small knife. With lightly floured hands, delicately roll each piece into a long log about ½ inch in diameter.

6. Get a bowl ready for the dumplings before you cook them, since cooking happens pretty quickly. Working with one log at a time, cut it into 1-inch pieces, and keep a towel handy to wipe off your knife if it gets sticky. Drop the dumplings into the boiling water and cook for about 2 minutes total; as soon as they start floating, they'll need to cook for about 1 more minute. They're done when they're pillowy and light in the center.

7. Use a skimmer or slotted spoon to pull them out of the pot and drop them into the bowl (dumping them into a colander might beat them up). Once the water in the pot comes back to a boil, repeat with the remaining dough. Toss all the cooked dumplings with the olive oil to prevent sticking.

8. To use in the paprikash, follow the preceding recipe from this point. Otherwise, to serve the dumplings, warm a bit of olive oil in a pan over medium heat, sear them for a couple of minutes per side, and sauce as you would pasta or gnocchi. If you're not serving them right away, you can refrigerate them in an airtight container for up to 3 days.

1 pound ricotta
1 gallon water
2 tablespoons plus 2 teaspoons Morton kosher salt, divided
4 sprigs fresh tarragon
2 eggs
  Grated zest of 1 lemon
1 teaspoon baking powder
2 cups all-purpose flour, plus more for dusting
1 tablespoon extra-virgin olive oil

II

REBELLION
AND
REDEMPTION

5

✦✦✦

A Butcher and a Baker

I got my first job in the food-service industry by lying about my age. I'd been earning a paycheck since I was ten, baby-sitting for my uncle's sister, who had triplets. I needed the money. "We can't afford that" is probably the thing my mom said most to me when I was growing up. Starting when I was thirteen, I bought my own clothes, deodorant, even food for the house. With the cost of all that, I knew I needed to find work that was more lucrative. So I went around to the businesses in my neighborhood, asking for a job. Everywhere I went they said no. Then I realized that they all thought I was too young. So I changed my line at the next shop I walked into, which happened to be a local butcher shop, and told them I was sixteen. It was plausible; I was already close to 6 feet tall and growing facial hair. They hired me on the spot.

Hall's Meat Market was a neighborly kind of place, the sort of store where local families shopped not only for brisket or steak

but also for necessities that they had run out of at home, such as juice or milk. My job was to sweep the floors, stock the coolers with sodas, wash dishes, and break down boxes. While I was doing all that, though, I was paying attention to the food. I'd watch as the butchers and cooks cut up meat and stirred mayonnaise into macaroni salad. When they weren't watching, I'd sneak over to the meat slicer and use it to shave off some bologna for myself to eat. I was always secretly tasting things.

The butcher shop was kind of a boys' club; the other employees were always giving each other a hard time. I was intimidated by all of them, and they took advantage of that. One afternoon, one of the butchers told me, "Go over to the Rite-Aid across the street and tell the lady behind the register that we need twelve feet of fallopian tubes, quick!" I ran over and asked for it, only to be yelled at by the woman behind the counter (who happened to live on our street and knew my mom).

That was par for the course. But those guys were the gateway to one of my first real culinary breakthroughs. One day, the main butcher, an overweight young man, was cooking lunch for himself. As I walked by him, I noticed that there was something in his frying pan I'd never seen before. It looked to me like marshmallows. But why would he be pan-searing marshmallows in hot oil? Soon all the butchers were crowded around the sauté pan, talking about scallops and why they loved them so much. One of the butchers threw a pinch of red-pepper flakes into the pan and turned the scallops in them before serving himself. He left to eat the scallops, never offering me a bite. I saw one of the other butchers rip a piece of white bread off a loaf and dip it into the cooking oil, though. When no one was looking, I followed suit, using a piece of bread to soak up some of the leftover oil, which had been infused with the flavor of the scallops and chili flakes. I shoved it into my mouth. My eyes lit up. *I love scallops,* I thought.

Two years later, I was having more such revelations at my next job, just across the street, at Woehr's Bakery. I vividly remember peering at the cake display and ogling its contents: Fruit tarts with pastry cream hidden inside and a slick of apricot glaze to make them shine. Black Forest cakes. Carrot cakes. Red-velvet cakes. I'd walk the aisles of the bakery as if it were an art gallery or a museum, in awe of what was on display. I approached the babka, rugelach, and croissant-shaped schnecken with reverence, and took care to memorize each item. "What is Sachertorte?"

customers would ask. I'd respond with "Oh, the Sachertorte is my favorite! It's a rich chocolate cake layered with a bright apricot filling and topped with dark-chocolate icing. A specialty of Vienna." I would pride myself on getting all the elderly ladies to love me for the way I would describe the food. "Oh, cream-cheese pound cake is my favorite!" I'd say. "I have a slice every day, and I bring it home for dessert sometimes! The cream cheese makes it extra moist, and who can resist the chocolate icing on top?"

We had many regular customers, from the owner of a landscaping company who'd arrive at five each morning for his cup of black coffee, to a schizophrenic gentleman whom everyone called "Vietnam Tom." He spent every day sitting on a bench in front of the bakery, wearing his old army uniform. Everyone knew him as a neighborhood fixture. Mostly, he'd smile and wave as people would drive by or come into the bakery, but sometimes he'd point his fingers like a gun and pretend to aim and pull the trigger at select cars. I'd sit with Tom out front, talking about aliens, or his hypothesis that everyone would soon be dead. He was a gentle presence, though. When he was angry with you, the worst he would do was turn his back and start whistling.

My charm with the bakery's customers was matched by my attitude with the other employees. Whenever I could, I'd spend time with Mr. Jackson, an elderly African American man, who would perch on a stool, decorating birthday and Bar Mitzvah cakes. He'd sculpt bright-pink flowers out of icing, or squiggly blue lines, or beautiful cursive text that read "Congratulations Zoe!" or "Mazel Tov Jonathan!" I spent so much time hovering over him that he began to teach me how to write in icing and chocolate. The doughnut man, Cleveland, a sweet guy in his early thirties, allowed me to watch as he dropped the doughnuts into the fryer and flipped them with long wooden chopsticks. I'd neglect my duties at the register so I could toss the crullers in cinnamon sugar and dip the doughnuts in chocolate glaze. Cleveland and I would also smoke weed together in the back, then come in and plunder the bakery in a fit of the munchies. That was the only hint the folks at the bakery got of my alternate life as a misfit teenager. At the bakery, I was all charm—because I had respect for people who knew how to cook and bake. Everywhere else in my life was trouble.

KIBBEH NAYEH

My time working at the butcher shop introduced me to cuts of meat I'd never encountered. I was fascinated by the big chunks of beef—flat-iron roast, London broil—in their cooler and learned that lamb had a different flavor altogether when the butcher would hand me a piece as he ground it and I'd taste it, raw. I wasn't afraid. The other butchers saw that, and it seemed to impress them—maybe that's what made them keep me around.

The biggest lesson I learned while I was there: when you have great raw meat, treat it with the respect it deserves. This classic Lebanese dish does that beautifully. Don't be intimidated or deceived by the long list of ingredients: it's mostly warm spices and fresh herbs, with texture from the bulgur and walnuts. Somehow, they all pull out the best of the meat. Malawach (recipe follows)—crisp, light, and buttery—is the ideal accompaniment, but if you can't make it, you can substitute paratha or roti bought from an international market.

Since you're eating the meat raw, pay close attention to quality, for reasons of safety as well as for taste; it's worth the extra trouble of going to a butcher shop that you trust (or, better yet, making friends with a farmer). Grind the meat yourself if you can, but if that's not possible, you can talk to the person at the butcher counter to be certain it's fresh.

Malawach (recipe follows) or store-bought paratha or roti, for serving
- ¼ cup water
- 2 tablespoons bulgur wheat
- 1 clove garlic, minced
- Grated zest of ½ lemon
- 1 tablespoon lemon juice
- 1 tablespoon pomegranate molasses
- 2 teaspoons white-wine vinegar
- 2 teaspoons Aleppo pepper
- 2 teaspoons za'atar
- ¼ teaspoon ground cumin
- ¼ teaspoon smoked paprika
- ¼ teaspoon ground coriander
- ¼ teaspoon ground allspice
- 1 teaspoon Morton kosher salt
- ¼ cup extra-virgin olive oil
- 2 tablespoons lightly packed fresh mint leaves, chopped
- 2 tablespoons lightly packed fresh parsley leaves, chopped
- ¼ cup chopped walnuts, toasted
- 1 pound ground beef sirloin, lamb leg, or a combination
- 1 tablespoon oil from harissa (page 389), optional

1. If you're making malawach, make the dough first, proceeding with that recipe until it's ready to fry, and then keeping it chilled.

2. Heat the water in a small saucepan until it starts to simmer (there's so little of it that this won't take long at all). Put the bulgur wheat in a small heatproof bowl, and pour the water over it. Cover with plastic or foil, and set aside until all the water is absorbed and the bulgur has cooled completely, about 15 minutes.

3. In a large bowl, combine the garlic, lemon zest, lemon juice, pomegranate molasses, and vinegar with all the spices and salt. Whisking all along, stream in the olive oil, then add the fresh herbs along with the walnuts and bulgur (if there's any excess water in the bulgur, drain it off).

(recipe continues)

4. Tip the ground meat into the bowl, and use your fingers to rake it all delicately together, until it's thoroughly combined but still has a loose, light texture. Don't work the meat so hard that it warms up.

5. Serve the kibbeh nayeh immediately. If you've got harissa, use your knife to make shallow crosshatches over the top and drizzle its oil all over; otherwise, do so with olive oil. Fry the malawach so that they're piping-hot; people should feel free to make a bit of a mess at the table, ripping them and using them to scoop up the meat.

 MALAWACH

YIELD: 8 MALAWACH

Of all the types of breads that come from Yemen—and there are many—malawach is one of my favorites because it's so much fun to eat. Fried flatbread with flaky, buttery layers: what's not to like? It goes hand in hand with kibbeh nayeh but is just as much of a treat drizzled with honey, jam, or rose tahini (page 393). The dough does take a bit of work—nothing too hard, as long as you're focused and patient—making it an excellent treat to try on a lazy day at home. The rewards are plenty.

- 4½ cups (540 grams) all-purpose flour
- 1 tablespoon Morton kosher salt
- 1 tablespoon sugar
- 1⅓ cups water
- 7 tablespoons ghee, room temperature, divided
- 1 teaspoon white-wine vinegar
- 6 tablespoons butter, softened
- 1 cup canola oil

1. Combine the flour, salt, and sugar in a large mixing bowl. Add the water, 1 tablespoon of the ghee, and the vinegar; stir with your hand or a wooden spoon until the liquid has all been absorbed.

2. Spill the dough onto a nonfloured work surface and knead for 2 to 3 minutes, until it's pliable and moist with all the flour incorporated but still looks rough and doesn't feel totally smooth. Place it in a clean bowl and loosely cover for 30 minutes.

3. Remove the dough from the bowl and knead it on the same surface for another 3 minutes or so; this time, it should be smoother. Divide it into eight even pieces and roll each one into a smooth ball.

4. In a small bowl, combine the remaining 6 tablespoons ghee with the butter, then use a pastry brush to paint a thin

(recipe continues)

layer of this mixture over your work surface. Working with one ball of dough at a time, roll it into a roughly 10-inch round (don't worry about making a perfect circle). Brush a layer of the ghee mixture all over the top of the dough, approximately 2 teaspoons per piece.

5. Tightly roll the dough like a jelly roll, then coil it around itself like a cinnamon bun. Repeat with the rest, then arrange them all on a plate or baking sheet, cover with plastic, and refrigerate until they're firm and well chilled throughout, at least 1 hour and up to 2 days. You may also wrap them tightly and freeze for up to 1 month, then thaw them completely in the fridge before proceeding.

6. When you're ready to fry the malawach, roll out each piece of dough into a roughly 9-inch circle on a clean, nonfloured work surface. Stack them between pieces of parchment, foil, or plastic wrap as you finish. This step will allow you to stay organized and focused when you start frying.

7. Line a plate or baking sheet with paper towels and set it off to the side; heat the oven to 175°F. Place a skillet over high heat and pour in the canola oil. Once it's smoking hot, add one malawach and immediately reduce the heat to medium. Cook for 1 to 2 minutes, until the bottom and edges are golden, then flip and cook for an additional minute or two. If, as you cook, the edges are browning faster than the top, carefully tilt the pan and baste a bit of oil over the dough, particularly if your skillet is on the larger side.

8. Move the fried malawach to the lined plate and keep them warm in the oven while you cook the rest, leaving the oil on medium heat for the rest of the process. Serve immediately, while the bread is still quite warm.

SPICY SCALLOP ROLLS

Ever since that first little taste of scallops in the butcher shop, I've loved them. This sandwich capitalizes on their buttery, meaty texture; it might remind you of a lobster roll, but the fresh flavors—jalapeño, cilantro, lime—are similar to those in Vietnamese banh mi. It's the best of both worlds.

1. Heat your oven to 450°F with a rack in the middle. If there's a tough muscle on the sides of the scallops, use your paring knife to remove it. Pat the scallops dry, and lightly sprinkle the tops with ½ teaspoon salt.

2. Line a plate with paper towels, and add 2 tablespoons oil to a large skillet over high heat. As soon as it starts smoking, carefully add each scallop (the oil may spatter a bit), leaving at least an inch between them, and decrease the heat just a bit, to medium-high, so the oil doesn't scorch. Make this in batches if you risk overcrowding the pan.

3. Don't bother the scallops—they'll stick to the pan until they're ready to flip. As they cook, they'll first form a crust on the bottom, and then color will start to creep up the sides as they turn opaque. When you can see a distinctly golden rim along the edges, just about ⅛ inch thick, flip, and cook the other side for 20 to 30 seconds to keep them medium-rare. Move the scallops to the lined plate, where they'll cool completely.

4. Mince 1 jalapeño. If the cucumber has seeds, scoop them out first, then cut it into roughly ¼-inch dice; you should have about ½ cup chopped. Thinly slice 2 tablespoons mint. Combine all these ingredients in a bowl with the scallion, mayonnaise, ginger, and remaining ¼ teaspoon salt.

5. Split the hot-dog buns, and brush or drizzle the center of each with about 1 teaspoon olive oil. Toast the buns, oiled side up, for 3 to 4 minutes, until the tops are toasted golden.

6. Slice the remaining jalapeño, and set it aside. Cut the scallops into quarters, and toss them in the mixing bowl until they're coated in the dressing; then divide them among the hot-dog buns. Serve the jalapeño alongside the rolls, with the lime wedges and the remaining 2 tablespoons fresh mint, encouraging people to add their own garnishes.

¾ pound sea scallops (10–20 count, about 12)
½ teaspoon plus ¼ teaspoon Morton kosher salt, divided
2 tablespoons plus 4 teaspoons extra-virgin olive oil, divided
2 jalapeños, seeds and pith removed, divided
¼ medium cucumber, preferably seedless
3 tablespoons lightly packed fresh mint leaves, divided
1 scallion, sliced
3 tablespoons mayonnaise
½ teaspoon minced fresh ginger
4 high-quality hot-dog buns
1 lime, quartered

YOGURT POUND CAKE WITH
CARDAMOM-LEMON SYRUP

YIELD: 1 VERY BIG CAKE

One of my very favorite dishes at the bakery was a cream-cheese pound cake. The cream cheese made it moister than a traditional pound cake, although, in making it myself, I've found that using yogurt instead maintains a more delicate crumb. The syrup, which you add to the still-warm cake, takes that moistness to the next level. It's understated, but magnifies many of the flavors that are already going on in the cake. At first, you'll feel that all that liquid can't possibly get absorbed, but it soaks right in without causing the cake to lose any of its structural integrity. You might even start adding a soak to the rest of your cake repertoire.

½ pound (2 sticks) unsalted butter, softened, plus more for the pan
3½ cups cake flour, plus more for the pan
1½ teaspoons baking powder
½ teaspoon Morton kosher salt
3½ cups sugar, divided
1 lemon
1 cup full-fat Greek yogurt, room temperature, plus more for serving
4 eggs
6 egg yolks
1 teaspoon vanilla extract
1 cup water
¼ cup extra-virgin olive oil, plus more for serving
8 cardamom pods, crushed
2 cups blackberries, halved

1. Heat the oven to 350°F. Generously grease and flour a Bundt or tube pan.

2. Sift the cake flour, and combine it with the baking powder and salt.

3. Add 2½ cups sugar to a large mixing bowl or the bowl of a stand mixer. Grate the zest of the lemon and rub all the zest into the sugar; reserve half of the lemon for the cake soak.

4. Add the butter and yogurt to the mixing bowl, and cream everything with an electric mixer or the paddle attachment of the stand mixer on high speed for 5 minutes. You want the mixture to be light in color, with plenty of air in it.

5. Add the eggs and the yolks one at a time, mixing between additions, followed by the vanilla. Don't worry: the batter will look broken and curdled, but that's okay. Gradually add the flour mixture, and beat on low until just incorporated. Scrape the batter into the prepared pan. Lift the pan a couple inches off the counter, and let it drop evenly; do this a few times, to get rid of any air bubbles in the batter.

6. Bake on the center rack for 50 to 60 minutes, rotating the pan once, after 30 minutes. The cake is ready when a knife comes out clean.

7. While the cake bakes, make the soak: Combine the remaining cup of sugar with the water and olive oil in a saucepan. Squeeze the lemon juice in, and drop in the lemon with the cardamom pods. Bring the mixture to a simmer,

(recipe continues)

then cover and remove from the heat until the cake is ready. (The oil and water will stay separate, which is fine.)

8. Once you've pulled the cake from the oven, let it cool for about 10 minutes; strain the syrup, and discard all the solids.

9. Use a thin knife to cut about sixteen deep slits all over the cake, then gradually pour the syrup all over, ¼ cup at a time, pausing between pours to let each one soak in. Let the cake cool completely in the pan before inverting it onto a cake plate or cutting board. Serve each slice with a dollop of yogurt, a drizzle of olive oil, and a pile of fresh berries.

 BLUEBERRY RUGELACH YIELD: 18 PASTRIES

Rugelach were another among my favorites at Woehr's Bakery, and I didn't discriminate between the fillings: raspberry jam, chocolate ganache, poppy seeds that had been ground up with a little bit of sugar. You don't see rugelach in many bakeries in the South, so whenever I get my hands on them, they still make me nostalgic for my years working at the bakery. There's almost nothing better than eating one warm out of the oven, an opportunity you'll rarely get unless you make the pastries yourself.

The filling can be made ahead (or, if you prefer, you can always substitute a cup of your favorite jam). The dough itself contains no sugar, getting all its sweetness from the lemon glaze and a swipe of simple syrup, so the filling really shows through. The only challenge is being patient between a few stints of chilling the pastries before baking, but you can do that completely on your own time.

1. To make the dough: Use an electric mixer or your stand mixer with the paddle attachment to whip the cream cheese, butter, and vanilla on medium speed until the combination is light and airy.

2. Add the flour and salt all at once. Mix, starting on low speed and gradually increasing to medium, until it's completely combined.

3. Dump the dough onto a lightly floured surface and shape it into a 7-to-8-inch square, about 1 inch thick. Wrap it tightly in plastic and refrigerate for at least 2 hours, until it's cool to the touch. This dough keeps well, so you can store it in the fridge days ahead, or freeze it and thaw it completely in the refrigerator when you're ready.

4. To make the filling: Combine the blueberries, ½ cup honey, grated zest of one lemon, and 2 tablespoons lemon juice in a saucepan over medium-low heat. Let it stew, stirring occasionally and breaking the berries apart with your spoon; decrease the heat if you're worried it'll scorch. Once it's significantly thicker, with slow, steady bubbles, combine the cornstarch and 1 teaspoon water to make a slurry, then whisk it into the berries.

5. After 50 to 60 minutes of cooking, the jam should be so thick that when you scrape your spatula across the bottom of the pan, it stays dry for just a moment before the berries crowd back in. Remove the pan from the heat and add the remaining 2 tablespoons honey. Let the jam cool completely before you fill the dough.

6. When it's time to assemble the pastries, if the dough is too hard to yield to your rolling pin, let it sit at room temperature for 15 or 20 minutes, until it's malleable but still very cold to the touch. Generously flour your work surface, a rolling pin, and the dough itself, then roll it into a rectangle about 12 by 18 inches, using a bench scraper or the side of your hand to push in and reinforce the edges so they stay neat and straight. Dust it with more flour if it seems likely to stick or tear.

7. Cut the dough in half along its width (making two 12-by-9-inch pieces), and spread the filling evenly in a very thin layer over both halves, leaving a ½-inch border all around. Make two 12-inch logs by rolling the longer side inward into a snug spiral. A bench scraper or thin metal spatula is helpful for manipulating the dough.

½ pound cream cheese, softened
½ pound (2 sticks) unsalted butter, softened
2 teaspoons vanilla extract
2 cups all-purpose flour, plus more for dusting
¼ teaspoon Morton kosher salt
3 cups blueberries
½ cup plus 2 tablespoons honey, divided
Grated zest of 1½ lemons, divided
3 tablespoons lemon juice, divided
1 teaspoon cornstarch
1 teaspoon plus ¼ cup water, divided
1 egg yolk
1 tablespoon milk
¼ cup granulated sugar
½ cup confectioners' sugar, sifted

8. Stick both logs, seam side down, on a plate or sheet pan, and cover loosely with plastic wrap. Refrigerate them for at least 30 minutes and up to 1 day, until they've firmed up.

9. When you're ready to bake, heat the oven to 375°F and line a baking sheet with parchment. Make an egg wash by beating together the egg yolk and milk.

10. Trim the ends from the dough and cut each log into nine slices (about 1¼ inches each), cleaning off your knife between cuts. Space the rugelach on the baking sheet just 1 inch apart, with the dough (not the spiral) facing up, and brush the egg wash over the tops. Bake for 40 to 50 minutes, rotating the pan after 20 minutes, until the tops are a deep, even gold.

11. While the pastries bake, make a simple syrup by combining the granulated sugar and remaining ¼ cup water in a saucepan over medium heat until the sugar dissolves. Separately, for the citrus glaze, combine the confectioners' sugar, grated zest of ½ lemon, and the last tablespoon of lemon juice; it should be pretty thick.

12. As soon as the rugelach are out of the oven, brush the simple syrup over their tops. Let them cool slightly before drizzling the citrus glaze over them, and use a thin metal spatula to carefully lift the cookies from the parchment.

6

✦✦✦

Arrested for the Munchies

I didn't mind breaking the law, and I enjoyed doing a lot of drugs. I fell in with a rough crowd when I was in eighth grade and began smoking cigarettes and weed, hanging out with drug dealers and older kids who carried guns, whenever I wasn't working at the butcher shop or the bakery. These were kids who, like me, were left on their own and seemed to have nothing better to do than chase trouble. We'd steal cell phones from people's cars and drive out to West Philly to trade them for an ounce of pot. We'd get into large brawls that included knives. We'd hang out in a park, drinking and smoking, and pick on a crackhead named Pookie who lived in the neighborhood. Every once in a while, just because we felt like it, we'd beat the crap out of Pookie. He was a big guy, six foot four and 250 pounds, but he was strung out on crack all the time and never fought back. We were like this roaming mass of negative energy looking for an outlet.

I was along for the ride but knew, on some level, that this wasn't who I really was. I just didn't feel I had many other options. I was angry, and I kept getting angrier, feeling shortchanged by life in general. Maybe that was because my family was so poor, yet so surrounded by money. I'd get picked up by a friend in his family's Rolls-Royce to go to their beachside mansion for the weekend. His dad would give us a wad of cash and tell us to have fun at the arcade. Then I'd come home to my bedroom, with its tiny little IKEA bed shoved in a corner, so short for my lanky frame that my feet hung all the way off the end.

I couldn't articulate why any of this bothered me. I would just shoplift, vandalize cars, run from the police, and take off to parties in New Jersey or Delaware, fueled by 40-ounce bottles of malt liquor. I stole my mom's car and went with a friend to Atlantic City for a couple of nights of complete debauchery, staying in abandoned houses and running out on the bill in restaurants. Eventually, I was pulled over by the police for driving without my headlights on at three in the morning. The city was so bright, I hadn't noticed. "How do I know you're not driving around casing houses?" the cop asked. *That's not a bad idea,* I thought to myself. He arrested us, and my mom had to make her way to Atlantic City to bail me out and drive me home. You'd think that would've woken me up, but I wasn't worried about disappointing her. All consequences from this mischief felt remote enough not to matter.

Food punctuated all of these bad deeds. We were always making pit stops for Italian hoagies, those sandwiches filled with layers of provolone and mortadella, pepperoni and salami. They'd put Italian dressing all over the hoagie, redolent with oregano and garlic, and I'd ask them to spread mayonnaise on the bread, too, with spicy banana peppers on top. I adored this sandwich, with all the meat and cheese, the juiciness of the vinaigrette and creaminess of the mayo, and the acidic crunch of the peppers. We'd go to the corner store, owned by a friend's Jamaican family. They were selling weed from the store—hanging out in the back room, we'd be surrounded by drug dealers and loaded guns—but they made a great Jamaican beef patty. It was a little like an empanada, filled with a meat ragù that was dosed with chilies and bright-yellow curry powder. We also ate a ton of cheesesteaks, and fries topped with mozzarella and baked in the pizza oven to become a gooey, delicious mess.

And then there were the Egg Wars.

The Egg Wars began after my friend Aaron's father, a Jewish real-estate developer, made it big and bought a large house with a massive basement that we teenagers took over. It became our drug-and-alcohol dungeon, filled with couches and bongs. We'd party there, then head upstairs, high, and raid his parents' refrigerator. Aaron's mom was from the Philippines and was a wonderful cook. She'd make curries and slow-cook chicken feet so that they'd be tender enough for her to chew off every little piece of meat. Even as a teenager, I was excited and happy to devour those chicken feet; I never gave it a second thought. And her fridge was always well stocked.

At some point, inspired by that abundance, we decided to have cooking competitions. We would look over the ingredients, salivating. So many options! Bacon, lettuce, leftover Chinese takeout, hot dogs, pickles, maple syrup, cheddar cheese, and eggs. We'd all grab what we wanted and run to different ends of the kitchen to prep. A stopwatch would be set for 20 minutes, and we'd have to perform. I'd whip up a hash of caramelized onion, potato, and bacon, which I'd serve over a circle of raw kale, with its crimped sides facing outward. Then I'd perch two poached eggs on top, and add a lemon slice shaped into a spiral to flank this glorious presentation. Meanwhile, my buddy would squirt maple syrup over bacon and put it in the microwave to dry and get sweet and chewy. That wasn't bad, I have to say, but I'd almost always win, out of sheer kitchen skills.

We'd usually eat the entire contents of the fridge, leaving behind only a half-bottle of yellow mustard and a mountain of dishes for somebody else to clean. It was always a giant mess. Eventually, Aaron's mom got sick of the routine and the dirty dishes. She called the cops on us. We were back downstairs in the basement when we heard someone scream, "Get on the floor!" The police were there, guns drawn, and they scared the crap out of us. We were arrested on the spot. Later, in court, we were lined up with some of our homemade bongs and bottles of malt liquor as evidence. I remember sitting in the courtroom next to a giant bong we'd made out of an old bargain pretzel bucket. The judge was serious with me; this wasn't my first time in court. "One more time getting in trouble and you'll be sent away to juvenile detention camp," he told me. He gave my mom a card with a number for the camp on it, and she kept it up on the refrigerator so I had to see it every time I grabbed some orange juice.

I was sentenced to community service and given the option of picking up trash in a public park or volunteering at a local hospital. I picked the hospital, and, in short order, managed to convince my superiors to transfer me to the kitchen. There I served my "punishment" enjoyably, dicing onions and chopping celery and carrots for hospital meals. Any repercussions of my actions had yet to feel real to me.

GREEN BUTTER

I f only I'd known this recipe back in the days of the Egg Wars, it would have made me the reigning champion. Pastrami—usually thinly sliced and piled onto your deli sandwich—achieves an entirely different level of good when you get it whole, sear it, and use it as the foundation for a pan of soft, crazy-creamy scrambled eggs. (Sliced pastrami will work just fine, if that's all you can get.)

1. Quarter the onion, then thickly slice it; chop the pastrami into ½-inch pieces. Combine them both with the butter, thyme, and salt in a large nonstick pan, then turn the stove to medium-low heat. Toss everything to combine and slowly caramelize in the pan for 15 minutes or so, stirring every so often.

2. Meanwhile, beat the eggs in a large bowl, then stir in the yogurt. Don't worry about getting it completely smooth— a little variation in texture is good. Set aside.

3. When most of the fat has rendered from the meat and the onions are just browning along the edges but still have plenty of texture and body, use a slotted spoon to remove them from the pan, leaving the fat behind. Discard the thyme.

4. Reduce the heat to low, and add the scallions; cook them until they're lightly softened. Pour the eggs into the pan in an even layer, and don't touch them for 30 seconds. Drag the wide edge of a rubber spatula all the way across the pan a few times, as if you were slicing a pizza, then leave the pan alone for another 30 seconds.

5. Continue this process of intermittent scrambling for 3 to 4 minutes, until the eggs are mostly set, with medium curds but still runny in some places. At this point, pinch the cream cheese into large chunks, and dollop it throughout the eggs; fold in the pastrami and onions. With your spatula, pull everything around gingerly until it's all incorporated but distinct creamy pockets still remain—another minute or so. Serve right away.

1 yellow onion
½ pound pastrami
2 tablespoons unsalted butter
1 sprig fresh thyme
1 teaspoon Morton kosher salt
8 eggs
⅓ cup Greek yogurt
2 scallions, sliced
2 ounces (¼ cup) cream cheese

ZA'ATAR TOAD IN THE HOLE

Toad in the hole is a great time-honored way of combining two of the great food groups—bread and eggs. It's fun to eat and fun to make, easy enough for a weekday morning but special enough for a Sunday. I learned the mayo trick from making grilled cheese; it allows the bread to get really crispy without burning (and its flavor fades to the background, so even people who reject it on their sandwiches will embrace it wholeheartedly). Mayo is also the perfect vehicle for za'atar, and together they create a great crust on the bread. A simple but bright tomato "salad" spooned on top provides a little extra dimension, and when you burst the egg's yolk with your fork, everything comes together in a perfect sauce.

1. Combine the tomato, scallions, olive oil, lemon juice, and kosher salt in a bowl. Set aside.

2. In a separate bowl, combine the mayonnaise and za'atar, and spread evenly over both sides of each slice of bread. Use a cookie cutter or a knife to cut a 2-to-3-inch hole in the middle of each slice. Discard the rounds, or keep them to fry with everything else.

3. Melt the butter in a large cast-iron or nonstick skillet over medium-high heat. Once the foam subsides, add the bread. Crack each egg into a bowl, then carefully tip each into the center of a bread slice. Do this in batches if you need to— leave plenty of space between the slices of bread, so you can flip them. Leave alone for 2 or 3 minutes, until the bottom of the bread is nicely browned. Use a thin spatula to loosen any stuck-on edges, then flip, and cook for another minute, just until the egg white is set. Once the bread is out, if you like, fry the removed rounds, about 1 minute per side, and keep them to serve atop the toast.

4. Spoon the tomatoes and scallions over each piece of bread, draining off any excess juice. Sprinkle a bit of flaky sea salt over the top, and eat right away.

1 small tomato, cored and chopped
2 scallions, sliced
1 tablespoon extra-virgin olive oil
1 tablespoon lemon juice
¼ teaspoon Morton kosher salt
½ cup mayonnaise
2 tablespoons za'atar
4 thick slices wheat or rye bread
1 tablespoon unsalted butter
4 eggs
Maldon or other flaky sea salt, to finish

Eggs poached in a spicy, savory tomato sauce: this dish serves itself. It's my go-to when I show up at someone's house and everyone is hungry. Chances are, there are eggs and a can of tomatoes on hand. Outside of that foundation, you can be as creative or as simple about adding anything else as you like.

Jerusalem artichokes, if you've never had them, taste and feel like a cross between potatoes and artichoke hearts; along with the fava beans, they make this dish special. They do need to be prepared separately, but you can do that in advance if it makes your life (and cooking timeline) easier. If you have trouble tracking either ingredient down, substitute any root vegetable—turnips, potatoes, even beets—for the Jerusalem artichokes, and a cup of shelled fresh or frozen beans, such as limas, for the fava beans.

Once you put pan to stove, the rest of the dish comes together quite quickly, so, for the sake of the vegetables' flavor and texture, make sure everything is prepped and ready to go. Dress it up or down with your favorite vegetables or meats—whatever's on hand—along with any herbs and spices you like. Tomatoes are the perfect backdrop. You'll need one egg per person, as few as two or as many as six. Part of the fun is making this dish your own, but one word of advice: try it with the zhoug, a spicy Yemeni green chile sauce, like the Middle Eastern approach to pesto. Its fresh, herbal heat is the perfect finishing touch.

Plenty of water, for the Jerusalem artichokes, fava beans, and an ice bath
1 tablespoon plus 2 teaspoons Morton kosher salt, divided
½ pound Jerusalem artichokes
1 pound fava beans in their shells
3 tablespoons extra-virgin olive oil
1 pint cherry tomatoes, halved
1 small red bell pepper, seeded and thinly sliced
1 small green bell pepper, seeded and thinly sliced
1 small yellow onion, thinly sliced
2 cloves garlic, minced
One 28-ounce can peeled whole tomatoes
1 egg per person
¼ cup zhoug (page 395)

1. Fill a large pot with the water and 1 tablespoon salt, and bring to a boil. Thoroughly scrub the Jerusalem artichokes; if they're large or unevenly sized, cut them into even chunks. Boil for 30 to 35 minutes, until they're about the consistency of a cooked potato, easily pierced with a knife but not falling apart. Drain, and when they're cool enough to handle, slice into little coins.

2. Fill another pot with water and bring it to a boil; meanwhile, prepare an ice bath. Cook the fava beans for 5 minutes, or until the outer shell puffs up and pulls away from the bean. The water in the pot will turn reddish, but don't freak out—that's normal. Shock the beans in the ice bath to stop the cooking, then shell them when they've cooled down. You should have about 1 cup beans.

(recipe continues)

3. Add the olive oil to a large enameled or stainless-steel skillet that has a lid (but don't use the lid just yet). Turn the heat to high, and when the oil is shimmering, pull the skillet off the heat and carefully add the cherry tomatoes; they'll give off a lot of smoke and may splatter. Place the pan back on the heat, and don't stir; you want the tomatoes to char lightly in a few places.

4. After a couple of minutes, when the tomatoes are starting to blister, stir in the bell peppers, onion, and garlic. Cook, stirring frequently, for 4 minutes or so, until all the vegetables are a little golden around the edges and the cherry tomatoes are melting into everything else.

5. Decrease the heat to medium, and add the Jerusalem artichokes, favas, and remaining 2 teaspoons salt. Roughly crush the canned tomatoes between your fingers, or chop them, and add them to the pan with their juice. Cook the sauce for a couple of minutes, until it thickens slightly.

6. Decrease the heat to medium-low, and use your spoon to make little divots in the sauce, one per egg. Crack an egg into each, cover the pan, and cook for 4 to 5 minutes, until the egg white is set but the center still jiggles. Dollop a spoonful of zhoug over each egg before serving.

SPECIAL SANDWICHES

YIELD: 4 OR 5 SANDWICHES, DEPENDING ON DESIRED POTENCY

Salami and butter make a classic sandwich in Europe, and herbs—plenty of fresh ones, plus the not-so-secret ingredient—make it special in more ways than one. (Omit the "green butter" and it'll still be amazing.) I'd suggest making this only in places where marijuana is legal, so *you* don't get arrested for the munchies.

1 tablespoon lightly packed fresh mint leaves
1 tablespoon lightly packed fresh basil leaves
1½ teaspoons lightly packed fresh oregano leaves
5 tablespoons unsalted butter, softened
   Grated zest of 1 lemon
1 teaspoon green butter (recipe follows)
½ teaspoon Morton kosher salt
1 very large baguette, or 2 small baguettes
8 ounces Italian salami, sliced

1. Mince the fresh herbs all together. With a fork, beat them into the softened butter along with the lemon zest, green butter, and salt.
2. Split the baguette lengthwise (cut off or eat the ends), and slather the butter inside. Layer the salami inside, and cut the baguette evenly into 5 sandwiches.
3. Have fun.

YIELD: 21 TEASPOONS
TOTALING
APPROXIMATELY
1000 MG OF THC.
USE 1 TEASPOON PER
5 SERVINGS TO YIELD
APPROXIMATELY
10 MG THC PER SERVING.

There are all kinds of ways to approach edibles, some tastier (and more powerful) than others. Using a slow cooker allows you to cook the butter low and slow without risk of burning, and the upshot is an incredibly potent fat that you can use in small quantities pretty much anywhere you want it—not only in sandwiches but also on toast and in scrambled eggs, brownies, or cookies—and it'll fit right in. Be careful: there's a range of THC from one strain of marijuana to another, but on average, about ¼ teaspoon of this stuff (or even less) will contain enough to do the job. If you've eaten edibles before, you'll know what's right; if this is your first foray, start with even less. Because this recipe is so potent and makes a relatively big batch, use a strain of marijuana you know you already like.

1. Heat your oven to 240°F. Break the weed buds apart into small, evenly sized pieces. Spread them across a rimmed baking sheet, and roast for 40 minutes.
2. Place the weed in your slow cooker's bowl with the butter and water. Cook on the lowest setting for 12 hours.
3. Strain the butter into a lidded container. (It will look murky! Don't worry, you didn't screw it up.) Refrigerate until the butter solidifies into a disc, naturally separating from the water. Pull out the butter, and throw away the rest.

¼ ounce high-quality marijuana
½ pound (2 sticks) unsalted butter
1 cup water

7

♦ ♦ ♦

Home Ec Hero

I signed up for Home Economics my freshman year of high school. It seemed like an easy elective and a good way to meet girls; it didn't really add up for me at that point that this class would allow me to cook. I may have been watching Emeril Lagasse and Paul Prudhomme preparing blackened redfish and dirty rice on TV at home, but it never occurred to me that I could *study* food.

I walked into class and met Donna Barnett. Her standard way of introducing herself to new students was to take a knife and do what she called her Benihana move: she'd flip the knife around in the air and stab it into a cutting board. "Don't ever mess with a woman who can handle a knife better than you can," she'd say, with a smile. She'd turn on James Brown to teach knife skills, chopping in rhythm to the music. All of that made quite an impression. There was something about her personality that immediately put me at ease. She was tough, but she was also easy to talk to; she seemed to understand where I was coming from more than most teachers. She didn't talk down to me.

I was definitely not a kid most teachers found easy to relate to: a big, tall teenager who emanated anger. I could be an imposing presence if I wanted to. I had a temper and liked to argue with teachers, and I would not hesitate to curse them out. But with Donna, I was different. Maybe this was because I could tell she was a great cook and I respected her talent in the kitchen. Maybe it was that she always treated me as if I was something more than a misfit; she didn't judge me. And I excelled in her class.

There were four kitchenettes in the classroom, each meant to hold four or five students. I always

chose Kitchen 4, the farthest from Donna's desk, where I could order the other kids around in the space, have them wash the dishes and do other menial tasks as we baked muffins and casseroles and put together salads. After a while, though, I wanted my own space. Donna recognized that and redistributed the other kids around the room, giving me my own kitchenette and freeing me up to pursue more complicated dishes. I cared about what I was doing in her class, unlike any other in school.

Eventually, Donna struck a deal with the other teachers to let me serve detention in her classroom whenever I got kicked out for talking back, fighting in the parking lot, or smoking in the bathroom. "Chop these onions," she would say, followed by "What the hell did you do this time?" I didn't mind telling her my problems and letting my guard down. My punishment was always constructive. She would plop down a pile of veg-

MAKING PIE CRUST
WITH DONNA

etables in front of me and tell me, "Half-inch dice, in the ziplock bag, pronto." Great. I was happy to do it. I enjoyed it, actually. "You're giving that kid a knife? You're crazy," the other teachers would say. But she knew what she was doing.

The final exam for Donna's class was to prepare a dish that everyone—all the students, as well as Donna—would taste. Most other kids made cookies or brownies from scratch, or their mothers' chili recipe. I decided, with a flourish, that I would make linguine with white clam sauce. It sounded fancy to me. Donna was hesitant—would my Conservative Jewish mother be scandalized by having her son cook a trayf dish? She didn't know that my family wasn't keeping kosher at home except around holidays. I convinced Donna to let me try to make it. The day of the exam, I pulled out a sauté pan and poured in some olive oil, a sprinkle of minced garlic, and canned clams, which were all we could afford. I added some clam juice and let it thicken into a sauce, enhancing it with parsley, butter, and lemon zest—which impressed Donna. She even snuck me a little bit of white wine for the sauce (we usually weren't allowed to use alcohol). I remember adding the dried linguine to a big pot of boiling water; it was my first time cooking any pasta other than Kraft macaroni and cheese. I tossed the long noodles with the clam sauce, and arranged it all on a large white platter. Each student took a forkful of pasta, and I made sure they all got some clams. *This is so much more sophisticated than some lame kiddie chocolate-chip cookies,* I thought to myself. Donna agreed: she gave me high marks.

LINGUINE AND CLAMS "CARBONARA"   YIELD: 4 TO 6 SERVINGS

I've learned a lot about pasta since making a version of this dish in high school Home Ec. Then all I had were canned clams and clam juice. Now I use fresh littlenecks, which give off plenty of their own juice, and turn to the same technique I'd use for a rich and creamy carbonara sauce. This method emulsifies the clam's juices around the pasta, bringing those flavors to the forefront. Use the best dried linguine you can find—not all dried pasta is created equal—or make fresh pasta from scratch (page 280) and cut it into linguine.

1. Put the clams in a large bowl. Cover with plenty of water and, if you're using it, the cornmeal, which will help the clams purge all the sand. Refrigerate for at least 1 hour or overnight.

2. Drain the clams, rinse well, and set aside. Combine 1 gallon water and 2 tablespoons salt in a pot, and bring to a rolling boil while you start on the sauce. If the water comes to a boil before you're ready to cook the pasta, cover with a lid and keep it on low heat.

3. Put 2 tablespoons olive oil in a large skillet over medium heat. Once it's warm, add the shallot, garlic, and red-pepper flakes. Simmer until fragrant, just about 30 seconds or so, before the color begins to change.

4. Add the wine and remaining ¼ teaspoon salt to the skillet, give them a good stir, then pile in the clams. Allow the wine to reduce by half before adding the lemon juice.

5. Cover the pan, and decrease the heat to medium-low. Check on the clams every couple of minutes, and move them into a bowl, one by one, as they open. If you see that one is only slightly cracked open, give it a friendly tap with your tongs or spoon; if it opens more, it's ready. If, after 10 minutes or so, any clams are still tightly shut, throw them away. Take the skillet off the heat to let the sauce cool, and pull the meat from the clams.

6. Add the linguine to the pot of boiling water, and cook just a minute or two shy of package instructions, so it's still al dente, typically about 8 minutes. Reserve ½ cup of the starchy cooking water, then drain the pasta.

7. With the skillet still off the heat, slowly whisk the egg yolks into the cooled sauce, followed by the clams (the eggs will cook as the sauce comes together). Swish in the pasta and reserved cooking water, toss to coat, and gently cook over low heat for a few minutes, stirring slowly and gently, until the sauce thickens and clings to the pasta. Be patient and let the low heat do its thing. Finish with the last tablespoon of olive oil and the butter, garnish with scallions, and serve right away.

2 pounds littleneck clams, scrubbed well
1 gallon water, plus more to cover the clams
1 tablespoon cornmeal, optional
2 tablespoons plus ¼ teaspoon Morton kosher salt, divided
3 tablespoons extra-virgin olive oil, divided
1 medium shallot, minced
1 clove garlic, minced
¼ teaspoon red-pepper flakes
¼ cup white wine
1 tablespoon lemon juice
1 pound linguine
3 egg yolks
1 tablespoon unsalted butter
2 scallions, sliced

8

✦✦✦

Wood Ovens and Butterflies

As I was fanning out some sliced mango for a fruit platter I was making in Home Ec, Donna told me she wanted to get me a job in a restaurant. "You should do this for a living," she said. "You could make a career out of this." I don't think I showed it, but I was thrilled. She was no-nonsense about it, in her usual way. She was getting me an interview, she said, with her friend Derek Davis, a well-established chef who owned three popular Philadelphia restaurants. And, Donna told me, "You're *not* going to embarrass me. You're going to show up on time. You're going to dress the right way. You are *not* going to screw this up." The truth was, I wanted to make Donna proud of me.

I was intimidated by the fanciness of Derek's restaurants, especially Kansas City Prime, his fine-dining steakhouse with a piano bar, elegant cuts of meat, and what, at the time, seemed very chic to me: crabmeat served in bright-blue stemware. During our interview, Derek drove me around in his SUV from restaurant to restaurant, introducing me to people. I was in a state of awe: *Here I am, with the head chef of a restaurant, and he thinks I'm important enough to drive me around in his car.* That feeling was magnified when I got the job.

The day I was to start work, I put on a chef's coat and white apron for the first time. I'd been assigned to work at Sonoma, a Cal-Italian restaurant that had a second-floor vodka bar boasting the largest selection in Philadelphia and a clientele of middle-aged housewives lined up for sour-apple martinis and neon-pink cosmopolitans. When I walked through the bar in my chef's whites, I felt as if I was suddenly a part of a world that, until that point, I'd seen only on television: the world of professional chefs.

I got to the kitchen and was told that, actually, I was needed at a different restaurant, a brand-new Tex-Mex place that Derek was opening called Arroyo Grill. I arrived there just in time for the tequila tasting.

Here I was, just a teenager, about to start my first shift on the line in a real restaurant kitchen, and the entire staff got served shot after shot of tequila. Some distributor or liquor representative was visiting, and kept pouring us drinks. We all got drunk. I was assigned to work hot apps with one of the cooks. My job was to pile up chips for nachos and hand him the plate so he could add the rest of the toppings. I was standing there as service was about to start, happily drunk and excited. Then the orders started coming in, and the other cook was like a machine. He was working the deep-fryer with one hand and flipping stuff on the griddle with the other. He was going a million miles an hour, and he knew exactly what to do at all times, his side towel perfectly folded. *I might be out of my league,* I thought to myself, but decided to do what I was told and continued piling chips.

After I'd spent only a short time at Arroyo, they transferred me back to Sonoma and put me to work in the prep kitchen. I cut the faces off soft-shell crabs and stacked them up; I peeled potatoes, cleaned the walk-in. My immediate boss was Don, the chef de cuisine of Sonoma, who, in my mind, set a new standard for cool. Thanks to Don, I realized that talented cooks weren't just mothers and grandmothers—or teachers like Donna. They could be, well, *dudes*. Who smoked cigarettes and drove Nissan Pathfinders, a car I came to equate with success, so much so that I asked Don how much money I'd have to make to buy a car like his. "I'm not gonna tell you that!" he scoffed at me, but he laughed good-naturedly. Don didn't take himself too seriously, even when he was angry. He yelled at me once for rinsing bell peppers underneath running water to remove their charred skin. "That takes off all the *flavor*," he told me. "You have to peel them by hand, carefully, rubbing off any char that's left on there."

The peppers weren't my only mistake. I was reamed out for not scraping the last of the Caesar salad dressing from the plastic container with a rubber spatula. Another cook threw a quart of cream in my face after I told him off. Mostly, though, I worked my butt off. I was promoted to the garde-manger station, which meant assembling salads and desserts. I remember gingerly making small dots of strawberry sauce on a plate and using a toothpick to shape them into hearts that would surround a giant creamy wedge of cheesecake, adorned with a sprig of mint. On a high shelf of my station were huge glass cake stands where we kept the seven-layer devil's-food chocolate-mousse cake (or some similar concoction), which was bigger than my head. I was so tall that the cake stand was directly at eye level for me. I spent every shift staring at that cake, wanting so badly to eat a piece. It was as if we were facing off, me and the cake, mano a cake-o.

One particular day at Sonoma was a turning point. Next to where I worked on garde-manger was the wood-burning-oven station. Every day, I watched the cook at the station pull thin-crust Neapolitan-style pizzas in and out of the oven and decorate them with toppings. One day, Don came over to the station. He dipped his hands in flour and started rolling out some dough with his hands, stretching it into a circle. He slicked the dough with olive oil, and I noted that he skipped the usual tomato sauce, instead dotting the pizza with fresh goat cheese before sliding it into the oven. When it came out, the crust a crackling brown and the goat cheese warm and starting to ooze, he added folds of cured salmon, a handful of arugula leaves, and a last drizzle of olive oil. I was mesmerized, watching Don lavish care on the pizza, his shoulders hunched forward, an almost balletic dance to his fingers as he arranged the ingredients. I got a funny feeling looking at that pizza, like butterflies in my stomach. It was as if I'd just kissed a girl I had a crush on. The pizza made me realize that this work, cooking, didn't have to feel like a job. It could be my life, the thing I *loved* to do. I called Donna as soon as I could after my shift. "I'm going to be a chef," I told her. "I want to be a chef."

STRAINING YOGURT FOR LABNEH

CAESAR SALAD, 1990S STYLE

Working at Sonoma was the first real line-cooking experience I ever had. That was where I was, 5 nights a week, while going to high school full-time during the day. I made a lot of Caesar salads during that time, and, to be frank, most of them were pretty boring. The goat cheese and roasted red peppers are a tribute to that time period, and together with the spiced croutons and anchovy-spiked dressing, they make this version something you want to eat all the time. Boquerones—marinated fresh anchovies—have a great, delicate brininess and firm texture, like night and day from cured anchovies, so don't be afraid of serving the fillets whole.

1. Cut the bread into 1-inch cubes (you should have about 3 cups' worth) and combine the paprika, salt, coriander, and cumin in a bowl that will be big enough to hold the bread.

2. Get the canola oil hot in a medium saucepan or large skillet over medium heat. Test the heat by dropping in a small piece of bread; if it audibly sizzles right away but doesn't burn, it's ready.

3. Add the bread to the pan, and give it a quick stir to coat it evenly with oil, then spread it in an even layer and leave it alone for a minute or so, until it builds a crust. Stir it periodically, waiting for it to crisp up and turn golden all over. Move it to the bowl with the spices, and give it a good jostle to coat with seasoning while it's still hot.

4. Roughly chop or tear the lettuce. Add it to your salad bowl, and toss with the peppers and dressing. Gently fold in the croutons, goat cheese, and boquerones immediately before serving.

3 slices rustic Italian bread
1½ tablespoons smoked paprika
¼ teaspoon Morton kosher salt
¼ teaspoon ground coriander
⅛ teaspoon ground cumin
⅓ cup canola oil
1 large head romaine or 2 or 3 heads Little Gem lettuce
3 roasted red bell peppers, seeded and sliced
¼ cup Caesar dressing (recipe follows)
2 ounces goat cheese, crumbled
12 boquerones

Like any self-respecting Caesar dressing, this has the velvety body of an aioli and a solid savory backbone, thanks, in part, to the mainstays anchovies and Parmesan. The Dijon mustard, white-wine vinegar, and Worcestershire sauce are a little more unexpected, but they round it out really well.

Combine all the ingredients except the oils in a blender on medium speed. With the machine still running, carefully and gradually stream in the oils and blend until you have a very thick, super-smooth dressing.

¼ cup finely grated Parmesan cheese
2 tablespoons lemon juice
1 tablespoon Dijon mustard
1 tablespoon white-wine vinegar
1 teaspoon Worcestershire sauce
½ teaspoon freshly ground black pepper
½ teaspoon Morton kosher salt
6 anchovies
2 large cloves garlic, chopped
1 egg
½ cup extra-virgin olive oil
¼ cup canola oil

SIMPLE CURED SALMON

Sonoma's smoked-salmon pizza is the dish that sparked my dream of becoming a chef, a realization that was as intimidating as it was exciting. This recipe is exciting but not at all intimidating. The method is as simple as mixing some spices and patting them on a side of fish (so make sure you use the best-quality salmon you can possibly find, with enough fat to carry the flavor, and make sure your fishmonger leaves the skin on but thoroughly scrapes away excess scales). It takes minutes to prepare; after that, you just have to wait. Beautiful, and far tastier (and less expensive) than its deli counterpart, it goes with anything.

1. With the skin facing up, glide the back of your knife along the length of the fish, from the tail end toward the head, to scrape away any lingering scales. Gently remove any pin bones with your fingers or some clean tweezers. Rinse the fish well, then pat it dry with paper towels.

2. Strip the leaves from the thyme, and combine them with the salt, sugar, orange zest and juice, coriander, and red-pepper flakes. This is the cure mix.

3. Pull out a roughly 2-foot-long piece of plastic wrap, and lay the salmon in the center, skin side up. Spoon about $^1/_3$ cup of the cure over the skin, then flip the salmon and rub the rest of the cure over the top, a little heavier on the thicker parts and lighter where it tapers off.

4. Tightly wrap the plastic around the fish, then wrap the whole thing in aluminum foil and refrigerate for at least 24 and preferably 36 hours.

5. Rinse the salmon under cold water to get rid of any excess cure. Pat it dry, and refrigerate it, uncovered, on a rimmed baking sheet or large rack, for at least 24 hours, so it can firm up.

6. When you're ready to serve, use a good sharp knife to cut very thin slices on a bias, stopping short of the skin. Serve with toast and your favorite soft cheese. If it's wrapped well, you can keep this for up to a week in the fridge.

2-pound side of fatty salmon, such as Atlantic, scaled
4 sprigs fresh thyme
1 cup Morton kosher salt
⅔ cup light-brown sugar
Grated zest of 1 orange
2 tablespoons orange juice
2 teaspoons whole coriander seeds, lightly crushed
½ teaspoon red-pepper flakes

½ cup heavy cream
½ cup pomegranate molasses
5 tablespoons unsalted butter
¾ cup sugar
2 tablespoons light corn syrup
⅓ cup water

Caramel—the deep, dark kind, with a little bit of burnt veneer over a heart of butter and sugar—is intense but simple, like each of its component parts taken to the logical extreme. Pomegranate molasses is the same way, syrupy yet not at all sweet, one of the few ingredients that can match the edge of burnt caramel. It's not just good on cheesecake: try it on ice cream, swirled into your yogurt, or rubbed on pumpernickel bread with butter as a late-night snack.

1. Melt the cream, molasses, and butter together in the microwave or in a small saucepan over low heat. When the butter is fully melted and the sauce is hot, pour it into a heatproof bowl and set it aside. You'll want it still to be quite warm when you add it to the caramel.

2. Add the sugar and corn syrup to a small saucepan, and pour the water evenly over them to moisten. Use short, shallow strokes to incorporate the ingredients without tracking sugar up the sides of the pan, then set the pan over medium-low heat and, without stirring, let it melt and turn amber; this should take 15 to 20 minutes. As it bubbles and darkens, you'll be tempted to stir, but I'm serious—don't. Otherwise, the sugar may crystallize. If you feel the need to mix them, just swirl the pan a couple times. You can multitask with this, but keep an eye on the pan and never stray too far— caramel tends to change slowly, slowly, and then *very* quickly the second it's neglected.

3. When the sugar is amber and bubbling like molten lava, immediately remove it from heat. Slowly and carefully—it'll bubble and hiss at first—whisk in the pomegranate molasses mixture. Don't worry if it seizes up at first; just keep whisking and it'll pull itself together.

4. Let the caramel cool completely before using it. Leftovers can be stored at room temperature for about a week, or for much longer in the fridge, then brought back to room temperature or briefly heated on the stove or in the microwave until it's easily pourable.

These give the cheesecake the crunch and texture that you're used to getting from a crust, allowing it to sing as a choir instead of a solo performer. (Make sure to use a very coarse sugar like turbinado, because regular brown sugar melts too easily to be a good substitute.) But don't limit them to that: they're great on yogurt with berries, or on their own as a snack, and they make perfect little gifts around the holidays.

¼ cup walnut pieces, toasted
¼ cup sliced almonds, toasted
¼ cup whole pistachios, toasted
1½ tablespoons unsalted butter, melted
¼ teaspoon orange blossom water
3 tablespoons turbinado or Demerara sugar
¼ teaspoon baharat (page 387) or pumpkin pie spice
¼ teaspoon Morton kosher salt

1. Heat the oven to 350°F, and line a rimmed baking sheet with parchment.
2. Coat the nuts with the butter and orange blossom water, then toss in the sugar, baharat, and salt.
3. Spread the nuts in an even layer on the parchment, with a little space between them all so they don't stick together, and bake for 10 to 15 minutes, rotating the pan every 5 minutes; you're looking for the sugar to be caramelized and crisped all over the nuts. Cool completely before using, and try not to eat them all in one breath.

9

✦✦✦

Trayf and Tribulation

Even though I was born in Israel, grew up with a religious mother, and went to a high school where the majority of students were Jewish, somehow, by the time I started college at the Culinary Institute of America, I didn't really know much about Jewish food. That became especially obvious when some friends and I decided to start a Jewish Culture Club at school, the first in the CIA's history.

Let me back up. When I began school there, I was still a little bit awestruck that I was even at the CIA. I'd been accepted (and had been able to afford to go) thanks in large part to the perseverance of mentors like Donna, who helped me and my mom

sort out scholarship applications and financial-aid forms. To me, the CIA was like a culinary Harvard. Its main building was an old and regal brick monastery on a campus in New York's Hudson Valley, dotted with apple orchards. Teachers here were called "chefs," and, unlike nearly all of my high-school teachers, none of them avoided eye contact with me when I passed them in the hallways. On one of our first nights on campus, new students were invited to the house of the college president, Ferdinand Metz. He asked our group of aspiring chefs, "What's the best kind of apple to use in an apple pie?" Other students called out answers; none of them were what he was looking for. I raised my hand and suggested that it took three different kinds of apples for different layers of flavor and texture. I got it right! I was so excited that I called Donna collect the next day to tell her.

To my surprise, I was starting to love being in school. We had academic classes like Gastronomy, where we studied the history of food and read about figures from Escoffier to Alice Waters, and Culinary Math, in which we learned about costing out food and how to read a profit-and-loss statement for a restaurant. Then there were the kitchen-based classes. We learned how to brunoise and julienne, how to make chicken stock and béchamel sauce. In Meat Fabrication, we'd butcher whole chickens and cows. Once, we broke down an entire pig, and then the chef in charge said, "All right, now you guys put it all back together." We clustered around the pig parts: "Well, I think the head goes here, and the tenderloin goes here, and the leg goes here. . . ."

And for someone who'd grown up without a lot of resources, eating whatever was immediately within reach, every day at the CIA brought new things for me to taste. I had sushi for the first time and was stunned by the smooth, clean flavor of the raw fish. That sense of revelation happened over and over again, with so many firsts: escargots bathed in a pesto cream sauce; risotto, each grain of rice still plump and tender; sweet and salty Korean short ribs. I dipped crusty baguettes into bright creamed watercress soup presented under sterling-silver domes in French Dining and felt as if I were royalty. I learned how to use chopsticks properly in Asian Cookery. Someone told me that hoagies were called po'boys in New Orleans; I'd had no idea.

I got mostly A's in my classes and even helped tutor my new friends. But I couldn't entirely evade my old habits. There was a kid named Sal in one of my classes who routinely ticked me off with his constant bragging. One day, I said something insulting to him and he jumped right across the table at me. The chef teaching our class had to break up the fistfight. That night, I slit all the tires of Sal's convertible Chrysler Sebring with my fish-fillet knife. Everyone knew I did it. And, unlike when I was in high school, my shenanigans caught up with me. Cutting Sal's tires almost cost me my degree; the only thing that stopped the school from expelling me was my excellent academic record.

I found some friends who bridged the old and the new Alon. We'd discuss whatever we were learning to cook, and then would go drive an old Jeep Cherokee into shopping carts in a grocery store's parking lot, as if we were at a demolition derby. Pushing a grocery cart around at 30 miles an hour and then hitting the brakes so that it would fly forward and smash into someone else's car—that was our idea of how to unwind.

For the first time in my life, though, I was close friends with other kids who were Jewish. Ross and Keven became my best pals; one year, Ross brought us home with him to New Jersey for Passover. We all went to services, and I was surprised at how much I enjoyed them. I began to ask myself what being Jewish was all about, whereas, before, going to synagogue had felt like a chore. It was then, on our way back to school after the holidays, that we decided we'd start a Jewish Culture Club.

I was a little bit hesitant to tell my new friends that when I was twelve, I'd been kicked out of Hebrew school. My dad had given me a pair of steel-toed boots (from the thrift store, no doubt), and I thought it was cool that they were strong enough to destroy things, so I walked around and kicked holes in the Hebrew school's drywall. They expelled me just before my Bar Mitzvah; I was already on the cantor's shit list for screwing around with the pronunciation of "amen" in the prayers I was supposed to be learning. I did memorize the prayers, though, and my Bar Mitzvah was held as planned. After the ceremony, however, my dad accused my grandfather—my saba—of stealing the money people were giving me. It was my typical family scenario.

That mayhem clearly prepared me to run a Jewish Culture Club. At our first meeting, about twelve people showed up, some dressed in Orthodox Jewish garb. I addressed the group and read the mission statement that Keven, Ross, and I had come up with. "We want to bring people together and teach them about the great foods of our heritage," the statement said, and went on to explain what an important cuisine this was, and how it was generally missing in our school's curriculum. For a moment, I felt like I was back in second grade, at show-and-tell, with my borekas, only this time I had a sympathetic audience! But then, just as in second grade, I blew it. "Imagine our first club party," I said. "The whole school will come! We'll set up tables and serve tabbouleh and tagine. We could even do something really cool—like roasting a whole pig!"

There was an uneasy silence in the room. One of my friends took over. This is how little I thought about my faith and food: I *knew* that most Jews who kept kosher considered eating pork products "trayf," forbidden—I just never really cared much about that. I was more excited to talk about *any* kind of food than to try to be culturally correct.

From that point forward, I started to pay attention whenever I heard or saw anything that might reflect Jewish culture. As a gift for starting college, my dad had given me an old television set from the 1980s, wrapped in chipped wood veneer, with a giant remote that had only four buttons. I took aluminum foil from the kitchen to make little rabbit-ear antennae, but even then I could really get only one TV channel. But that channel played *Seinfeld* reruns constantly, and someone on *Seinfeld* was always mentioning chocolate babka or inhabiting a stereotypical Jewish identity. It seems funny now, but a lot of my cultural education came from *Seinfeld.*

A less humorous side of my Jewish education came when we were putting up flyers around school for our club meetings. The morning after we'd taped up posters, I came home to discover that the one I'd put on my own dorm-room door had been marred by a piece of tape with a huge swastika on it. The same thing happened to Keven. We never told the school; we didn't want to make too big a deal out of it and have that be what attracted attention to the club. I remember calling my mother, though, who then told Saba, who happened to be visiting from Israel. He suggested he would get his "friends" to "deal with the situation." My mother and I had to beg him not to do anything. With renewed seriousness, Keven, Ross, and I went ahead with our Jewish Culture Club meetings, and the anti-Semitism gradually died off. It intensified our sense of ourselves as a group, however: suddenly, cooking Jewish food together felt like a substantive act, born out of a kind of adversity.

The small rituals of making food for Jewish holidays grew on me. We'd make latkes together for Hanukkah, shredding potatoes on a box grater, mixing them with onion, flour, and eggs, and pan-frying them until crisp. We organized a kosher cooking demonstration in the school's theater, the first time something like that had happened on campus. We had to go through the whole process of making the demonstration kitchen kosher-friendly—boiling spoons and whisks, having a rabbi come to oversee the process. I'd never learned how to do that before.

Keven and I were eventually invited to represent Israel at a food festival in Yonkers, New York. Different countries were represented by different booths, each of them an elaborate production. Russia had a snow machine, which fake-snowed all over the cooks as they were preparing their food. Morocco included tagines and rows of spices like you'd see in a souk. Israel was a desertscape, with a mural that prominently featured a camel. We decided to make up a fancy incarnation of falafel and pita, hummus and tabbouleh. Now it seems laughable to me. We made honey-wheat pita bread. Out of that, we produced doll-sized pita cups, filled them with a dollop of roasted-red-pepper hummus, and topped the whole concoction with a mini-ball of falafel, which, I'm sure, was stuffed with something that had a double-barrel name. It may have been food I'd find needlessly fussy now, but at the time it felt as if I was starting to find a piece of myself. I'd never thought about the familiar foods of my childhood as "Jewish" until then, and I found a growing resonance in understanding these dishes to be the food of my people, my roots. It was cooking that made me embrace being Jewish.

When I was growing up, my immediate family was not concerned about keeping kosher, except around Passover. I grew up eating bacon cheeseburgers without a second thought. Still, when our new Jewish Culture Club at the CIA had its first meeting, I raised some eyebrows with my suggestion that we roast a whole pig. I'd just been thinking it'd be a good activity for a party.

If you want, you can simply omit the bacon and toast the pecans in a 325°F oven. And if you don't have baharat, which is a beautiful, intense spice blend, you can replace it with pumpkin pie spice. Instead of the typical cottage cheese filling, I use a béchamel and custard to make this kugel especially smooth and creamy, equally good warm or cold the next day. Custards are delicate and should be cared for, so mine is baked in a water bath, creating a gentle, even heat that leaves you with a wonderful, rich texture. Don't let the fancy-sounding words deter you—there's no secret or magic to any of them. Both sweet and savory, this side dish is equally at home on a dinner table or for dessert; try serving it alongside bagels and lox or brisket and latkes.

- 12 tablespoons (1½ sticks) unsalted butter, divided, plus more for the pan
- 2 yellow onions, finely chopped
- 2 tablespoons minced fresh ginger
- Zest of 1 orange
- ½ cup orange juice
- ¼ cup Cointreau
- 2 tablespoons plus 2 teaspoons Morton kosher salt, divided
- 1½ teaspoons baharat (page 387)
- 3 tablespoons plus 1 cup all-purpose flour, divided
- 2 cups milk
- ¼ cup honey
- 10 ounces bacon, finely chopped
- 1 cup chopped pecans
- ⅓ cup light brown sugar, packed
- 3 quarts water, plus more for a water bath
- 1 pound dry fusilli noodles
- 3 eggs
- 2 egg yolks
- 3 tablespoons granulated sugar, plus more for dusting
- 1½ cups sour cream

1. Heat the oven to 350°F with a rack in the bottom. Pull out a 13-by-9-inch baking dish or a 2-to-3-quart casserole dish as well as a larger, deep roasting pan that will hold it; set them both aside for later.

2. To make the orange béchamel: Combine 8 tablespoons of the butter in a saucepan with the onions and ginger over medium-low heat. Cook, stirring occasionally, until the onions are soft and translucent but no color has formed, 15 minutes or so. Remove the pan from the heat and stir in the orange zest and juice, Cointreau, 2 teaspoons of the salt, and the baharat. Return it to medium-low heat and simmer for 5 minutes or so, until most of the liquid has reduced.

3. Use a whisk to gradually incorporate 3 tablespoons of the flour, then whisk in the milk and honey. Bring the sauce to a simmer and continue to cook for 10 minutes, whisking frequently to ensure that it doesn't stick to the bottom of the pan. Remove from the heat and cool completely.

(recipe continues)

4. Fry the bacon in a skillet over medium heat, stirring frequently. After about 10 minutes, when the fat has rendered and the bacon is golden and crisp around the edges, stir in the pecans and toast them in the bacon's fat for another 2 minutes or so. Take the pan off the heat and add the brown sugar and remaining 4 tablespoons butter. Stir until all the butter melts and set aside. Once it's cooled to room temperature, carefully stir in the remaining flour until it's thoroughly combined.

5. In a large pot, combine the water with the remaining 2 tablespoons salt and bring to a boil over high heat. Cook the pasta until it's fully tender (softer than al dente) but not falling apart, 10 or 11 minutes. Strain and reserve.

6. With a handheld mixer or a stand mixer with the whisk attachment, beat the whole eggs, yolks, and granulated sugar together on high speed for about 5 minutes, pausing occasionally to scrape the sides of the bowl. You're looking for the mixture to be pale and thick; when you lift the beater, it should fall in ribbons and not drip. Mix in the sour cream until it's fully incorporated, then do the same with the orange béchamel. Fold in the cooked pasta by hand.

7. Grease the casserole dish with butter and coat the inside with a thin, even layer of granulated sugar, shaking out any excess. Pour in the noodles and evenly spread the bacon and pecan mixture over the top. Set this dish into the larger roasting pan and pour hot water all around it so comes about halfway up the sides. Bake for about 1 hour, until a knife inserted in the center comes out clean and dry. Kugel can be served warm from the oven, at room temperature, or straight out of the fridge, and it will keep for a couple of days.

Hummus wasn't always ubiquitous, the way it is now. I can remember when you could buy it only at Middle Eastern grocery stores; now people are seasoning it with sriracha, mixing it with guacamole, making it with black beans—you name it. With its simple flavors and the creaminess from tahini, it's not hard to like. But when's the last time it was so good you wanted to eat it with a spoon? This one is the ticket. You'll see several details that you may not have encountered in past hummus-making adventures—baking soda plays a prominent role, and a fine-mesh strainer comes in handy—but those steps go the extra mile to make it something people remember and celebrate. At my restaurant Shaya, we treat it like a blank canvas and top it with everything from lamb ragù to seasonal vegetables. The simplest way to dress it up is with a big dollop of prepared tahini (page 392), but that's hardly necessary.

4½ quarts water, divided
3 teaspoons baking soda, divided
1½ cups dried chickpeas
7 cloves garlic, lightly crushed
¼ cup raw tahini
2 tablespoons lemon juice
1½ teaspoons Morton kosher salt
½ teaspoon ground cumin
3 tablespoons canola oil
2 tablespoons hot water
5 tablespoons extra-virgin olive oil, divided
¾ cup prepared tahini (page 392), optional
¼ cup lightly packed fresh parsley leaves, chopped
½ teaspoon Aleppo pepper

1. In a large bowl, combine 1½ quarts water and ½ teaspoon baking soda; add the chickpeas and soak overnight.

2. Heat the oven to 400°F. Drain the chickpeas, and toss with 2 teaspoons baking soda, then spread in a single layer on a rimmed baking sheet, and roast until the beans have visibly dried, 10 to 15 minutes.

3. Move the chickpeas to a large sieve or colander; with cold water running over the chickpeas, start roughing them up with your hands to loosen the skins. You can grab a small handful and briskly run them between your palms, or pinch them between your fingers (don't worry about removing and discarding the skins yet). The more you do now, the more will come off during cooking, so take some time here and don't worry if they split. It's good to be thorough—this is like giving them a deep-tissue massage to loosen everything up.

4. Combine the remaining 3 quarts water with the remaining ½ teaspoon baking soda, this time in a pot. Add the chickpeas, and bring to a boil over high heat, then reduce the heat to medium. With a small sieve or slotted spoon, skim away the foam and loose skins from the top of the water and discard. It may be helpful for you to reserve

the discarded skins in a bowl to track your progress; with enough persistence, you're aiming to have about ¾ cup of skins by the time you're finished.

5. Every couple of minutes during the cooking process, strain away the skins by plunging your sieve deep into the pot and giving a good stir, then using the sieve to catch the swirling skins, as you would fish for minnows. It's okay to beat the chickpeas up a little against the side of the pot to speed this along. Repeat this process as much as you have the patience to do (you won't get them all, so don't drive yourself insane), until the chickpeas are just becoming tender, in 20 to 25 minutes.

(recipe continues)

6. When the chickpeas are still sort of "al dente," give them one last skim to trap any skins, then add the garlic. Cook for another 25 to 30 minutes, until the beans are super-creamy. Drain, and let them sit in the strainer for a few minutes, so any extra moisture can evaporate.

7. Combine the chickpeas in a food processor with the raw tahini, lemon juice, salt, and cumin. Process for several minutes, until the mixture is incredibly smooth. With the machine still going, stream in the canola oil, hot water, and 2 tablespoons olive oil. Let it rip—there's no way to overprocess this stuff, and you want it to be as light as air.

8. Serve the hummus at room temperature. I like to spread it in a wide, shallow bowl, where I can smear it up the sides and show off the topping. Use the back of your spoon to make a well in the center, and fill it with prepared tahini if you're using it. Drizzle with the last 3 tablespoons olive oil, and scatter the parsley and Aleppo pepper on top.

SHORTCUT HUMMUS

YIELD: ABOUT 1 QUART

Though I prefer to make hummus with dried chickpeas, which taste better and give you more control over texture, this is how I make hummus in a pinch—no advance planning needed, and a lot fewer steps once you get started. It also makes a *lot* of hummus, so it's a great dish for a party. In true shortcut fashion, there's no big garnish here, but feel free to top it as you would classic hummus (preceding recipe), or with anything else you'd like.

1. Drain the chickpeas, and rinse them well. Gently—since they're already soft—massage them in your hands to loosen the skins so that they slip off in cooking.

2. Add the chickpeas (skins and all) to a pot with 1½ quarts water. Bring it to a boil over high heat, then reduce the heat to medium. With a slotted spoon or small sieve, periodically skim away any of the skins that have floated to the top over the course of 10 or 15 minutes. If you'd like to track your progress, reserve the skins in a measuring cup, aiming to have about ¾ cup of skins by the time you purée the beans. The more time you take here, the smoother the results will be.

3. Meanwhile, combine the lemon juice and garlic, and let

Two 15-ounce cans chickpeas
1½ quarts plus 6 tablespoons water, divided, plus more as needed
2 tablespoons lemon juice
1 clove garlic, crushed
¼ cup extra-virgin olive oil, plus more for serving
¼ cup canola oil
2 tablespoons raw tahini
1½ teaspoons Morton kosher salt
¼ teaspoon ground cumin

them steep for at least 30 minutes. Fish out the garlic before proceeding.

4. Drain the chickpeas, and combine them in a food processor with the garlic-infused lemon juice, 6 tablespoons water, olive oil, canola oil, tahini, salt, and cumin. Process for at least 5 minutes, until the hummus is very smooth and light. If you find that it's still thick and grainy, add more water 1 tablespoon at a time, with the processor running, until it smooths itself into the consistency of buttercream frosting.

5. Serve at room temperature, drizzled with more olive oil if you like.

ALWAYS EAT HUMMUS WITH PITA BREAD (PAGE 302)

SHAVED CABBAGE SALAD WITH
ORANGE BLOSSOM VINAIGRETTE

Most often, you might buy orange blossom water for a dessert or a cocktail, but it's as friendly to your first course as it is to your last. It's the "secret ingredient" in this dressing, transforming a seemingly bare-bones slaw into something that makes you want to keep coming back for more. See if you can get your dinner guests to put a finger on what makes it so special.

¼ cup extra-virgin olive oil
1½ tablespoons lemon juice
1 tablespoon rice wine vinegar, preferably seasoned
2 teaspoons honey
2 teaspoons Morton kosher salt
¼ teaspoon orange blossom water
½ small head red cabbage (about 1 pound)
½ small head green cabbage (about 1 pound)
½ cup lightly packed fresh parsley leaves, chopped
¼ cup lightly packed fresh mint leaves, chopped

1. Put the olive oil, lemon juice, vinegar, honey, salt, and orange blossom water (see next step for a note about timing) in a large salad bowl, and whisk to combine. There's no need to make a perfect emulsification.
2. Remove the outer leaves and any brown bits from the cabbages, and trim out the stems and cores. Thinly slice them, and toss with the parsley, mint, and dressing. This won't keep for too long without the orange blossom flavor's becoming overpowering, so, if you're making it ahead of time, don't add the orange blossom water until just before you toss the salad.

BRIGHT GREEN FALAFEL

These are a far cry from the falafel that Keven and I made when we were in charge of the Israeli booth at that food fair. They have the vibrant flavor and texture of the fresh herbs themselves, and if you've only ever had dense falafel, these will seem like feathery clouds in comparison, thanks to the egg whites. (If you're looking for a vegan version, you can omit them and still have great results.) They're great with so many things: Swaddle them in a pita (page 302) with harissa (page 389), tumble them into a simply dressed salad, or dip them into tzatziki (page 162). My favorite way is to drizzle the tops with prepared tahini (page 392). As with all deep-frying, you'll want to have a thermometer for safety's sake.

1. Put the chickpeas in a large bowl, and submerge in water. Soak overnight.

2. In the bowl of your food processor, pulse the parsley a few times, until it's roughly chopped. Drain and rinse the chickpeas, then add them along with the onion, lemon zest, ¼ cup water, flour, salt, baking powder, and spices. Process until the mixture is all the same color and starting to pull together.

3. Whip the egg whites to stiff peaks with a whisk or mixer. Fold the whites into the chickpea mixture, and chill for at least 1 hour.

4. Clip a thermometer to the side of a heavy-bottomed pot or Dutch oven, and add enough canola oil to come about halfway up the sides of the pot. Bring to 350°F over medium-high heat. While it warms up, line a plate or cooling rack with paper towels.

5. Working in batches of six to eight—just enough so they'll have plenty of space in your pot—shape the dough into golf-ball-sized pieces; it will be pretty loose but should still hold together. Use a slotted spoon to lower them carefully into the oil, one at a time, and fry each batch for about 4 minutes. After about 1 or 2 minutes, if they're sticking to the bottom of the pan, nudge them loose with your spoon. These will look done before they're completely cooked through, so be patient and let the crust become a very deep,

(recipe continues)

1⅓ cups dried chickpeas
¼ cup water, plus plenty for soaking the chickpeas
1 quart lightly packed fresh parsley leaves (from about 2 bunches)
¼ yellow onion, chopped
 Grated zest of 1 lemon
1 tablespoon all-purpose flour
2 teaspoons Morton kosher salt
¾ teaspoon baking powder
½ teaspoon ground cumin
¼ teaspoon ground cardamom pods
¼ teaspoon cayenne pepper
2 egg whites
2 to 3 quarts canola oil

burnished brown. Cut into one—it should be firm, the same consistency throughout.

6. Once the falafels are cooked, keep them warm in the oven while you cook the rest. Serve warm on their own or with any of the suggestions mentioned in the headnote.

10

✦✦✦

Vegas or Bust

On my first day of work in Las Vegas, I realized I was in the culinary equivalent of Disneyland . . . and Keven and I had all-access passes. We were the only two externs at the Rio, a Las Vegas casino with twelve restaurants (featuring everything from a whole wall of bagels at the Jewish deli to handmade dim sum at the fine-dining Chinese restaurant), room service, banquets, and two thousand employees in the food-and-beverage department alone. Our job was to bounce around between various restaurants, spending a week here, a few weeks there, soaking up as much information as we could.

I'd managed to get there only because of successfully faking a mandatory drug test. Every Culinary Institute of America student has to do an 18-week externship in a restaurant. Because my family was poor, I had to find one of the few that paid a decent wage; I couldn't afford to work for free in some fancy New York City restaurant. Keven had offered to let me come and live with him and his parents in their Las Vegas mansion so I could work in a casino, but I failed a surprise drug test from the MGM Grand. I was, after all, still smoking weed out of my dorm room window nearly every day. In a panic, I found out that a certain shampoo could strip your hair of any evidence of drug use. I used it many times. It almost destroyed my hair, but it worked! I passed—which I found out only *after* moving to Las Vegas with Keven—and the Rio Casino hired me. The gamble had paid off.

Our gatekeepers to the Rio were Chef Watch Chumphol and Chef Kenny Bayless, the assistant executive chefs of the casino. They were quite a pair. Chef Watch was Thai, a stocky guy with a head of curly black hair, a thick accent, and a no-nonsense attitude. He was the technician; there was nothing he couldn't cook brilliantly. Chef Kenny was the motivational speaker of the two, and the one who could be sympathetic, like an older brother. He was soft-spoken—unless he was yelling at you. In fairness, they yelled at us—and everyone—a lot. They weren't sweet men. You could tell they were in a good mood when they were making dirty jokes. They proved their points in a macho way, cursing us out, but they liked us. There was an unspoken respect, beneath the shouting, that I learned about in the Rio's kitchens. If someone was known to be a great cook—or a young cook who had a lot of potential—the chefs might yell at him or her, swear, and throw stuff. But these were signs of affection. Keven and I knew Chefs Watch and Kenny loved us because they were always swinging by the kitchens, asking us what we were working on, and then telling us how terrible we were, that our cuts didn't look right. They'd taste something and spit it out in the trash can. They were dramatic about it, but it was motivating, not threatening. We'd put our heads down and say, "Yes, Chef!" with a smile.

We were rewarded with responsibility and attention for being their whipping boys. They'd ask us to manage the menu for a pool party over at Caesar's. Chef Watch would share the Thai food he made for himself with us. I fell in love with his congee, a creamy rice porridge studded with Chinese sausage, bok choy, and scallions, drizzled with a little mushroom-flavored soy sauce. Watching him make pad thai—thin rice noodles in a delicious tangle with shrimp, snow peas, scrambled egg, and spicy chilies—I learned how to add layers of flavor to food. He taught me how to build the perfect shellfish stock using the heads of lobsters and shrimp shells. He and Kenny would invite us to eat family meal with them, sitting in the formal dining room at Antonio's, the Rio's fancy Italian restaurant.

Antonio's was the domain of Chef William Chinook, whom Watch called "Chef No Neck." It was true: Chef William was so obese that his head seemed to rest directly on his shoulders. The nickname stuck, whether he liked it or not. Chef William was a temperamental guy, a quality made more intense by the daily rounds of painkillers he took for his back and knee problems. Each day, his moods would go up and down—he'd go from jovially patting you on the back to being confrontational and putting you in your place. He could totally lose it on you. But he took me under his wing and taught me the art of cooking some dishes that would leave me forever enamored with Italian food.

He taught me the method for a perfect osso buco, one so

tender the meat slips from the bone as soon as you touch it with your fork. He'd take a center-cut veal shank, which would make a beautiful ring of meat and bone around the marrow when it was finished, and braise it with a beef demi-glace, Marsala wine, and herbs, and reduce that sauce for hours before finally serving it on a bed of saffron risotto that was dotted with green peas. I remember scooping out the marrow from the bone, like the distilled essence of beef, and folding that into the golden and floral risotto. A little bit of vibrant green gremolata—a chiffonade of parsley and lemon zest, jazzed up with a peppery olive oil—cut through all the richness. That single dish educated me about so many gradations of flavor. For all of Chef Willliam's moodiness, he was tender with his cooking, and he'd take the time to talk to me about it. You could feel how much he loved it.

Those 18 weeks at the Rio took Keven and me all over the

culinary map. We spent a week at the sushi restaurant, training on the hibachi station, where we had to learn to flip eggs on a spatula, turning it to crack them midair, and have the eggs land on the griddle so we could make fried rice. In a New Orleans–themed restaurant, I spent so many hours cleaning portobello mushrooms and soaking them in cheap balsamic vinegar that my fingers turned black.

One of my final rounds was with Chef Jean-Louis Palladin at his restaurant, Napa. He was one of the pioneers of modern French cooking in America, famous to cooking geeks like me, and I was more than a little wide-eyed around him. He was quiet, for the most part. He wouldn't call out the orders; he'd just be there, wiping the rims of plates, arranging the garnishes on the food, and putting plates up for the servers to take. Near the end of service every evening, he would silently scrub down his station—which stuck with me, the head chef doing his own cleaning—and sit down in the dining room for dinner. We would have to cook for him, never knowing what he might order from the menu. It could be the smoked-salmon consommé, which we siphoned out of a stockpot using a small, clear hose. Or it might be a dish of linguine that had small baby eels folded into it, or a crab cake roasted in the wood oven, bound together with scallop mousse instead of mayonnaise.

I worked the fish station, which felt like a huge honor for a CIA extern. I'd be searing salmon, poaching asparagus spears, and grilling eggplants, which were scooped out to make eggplant "caviar." During service, Chef Jean-Louis would quietly walk around, looking at how we were plating things, tasting sauces. I'd heard about his getting angry but only saw it once. A salad had ended up in front of him with a wilted green on it. He picked up the offending piece of lettuce, walked back to the cook on garde-manger, and threw it at him. It stuck to his face for a second. "Never serve a piece of shit food like this in my restaurant again, you fucking piece of shit!" he yelled, in his French accent. *Oh man,* I thought to myself. *I do not want that happening to me.* But even as I ducked my head down, I was thinking: Chef Jean-Louis's anger was different. He wasn't being macho like Chef Kenny or Chef Watch, or moody like Chef No Neck (er, Chef William). He was so focused on the perfection of the *food* that it was the only thing that could make him truly angry.

ROASTED MARROW BONES WITH GREMOLATA AND BRIOCHE

YIELD: 6 TO 8 SERVINGS

One of the best parts of the osso buco that Chef William taught me to make was the marrow: rich, fatty, its flavor the very soul of beef. I braised hundreds if not thousands of veal shanks in that Vegas kitchen; occasionally, I'd sneak a bone out of one of the braising pots and let the meat *accidentally* slide off, rendering it unservable. I'd then scoop out the hot marrow with some of the meat's own gravy and slather it on a

fresh baguette with a little sea salt and lemon juice. That's how I fell in love with marrow.

You don't need to roast a whole shank just for its marrow center, though. Ask your butcher for marrow bones, long and split down the middle, which you broil and very quickly transform into one of the most delicious and effortless dishes your kitchen's ever seen. Serve this to company and I guarantee they'll be talking fondly about it long after they leave. I was really into brioche and toast points back then—to me, they seemed like the height of sophistication, both literally and figuratively rich—and though they no longer figure in my regular cooking, the toasted brioche triangles really are the perfect little vessel for buttery marrow.

1. Heat the oven to 450°F with a rack in the center of the oven. Toast the brioche slices side by side on a baking sheet until they start to crisp up and get a bit of color, just 3 or 4 minutes. Flip the slices on the sheet, and toast for another 3 minutes. Let the bread cool, then cut each slice into four triangles.

2. Turn on your broiler and set a rack about 6 inches beneath the heating element. Arrange the bones on a rimmed baking sheet with the marrow side up, and sprinkle 1½ teaspoons salt evenly over the tops. Broil for 16 to 24 minutes, checking on them roughly every 8 minutes because broilers vary so much in strength. You're looking for the fat to be bubbling and deeply golden all over; the very edges of the bones should be dark brown.

3. While the bones are in the oven, make the gremolata: combine the herbs, garlic, lemon zest and juice, olive oil, and red-pepper flakes with the remaining ½ teaspoon salt.

4. To serve: Move the bones to a separate platter and let them cool slightly before spooning the gremolata over them in a generous, even layer. Don't be shy; the bright acid and spices really cut through and liven up the rich marrow. Use small spoons to scoop the marrow from the bones and spread it over the toast points.

Six 1-inch slices brioche
4 pounds center-cut marrow bones, halved lengthwise
2 teaspoons Morton kosher salt, divided
½ cup lightly packed fresh parsley leaves, finely chopped
½ cup lightly packed fresh cilantro leaves, finely chopped
½ cup lightly packed fresh mint leaves, finely chopped
2 cloves garlic, minced
Grated zest of 1 lemon
¼ cup lemon juice
2 tablespoons extra-virgin olive oil
¼ teaspoon red-pepper flakes

LOBSTER GREEN CURRY

YIELD: 8 TO 10 SERVINGS

One of my most memorable experiences with lobster happened while I was working in Las Vegas. I was in the kitchen at Antonio's Italian Ristorante on an evening when a very wealthy customer had booked our private dining room. The gentleman had hired a bunch of strippers to dance on the table, prompting all the cooks to hover around the door, trying to peek in. The waitstaff came back to the kitchen and told me that the customer had ordered the biggest lobster we had.

The casino had its own internal seafood shop, which fueled all of its restaurants, and when I called, they told me they had a 25-pound lobster. *Twenty. Five. Pounds.* If it had been up to me, I would have told the customer that we only had a 2-pound lobster, and set this big guy free in the ocean. But when in Vegas, you give the high rollers what they want. It showed up in our kitchen, several feet long. I felt bad killing it, not only because it must have been several decades old, but also because I knew that lobsters that large don't taste very good.

This postmortem homage is based on some other things I picked up in Vegas (and it happens to be green, like that high roller's money). By teaching me about Thai food, Chef Watch Chumphol introduced me to so many fundamental culinary concepts that have made me a better cook. When it came to layering flavors, he was the master, and there are few better examples than a good curry. Starting with a good curry paste—Mae Ploy is my favorite—goes a long way to making this special, and you toast it with all the other aromatics to make the most of it. (Lime leaves, available in most Asian markets, can be omitted if you can't find them.) As is, it's got a spicy kick; if you prefer something on the milder side, decrease it by 1 or 2 tablespoons. I, for one, love the baseline of heat that butts up against the cooling cucumbers and herbs that you add at the last minute. It's even better with a cold beer on the side.

The curry recipe is part and parcel with the lobster stock that follows (next recipe), so take note that it requires a little bit of extra choreography. If you don't want to go through that process, substitute seafood stock and 2 pounds of raw, shell-on shrimp for the lobster.

VEGAS OR BUST · 129

1. Use the recipe that follows to make lobster stock. Reserve all the parcooked meat and 2 cups of stock. (You can make this a day in advance and refrigerate them both, or leave them covered at room temperature if you're proceeding right away.)

2. Heat the canola oil in a large pot over medium heat. Add the lemongrass, ginger, and garlic, reduce the heat to low, and toast for about 30 seconds, just until fragrant, before the garlic builds any color. Scrape in the curry paste, and continue to toast until it's smooth and super-fragrant.

3. Increase the heat to medium. Stir the coconut milk well (it tends to separate), and add it to the pot; squeeze in the lime juice, and drop the lime in, too. Cut the raw potatoes into 1-inch chunks, and add them with the bell pepper and onion.

4. Stir in the stock, sugar, 2 teaspoons salt, fish sauce, and lime leaves, and decrease the heat to low. Cook for 35 to 40 minutes, until the flavor is toasty and complex and the potatoes are tender. You don't need to reduce or thicken the stock; you just want to build flavor. At this point, you can cover the pot and keep it over the lowest flame until you're ready to serve.

5. Meanwhile, prepare the rice: Bring the water and the remaining 1 teaspoon salt to a boil in a saucepan over high heat. Once it's boiling, add the rice, cover, and reduce the heat to low. Cook for about 15 minutes, until it's tender, then remove the pan from the heat and keep it covered. Fluff with a fork, and set aside.

6. A few minutes before serving, add the lobster meat and all its juices to the curry pot. Poach for 4 to 5 minutes, just until the meat is opaque, tender, and firm—make sure you're in control of the heat so it doesn't boil. Serve over rice, garnished with the cucumber, peanuts, mint, and basil, alongside a cold beer.

2 cups lobster stock (recipe follows)
¼ cup canola oil
2-inch stalk lemongrass, very finely minced
1-inch knob fresh ginger, peeled and minced
1 clove garlic, minced
¼ cup green curry paste
3 cups coconut milk
1 lime, halved
1 pound Yukon Gold potatoes
1 green bell pepper, seeded and thinly sliced
1 yellow onion, thinly sliced
1 tablespoon sugar
1 tablespoon Morton kosher salt, divided
1 teaspoon fish sauce
5 lime leaves (fresh or frozen)
3 cups water
2 cups jasmine rice
Parcooked lobster meat from lobster stock (recipe follows)
1 medium cucumber (preferably seedless), chopped
½ cup roasted peanuts, chopped
½ cup lightly packed fresh mint leaves, chopped
½ cup lightly packed fresh basil leaves, preferably Thai basil, chopped

Lobster meat is so treasured, but its shells are equally valuable, and putting them in a stock allows you to make the most of the whole animal. By only partially cooking the lobster now, you avoid the common pitfall of overcooking it later, when it's added to your curry (or risotto, or seafood soup . . .). You also lose less of the shells' sweet, salty flavor this way; instead, you concentrate it into a huge batch of stock that takes less than an hour to cook.

There is a flip side: this method uses techniques that may not already be in your repertoire. The rhythm might feel difficult, if only because it's new. By all means, you can simplify things by forgoing the lobster altogether, using shrimp and your favorite seafood stock for the curry. The way I see it, though, if you're treating yourself and loved ones to lobster, this two-part recipe offers a great learning opportunity that you can apply to the rest of your cooking, and pays off with restaurant-quality food.

1. Set the lobsters in a large stockpot, and cover with the water, making sure they're completely submerged. If they're not, add more as needed. Remove the lobsters, and set them off to the side.

2. Squeeze the lemons into the pot, drop them in, then bring the water to a boil. Remove the pot from the heat, and immediately nestle the lobsters inside; cover, turn off the heat for 3 minutes, just long enough so the shells start to lighten in color. Pull the lobsters out, and reserve the cooking liquid in your pot. Don't freak out if their nerves are still twitching slightly. Rest assured, they're completely dead.

3. When the lobsters are cool enough to handle, start to break them down, working directly over your stockpot or a rimmed cutting board the whole time, to capture any errant juices. First hold the head in one hand and the tail in another, then firmly twist them apart to separate; don't be afraid to use some elbow grease.

4. Remove the two large claws by firmly gripping and twisting them right from the joint where they meet the body, still taking care to capture the juices that escape as you work. Drop the heads, along with any roe or fat, into the pot.

5. To separate the knuckles from the claws, use a seafood cracker or cover the claws with a dish towel and loosen the joints by banging once or twice with a meat mallet or the

Two 2-pound lobsters
1 gallon water, or more as needed
2 lemons, halved
2 stalks celery, roughly chopped
1 yellow onion, roughly chopped
1 tablespoon Morton kosher salt

bottom of a heavy saucepan. Use your fingers or the tip of a paring knife to extract and reserve every bit of meat, reserve it, then add the shells to the pot.

6. Grab the smaller part ("thumb") of the claw with your towel, and pull it firmly from side to side until it loosens enough so you can pull out the meat. (Don't worry too much if it doesn't come away in one very neat piece.) The meat will be limp and undercooked, but it will finish cooking in the curry. Crack open the large part of the claw the same way you did the knuckles; reserve that meat, too, and drop the empty shells into the stockpot.

7. Flip the tail upside down and use kitchen shears to make two cuts around the underside, along the edges where it meets the harder shell. Peel it open to pull out the meat, chop that into bite-sized pieces, and reserve; then it's into the stockpot for that shell, too.

8. Cover and refrigerate all the lobster meat. To make the stock: Add the celery, onion, and salt to the stockpot with the shells and cooking liquid. Bring to a boil over high heat, skimming away any foam as it rises up. Reduce the heat to medium, and simmer for about 45 minutes, skimming occasionally, until the liquid is pretty clear, with a full, briny flavor. Strain, and let cool before using or freezing.

II

✦ ✦ ✦

Steak for My Saba

had graduated from culinary school, had my first real cooking job back at Antonio's Italian Ristorante at the Rio Casino in Las Vegas, and I wanted to show my grandfather my talent. I wanted to impress him. And here my saba was, demanding that I cook his steak well done, sucked dry of all its juices. But: I would cook it however he wanted. I knew this steak was a significant one for us.

•

I HAVE SO MANY MEMORIES of my grandfather. In one, I'm seven years old, sitting in the back of a car speeding toward the touristy area of Philadelphia. The windows are up, and a thick cloud of Camel cigarette smoke fills the car. The Wham! hit "Wake Me Up Before You Go-Go" is blasting on the stereo, and my grandfather is singing along, even though he doesn't really speak English. He's dancing in his seat, chain-smoking. We're on the verge of crashing the car. I am enthralled. This guy, I think, is a total badass.

My saba made a big impression on me during his visits from Israel. He was a large guy, with a big nose and a head full of curly black hair. To me, he seemed to be about twenty feet tall, full of life, and indestructible. His shirtfront pockets always contained three things: a pack of cigarettes, a mini-screwdriver, and a pocket protector. He worked as a taxi driver in Jaffa for years (before becoming a computer programmer and then a hardware-store owner; hence the pocket protector and screwdriver), and he would drive with an Israeli taxi driver's mania, even in Main Line Philadelphia. Here was a man who crashed almost every car he drove, who loved watching spaghetti Westerns, and who pulled shrapnel out of his leg with tweezers while we kids would sit around the living room and watch in awe.

The shrapnel had ended up in my saba's leg during the Israeli War of Independence in 1948. Jews came from all over Europe to fight for Israel, and he was one of them. He narrowly escaped the concentration camps of World War II. He lived in Sofia, Bulgaria, and his country sided with Germany; Jews in Bulgaria faced the kind of social and legal restrictions that were a hallmark of Nazi-aligned areas. In 1943, Hitler ordered the removal of Bulgarian Jews to the death camps. But Bulgaria's King Boris III, under public pressure, halted the deportations. The Jews in Sofia—my grandfather among them—were spared; those from Macedonia, Thrace, and other parts of Bulgaria weren't so fortunate. In 1948, after World War II, my saba went to Jerusalem, where a bomb exploded very close to him. While lying in a hospital bed, he was able to negotiate a deal with the doctors to save his leg. I can see him now saying, "Fuck, no! You're not cutting off my leg!" I can picture him then turning his head in the other direction and flirting with the beautiful Bulgarian pharmacist who would later become my grandmother and teach me how to cook.

Some of my strongest memories of Saba's visits involve food. While cleaning his long cigarette pipe at the dining table, he would carve beef salami into rounds and shingle the slices on a baguette with cream cheese. Every time my saba came to visit, he would take us out to restaurants and introduce me to new foods—from a lobster that seemed almost as big as me, to my first bite of skate, that tender, mild fish—that my family had never had the money to eat. My mom was struggling to get by; TGI Friday's was the location of our birthday dinners every year. And so my saba's visits brought the luxury of eating out, of getting ice cream, and of finding candies from Israel hidden for me in his and my safta's suitcases.

Later, when I was getting in trouble as a teenager, I knew my saba would hear about it from my mother. My family got more worried every time I got arrested, every time I got kicked out of school, or got caught in Atlantic City at 2:00 a.m., drinking on a Tuesday. When he came to visit me in Las Vegas, it was my opportunity to show him just how far I'd come from those days.

I was proud of my setup in Las Vegas. I had a little apartment just behind the Gold Coast Casino. At night, I'd have to keep my blinds closed, because the lights reflecting off the building lit up my bedroom like Yankee Stadium. Antonio's was the kind of place that has fake marble columns and a ceiling painted to resemble a blue sky dotted with clouds. I'd cooked there for everyone from Pat Morita, the actor who played Mr. Miyagi in *The Karate Kid,* to the boxer Oscar De La Hoya and, even, one night, Joey Buttafuoco. I had my saba come in for dinner when he arrived. I was sure he would be impressed, especially when I proudly told him there would be no bill. He was mortified. We gave away free food all the time at the casino, so I couldn't understand why he was so upset. In my saba's world, though, nothing came for free. He thought I would be fired for stealing food. I was embarrassed at the time, but as I look back on it now, I think this was one of the great lessons I learned from him: You're not as important as you think you are. A restaurant is a job, not a playground.

I had one more meal during Saba's visit with which to redeem myself, and decided to cook him dinner personally in my apartment. I'd recently been given my first cast-iron pan and was excited to show him a steak recipe I'd just learned, which came with sliced potatoes that were fried until crisp and seasoned with chili flakes. He sat at the table, breathing heavily, as I prepped the food. We'd walked from the Las Vegas Strip after catching the water show at the recently opened Bellagio casino. He asked me to take him home; he could hardly breathe after walking so far. He'd been diagnosed with lung cancer and had a lung removed, but his declining health hadn't really sunk in for me until that moment. Seeing fragility in this person I'd always known as a beast of a man was eye-opening. As I flipped the steak in the pan, I realized why he'd come to visit. I cooked that steak well done for him, as he'd asked, even though I knew it would ruin the meat. He told me how much he loved the food, how proud he was of me, but the recognition felt melancholy to me now. That steak dinner was our final meal together.

2 boneless 14-to-16-ounce ribeyes
1 teaspoon Morton kosher salt
2 tablespoons canola oil

hat final meal I cooked for my saba—steak and potatoes—inspired all the recipes in this chapter, the meal I would make for him if I could get a do-over. Cooking a good steak doesn't take much fanfare, but it will teach you a few lessons that improve the rest of your cooking. Pre-salting gives the seasoning time to work its way through the meat, and letting it rest in the fridge (ideally, for up to a day) helps it dry so it gets a better crust the moment it hits the pan. Both steps boil down to thinking ahead, and they do wonders to intensify everything that's already great about this cut of beef. Cooking it in blazing-hot oil gives that really hard sear, providing it with lots of flavor, which is perfectly offset by chimichurri (recipe follows) but needs nothing else.

1. Use a paper towel or dish towel to pat the steaks dry on both sides. Sprinkle ¼ teaspoon salt on each side of each steak, and give it a pat to make sure it sticks. Refrigerate the steaks on an uncovered plate for at least 1 hour and up to a day.
2. Before you cook, let the steak sit at room temperature for 20 minutes or so to take off the chill.

(recipe continues)

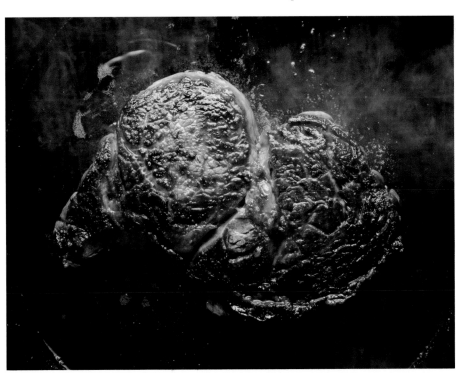

3. Set a large cast-iron skillet over high heat until it's blazing-hot, then add the canola oil. If the steaks won't fit in the skillet without crowding, add only 1 tablespoon of oil now and save the other for the second steak, and heat your oven to 175°F so that the first steak stays warm while you cook the second. Allow the oil to get smoking-hot.

4. Lay the steak or steaks in the skillet side by side, and immediately decrease the heat to medium. Leave them alone for 5 to 8 minutes, depending on how thick they are. You should see a deep-brown crust climbing about ¼ inch from the bottom for medium-rare, or a little higher if you prefer a more well-done steak. Flip and cook the other side for another 3 to 5 minutes, until the other side is deeply browned as well. Again, cook for an extra minute or two if you like.

5. Let the steaks rest for at least 5 minutes on a plate, so the juices can settle in. (If you're worried about the steaks getting cold, keep them in a warm oven.) Slice the steak thinly and on a bias to serve, preferably with chimichurri on the side (recipe follows).

ZA'ATAR CHIMICHURRI

YIELD: ABOUT 1 CUP

In Israel, steak is typically eaten with something acidic, like lemon or tomato. With the earthy za'atar, this is my spin on chimichurri, the staple sauce in Argentina, where steak is practically its own food group. If you're like me, you'll keep finding excuses to eat it on other things, from salads and roasted vegetables to fish, scrambled eggs, even toast. Just make sure you wait to add the lemon until just before you're ready to serve, to keep the green herbs tasting bright and lively.

Chop the parsley and cilantro together. Add them to a bowl with the garlic, za'atar, salt, and red pepper, then stir in the olive oil. Shortly before it's time to eat, stir in the lemon juice. This is best eaten when it's very fresh.

1 cup lightly packed fresh parsley leaves
¾ cup lightly packed fresh cilantro leaves
½ clove garlic, grated or minced
2 teaspoons za'atar
¼ teaspoon Morton kosher salt
¼ teaspoon red-pepper flakes
½ cup extra-virgin olive oil
2 tablespoons lemon juice

BRUSSELS SPROUTS WITH CARAWAY AND TAHINI

All the best things you can say about potatoes as a side-kick to steak, you can also say about Brussels sprouts: they're hearty enough to hold their own, and they soak up the best of what's around them. My favorite way to cook them is hard and fast; it gives you so many textures, from the crisped-up outer leaves to the still-crunchy center. This is also one of the fastest ways to prepare them. I love adding tahini, which under-scores the sprouts' natural nuttiness.

¼ cup extra-virgin olive oil
1 teaspoon ground caraway seeds
¼ teaspoon ground allspice
¼ teaspoon red-pepper flakes
Grated zest of 1 lemon
2 teaspoons Morton kosher salt, divided
1 tablespoon lemon juice
1 clove garlic, crushed
2 pounds Brussels sprouts
¼ cup raw tahini
3 tablespoons water

1. Heat the broiler, and set a rack in the middle of the oven. In a large bowl, combine the olive oil, spices, lemon zest, and 1½ teaspoons salt. Separately, combine the lemon juice and garlic clove, and set aside to steep for at least 30 minutes.

2. Trim the stems from the sprouts and halve the sprouts lengthwise (quarter them if they're big). Toss them in the large bowl with the seasoned olive oil, and spread them on a rimmed baking sheet until they're evenly coated with the spice. It's okay if there are loose leaves—those are the ones that will crisp up the most.

3. Broil for 5 or 6 minutes; when the edges are deeply caramelized, give everything a good stir, and broil for another 4 to 5 minutes, until the sprouts are uniformly golden with some deeply charred edges.

4. Remove and discard the garlic from the lemon juice. Whisk the juice with the tahini, water, and remaining ½ teaspoon salt. Transfer the sprouts to your serving dish, and drizzle the tahini sauce over the top.

CREAMY BAKED FENNEL

In the Lombardia region of Italy, fennel cooked slowly in cream is a common accompaniment to steak. It's not too far off from the Pernod-spiked creamed spinach you might find in old-school steakhouses here in the States. There's something about this trifecta of flavors—cream, vegetables, and anise-y sweetness—that just makes sense. As the cream cooks down in the oven, it reflects the fennel and herbs back at you, making a warming and rich complement to the meat.

2 fennel bulbs, with their fronds
¼ cup plus 2 tablespoons extra-virgin olive oil, divided
3 sprigs fresh thyme
5 fresh sage leaves
2 medium shallots, chopped
½ cup white wine
1¼ cups heavy cream
1½ teaspoons Morton kosher salt
1 teaspoon sugar
1 cup fresh breadcrumbs
½ cup raw pecans or walnuts, finely chopped
¼ cup grated Parmesan cheese
½ teaspoon red-pepper flakes
Grated zest of ½ orange

1. Heat the oven to 400°F, and set a rack in the middle of the oven. Trim the stems from the fennel, and quarter the bulbs lengthwise. Reserve the fronds as garnish.

2. Get ¼ cup olive oil hot in a large skillet over medium heat. Add the fennel, and leave it alone for 8 to 10 minutes, long enough to build a deep-golden crust on that side; decrease the heat a bit if it starts to scorch or smoke. Flip each piece to the other flat side, and cook for another 5 or 6 minutes, until that side is browned, too. Nestle the fennel into a deep, round casserole dish (it's okay to stack the pieces) and set aside.

3. Strip the leaves from the thyme, and chop them along with the sage. Add the shallots and herbs to the hot pan, and sauté until the shallots are golden along the edges. Stir in the wine, and reduce by about half; then add the cream, salt, and sugar. Bring everything up to a good simmer for a couple of minutes, until it's thickened a bit more.

4. Pour the pan sauce over the fennel, and bake for 50 minutes to 1 hour, until the fennel is very tender and the liquid has reduced by enough that there's not a lot of bubbling left in the dish.

5. Heat your broiler. Strip the tender fennel fronds from their stems, give them a rough chop, and mix them with the breadcrumbs, nuts, Parmesan, pepper flakes, orange zest, and remaining 2 tablespoons olive oil. Spread this evenly over the fennel, and broil for 2 minutes or so, until the top is nicely colored. Serve.

VEGETABLE "POT ROAST" WITH DUQQA

This dish is one big paradox: It's for anyone who, like me, secretly (or not so secretly) likes the juicy, flavorful vegetables at the bottom of the pot roast as much as the meat itself. It's hearty but light, savory but bright, with a lot of great texture from the waxy potatoes and crunchy duqqa. It'll also make your whole kitchen smell like heaven. It needs a while in the oven—probably longer than you're used to cooking vegetables—but every minute goes toward building those bold, complex flavors. It's a wonderful side dish anytime, a natural next to a ribeye (page 137), and an equally satisfying and impressive entrée for the vegetarians at your table. (You can use four Kalamata olives instead of the anchovies.)

1 head celery
2 pounds new or Yukon Gold potatoes
1 pound parsnips or carrots, peeled
2 lemons
½ cup extra-virgin olive oil
¼ cup whole-grain mustard
5 fresh sage leaves
4 anchovies or Kalamata olives
4 cloves garlic, thinly sliced
1 tablespoon celery salt
1 teaspoon Morton kosher salt
1 teaspoon red-pepper flakes
½ cup vegetable broth
⅓ cup duqqa (page 388)

1. Heat the oven to 375°F with a rack in the center of the oven. Use a large rectangular baking dish as a stencil to cut a piece of parchment.

2. Pull off the celery's light-colored, tender inner leaves and keep them in the fridge for the time being; discard the tougher outer leaves. Cut off the root and tips, then slice the stalks diagonally into 1-to-2-inch pieces. Cut the potatoes and parsnips into 1-to-2-inch chunks (roughly the same size as the celery), cut the lemons in half, and toss everything together in the baking dish.

3. Combine the olive oil, mustard, sage, anchovies, garlic, salts, and red-pepper flakes in a large pan, and cook this mixture over medium-low heat for a few minutes, until the anchovies have melted and the garlic has built a little color.

4. Remove the pan from the heat, and add the vegetable broth; then pour the mixture evenly over the vegetables. Press the parchment on top to hold in all the moisture, wrap the pan tightly in 2 overlapping sheets of foil, and bake for 1½ to 2 hours, until the vegetables are super-tender but still have some integrity.

5. Remove the foil and parchment, and increase the heat to 500°F. Bake for another 20 to 30 minutes, until the edges of the vegetables are deeply colored. Sprinkle the reserved celery leaves and the duqqa evenly over everything right before you serve.

✦ ✦ ✦

12

Boss Man

When I moved there, St. Louis was a city that was in love with its steak and baked potatoes. The Harrah's Casino in St. Louis—where, at age twenty-one, I'd just landed the job of executive chef at a brand-new location of Antonio's Italian Ristorante—was a very different casino from the one in Las Vegas. No fine-dining Chinese restaurant, no caviar, no giant lobsters. Instead, there was the Range Steakhouse, which was famous for its 72-ounce prime rib. It was pretty much as if a cow had jumped onto the plate, died, and been baked to medium under the hot sun. When I took over, I intended to blow diners' minds with my sophisticated Italian cooking.

Some of the food at my incarnation of Antonio's was good. When we first opened, I served a lot of what I'd learned in Las Vegas from Chef William—Chef No Neck. I made his soup of shallots, red onions, white onions, leeks, and scallions, stewed down with chicken broth and Marsala into creamy bliss. We'd pour that into a hollowed-out roasted onion, add a piece of crusty ciabatta on top, and then melt a layer of aged provolone over it all, until the onion was topped with a bubbly, golden-brown lid. We made Chef William's osso buco, so tender that only a piece of butcher's twine held it together. Many of our customers had never before encountered a bone-in veal chop Milanese. Pounded until very thin and just lightly breaded, seasoned with salt and lemon juice, it gave you the perfect bite: the slight crunch of the breading, the snapping tartness of the lemon, all a gorgeous complement to the mild veal within.

FIVE DIFFERENT
ALLIUMS FOR
ONION SOUP

I started to get more creative, to break out of the recipes I'd learned in Las Vegas. I was trying to be innovative and, caught up in my success as a mere twenty-one-year-old, I believed I could do no wrong. The veal chop stopped being breaded and became grilled with melted cheese and sugary caramelized onions. A Chilean sea bass that used to be stewed in a rich tomato sauce with onions, capers, olives, and spicy chilies began to be served over a citrus beurre blanc with fennel. I took an innocent little rainbow trout and stuffed it with wild rice, adding insult to injury by drizzling it with arugula coulis and roasted-red-pepper aioli. I put truffle oil in all sorts of superfluous places.

On one evening, I must have had my mother visiting, because it was my first time eating in Antonio's dining room. We had a dish that I'd kind of stolen from Chef Jean-Louis Palladin, one I'd made while working the fish station in his restaurant in Las Vegas. It was asparagus shaved very thin—"asparagus fettuccine," he'd called it—tossed with lemon-infused olive oil, and topped with a pan-roasted piece of wild salmon. I tried to re-create a version of the dish with tiny, gumdrop-sized gnocchi and an asparagus sauce as a base. This one night, I was sitting in the dining room, watching everyone eat and listening in on their conversations. I saw someone eat the gnocchi and then exclaim, "These are horrible!" It was like a knife to my heart. I was completely defeated. I didn't know at that time that allowing my potatoes to cool while making my dough would turn the gnocchi starchy and gummy. But, instead of saying to myself, "Well, what's wrong with the gnocchi? How can I make them better?" I just took it off the menu. I was, like, "*Screw gnocchi,* I'm just going to do something else." In so many ways, I was still a child when it came to food.

Because of that, I completely missed out on the wealth of Italian food that was right under my nose in St. Louis. There were lots of Lombardian and Sicilian immigrant families serving classic Italian American fare at places called Gino's, Charlie Gitto's, and Gian-Tony's. I would go eat at these places and judge them on technique and on what the restaurant looked like; I would sneer at how all their menus were the same. They each had their chicken Parm, their shrimp with angel-hair pasta, their toasted ravioli, breaded and deep-fried and served with a little ramekin of marinara sauce. Why couldn't they be more creative? I was happier at the nearby Italian import shops, where I could muse about the wonders of what I could accomplish with twenty-five-year-old balsamic vinegar and bottarga, the cured eggs of mullet.

Somehow, with my rapid rise from extern set loose in the kitchens of the Rio Casino to chef in charge of Antonio's in St. Louis, I'd gone from thinking of myself as the eager learner to the expert.

This did not exactly sit well with some of the folks in my kitchen. There were some cooks who'd been working a line for years and were far more experienced than I was. At the beginning, we'd had a decent rapport. But as I began breaking away from the classics on the menu and cooking whatever I wanted, I could feel the relationships in the kitchen start to break down, a rumbling from below. "Why are we cooking this?" they'd ask. Or "This dish isn't working out." Instead of working with them on it, I'd get frustrated and yell, "The dish is fine! The servers just need to explain it better!" One day, I called Chef William to ask him what to do about a sous-chef who'd been undermining my authority. "Pull him into the walk-in and tell him you're going to make his life a living hell," he suggested. I tried it out. "Are you serious?" the sous-chef asked me as we both shivered in the walk-in fridge.

Thank goodness for Octavio.

Octavio Mantilla was the general manager for Antonio's, who'd moved from New Orleans to St. Louis to open the restaurant with me. He was a decade older than I was, shorter, and Nicaraguan. Like me, he was an immigrant to the United States, having arrived in Louisiana when he was thirteen. He'd already been working in the hospitality industry for years and knew how to handle both the restaurant's employees and the higher-ups at Harrah's, becoming my corporate diplomat and my guide for how to be less of a jerk to my staff. He would never get in the middle of kitchen conflicts and try to fix things. Instead, he had this way of allowing a problem to get to a point at which I was frustrated enough to talk it out with him. Then he'd gently offer me wisdom about how to navigate the situation. It helped me out with my people skills.

Even as I was making unnecessarily froufrou food, the irony was that I kept getting good press. And the more I got preferential treatment for my work ethic and my passion, the more it went to my head. I'd stopped *studying* food and was trying to *create* food . . . and what I made suffered. I couldn't even admit it to myself.

FIVE-ONION SOUP WITH PROVOLONE TOAST

This is one dish dating back to my days at Antonio's that I love just as much today. During that time in my life, I was making lots of culinary mistakes. This was never one of them; it's always been a warm friend I could count on. At the casino, we served it in a colossal onion that had been hollowed out and roasted—an edible soup bowl—but that gimmick is not necessary to enjoy it. For me, it's a lesson in patience: you *could* rush or skimp on it, but the payoff would be nowhere near as great. Give it some time (plus plenty of butter), and all the alliums melt together and sweeten.

1. Wash the leeks thoroughly to remove any grit. Melt the butter with ¼ cup olive oil in a heavy-bottomed pot or Dutch oven over medium heat, then add the leeks, onions, shallots, and scallions; give them a good stir so they're evenly coated with the fat. Decrease the heat to low, and slowly cook, stirring occasionally, until all the alliums are melting but aren't showing any color, 50 minutes to 1 hour.

2. Stir in the flour until it's fully incorporated, then add the stock, cream, Marsala, salt, and white pepper. Increase the heat to medium, and simmer for another 25 or 30 minutes, until the whole thing is very thick and rich. Stir it regularly, since the flour can scorch on you if it's left unattended.

3. When the whole soup is very thick and most of the water has cooked out, stir in the Parmesan, basil, Worcestershire, and Tabasco, and remove from the heat.

4. Meanwhile, heat the oven to 400°F. Arrange the bread on a baking sheet, and drizzle the last 2 tablespoons olive oil over it; toast in the center rack of the oven for 8 to 12 minutes, until the croutons are very crisp and golden. Take the pan out of the oven and turn on the broiler.

5. Tile the bread over the soup, and drape the provolone so the slices overlap in a layer to cover the pot. (If you prefer, you can instead ladle the soup and layer the toasts in individual bowls.) Broil for 2 to 3 minutes, until the cheese is freckled brown, and dive in.

2 leeks, white and light-green parts only, thinly sliced
1 stick unsalted butter
¼ cup plus 2 tablespoons extra-virgin olive oil, divided
2 white onions, thinly sliced
2 red onions, thinly sliced
6 to 8 shallots (about ¾ pound), chopped
2 bunches scallions, thinly sliced
¼ cup all-purpose flour
1 quart chicken stock
1½ cups heavy cream
¼ cup dry Marsala or red wine
1 tablespoon Morton kosher salt
½ teaspoon ground white pepper
⅔ cup finely grated Parmesan cheese
16 fresh basil leaves, torn
1 tablespoon Worcestershire sauce
1 teaspoon Tabasco sauce
8 slices ciabatta or baguette
8 slices provolone cheese

Despite my angst over the failed gnocchi in St. Louis, I did eventually learn how to make them well. The lesson I took from them is: face your fears and conquer the food that intimidates you most; you may not win the first battle, but you'll win the war!

The key is to commit to the process. Be precise about the weight of your peeled potatoes (too much or too little will alter the final texture); use a potato ricer or food mill, and work rapidly, while everything is warm, since the starches get gummy if you beat them up or allow them to cool. Therefore, it's crucial to get your ingredients and equipment ready to go before you start. Take those little steps, be sure not to overwork the dough, and you'll get the lightest, fluffiest gnocchi you've ever had.

Because time is of the essence whenever you cook potatoes, you get the best results when you make a relatively small batch—this recipe makes four portions. But because the gnocchi can be made in advance, you can make two or three batches, then sauce them all at once. Each batch will get easier, as the process becomes more intuitive. For all that focus, I like to pair this with something effortless that allows the gnocchi to really shine. Look no further than my fast tomato sauce (recipe follows). Other great options would be brown butter or even a really good olive oil.

- 1 gallon plus 2 quarts water, divided
- 2 tablespoons plus ½ teaspoon Morton kosher salt, divided
- 2 or 3 large Yukon Gold potatoes (18 ounces peeled)
- 4 tablespoons unsalted butter, softened
- 4 egg yolks
- 1⅓ cup (160 grams) all-purpose flour, preferably White Lily, plus more for dusting
- ¼ teaspoon finely grated nutmeg
- 2 teaspoons extra-virgin olive oil, plus more for serving
- 1 recipe fast tomato sauce (recipe follows)
- ½ cup finely grated Parmesan cheese

1. Heat the oven to 400°F. Fill a pot with 1 gallon water and 2 tablespoons salt, and let it come to a boil. Cover the pot and leave it on low heat, so it's ready when you need it.

2. Peel the potatoes, and measure out exactly 18 ounces. Cut them into eighths, place them in a large ovenproof pot or saucepan, cover them with 2 quarts cold water, and put the pan over high heat. Once the water boils, decrease the heat to medium, and simmer until the potatoes are easily pierced with a fork, 10 to 12 minutes.

3. Drain the potatoes, and place them back in the ovenproof pot. Bake until they're rid of excess moisture, 4 to 5 minutes. While they bake, use a fork to beat together the butter and yolks until they're as smooth as you can get them; set the bowl aside.

(recipe continues)

4. As soon as the potatoes are out of the oven, pass them through a ricer or food mill into a large bowl, making sure you scrape the bottom. Fold in the butter mixture until it's incorporated, then add the flour, nutmeg, and last ½ teaspoon salt all at once, using your spatula to cut these ingredients in with minimal stirring. It'll look crumbly, almost like pie crust.

5. Generously flour an unrimmed baking sheet and your work surface. Dump the dough onto the surface, and gently press it into a ball. Cut it in quarters, and work with one piece at a time, leaving the rest covered with a dish towel to stay warm.

6. Roll each piece of dough into a long, skinny log, about ¾ inch wide; dust with flour as you work, to prevent it from sticking. With a floured paring knife or bench scraper, cut the dough into ¾-inch dumplings, keeping the blade clean as you work. Add all the dumplings to the baking sheet, and repeat with the rest of the dough, working quickly so the potatoes don't get too starchy as they cool.

7. Shape the gnocchi, one at a time, by pressing the dumpling between the pad of your thumb and a gnocchi board or the back of a fork. Roll it steadily, parallel to the board's ridges or the fork's tines, so it curls around itself.

8. Gently drop the gnocchi from the baking sheet into the boiling water. A bench scraper or wide spatula can help you make sure they aren't misshapen in transit. Watch for them to float—should be about 1 minute—then cook for another 30 seconds. They're done when the centers resemble pound cake, with the same consistency throughout. Drain, and toss with the olive oil.

9. At this point, you can add the gnocchi to the sauce and eat them, or refrigerate them in an airtight container for a day or two. To reheat: Drop them into boiling water for about 20 seconds, just until they're warm all the way through, before adding sauce; reheating them this way restores the light, fluffy texture. Top with plenty of Parmesan to serve.

FAST TOMATO SAUCE

YIELD: 4 SERVINGS

½ cup extra-virgin olive oil
1½ pounds tomatoes, cored and roughly chopped
3 cloves garlic, thinly sliced
9 fresh basil leaves, torn
¾ teaspoon Morton kosher salt
¾ teaspoon red-pepper flakes

This is my go-to pasta sauce, as fast as it is delicious. Make it with the best in-season tomatoes you can find—the screaming-hot oil allows you to hold on to their fresh, raw sweetness and acidity while concentrating them into a thick sauce. Needless to say, this sauce is good on any pasta you feel like making, so don't limit it to showstoppers like gnocchi. Just be sure you wear an apron, so you don't get tomatoes and oil splattered on your clothes!

1. Pour the olive oil into a large skillet with high sides or a Dutch oven over high heat, and cook until it's smoking-hot. Being extremely careful, add the tomatoes and garlic; they will give off a lot of smoke as soon as they hit the oil, so it's easiest to have the tomatoes on a flexible cutting board or in a bowl that you can dump from.

2. Use your spoon to spread the tomatoes in a single layer, then add the basil, salt, and red pepper. Give everything a good stir, and cook another 4 to 5 minutes, until the sauce thickens.

CHICKEN MILANESE WITH WATERCRESS AND LEMON

YIELD: 4 SERVINGS

The term "Milanese" is used to describe the breaded veal chop that's a signature dish of Milan, a close cousin to schnitzels from Austria. When my mom made schnitzels, she would use chicken breasts. They taste great in this preparation and cost a fraction of the price. If you can't find watercress, get arugula—you want something with a little bite to cut through the rich crust of the meat.

1. Place a chicken breast on a long sheet of plastic wrap, and splash it with a dab of water to keep it slick, then pull the plastic over it to cover. With a meat mallet or heavy rolling pin, pound it outward until it's an even ½ inch in thickness. Repeat with the others.

2. Place the flour in a wide, shallow bowl. Beat the milk and eggs together in a second bowl; in a third, season the breadcrumbs with the sesame seeds, hawaij, and salt, and mix well. Separately, line a large plate with paper towels.

3. Set the olive oil and butter in a large skillet over medium-high heat. Drop a small piece of bread into the oil to test the heat—it's ready when it toasts golden right away; if it turns dark too fast or if the oil spatters wildly, turn the heat down a bit before adding the chicken.

4. Dredge a piece of chicken in the flour, coating all sides and shaking off any excess. Do the same thing in the milk and eggs, then dip it in the seasoned breadcrumbs. You want a light but even coating, so resist the urge to cake it on.

5. Drop the chicken into the oil, and leave it be for 2 or 3 minutes, until the bottom is deeply golden and crisp. (You can cook multiple pieces of chicken at a time, as long as the pan isn't crowded.) Flip the chicken, and cook, undisturbed, for another 2 minutes or so. Moderate the heat as needed: you want it to be hot enough to create a crust but low enough so that you're in control.

6. Move the chicken to the lined plate, and repeat until all the pieces are cooked. Pile ¼ cup watercress or arugula on each piece, and serve with a lemon wedge, which people can squeeze themselves. Eat while it's hot.

4 boneless, skinless chicken breasts (1 to 1½ pounds)
Water, for pounding the chicken
½ cup all-purpose flour
¼ cup milk
2 eggs
1 cup fresh breadcrumbs
¼ cup white sesame seeds, toasted
2 tablespoons hawaij (page 390) or yellow curry powder
1 teaspoon Morton kosher salt
½ cup extra-virgin olive oil
1 tablespoon unsalted butter
1 cup fresh watercress or arugula
1 lemon, quartered

13

✦✦✦

Safta's Last Lutenitsa

Cooking kettles of macaroni and cheese for five thousand people and managing the economics of a salad bar were not what I'd had in mind when I decided to become a chef. Now here I was, in charge of the buffet at another location of Harrah's Casino, this one in New Orleans. The pay was good, better than I'd ever had before. But most of my job was far from the kitchen. I oversaw the four hundred employees who were charged with keeping food available to Harrah's customers 24 hours a day, 7 days a week.

My archenemy at the time was the chocolate fountain on the dessert bar. It was constantly overflowing, jammed with diners' strawberries and pretzel rods. And if the chocolate fountain wasn't working properly, I would hear about it promptly—and with great passion—from our elderly female customers. Solving problems at the dessert bar, breaking up knife fights between dishwashers, figuring out graceful ways to scold diners who had stuffed pork chops from the buffet into ziplock bags in their purses—this was my job. It was so far from the cooking I loved. I'd spend every night off as a volunteer on the line at Restaurant August, the flagship of Chef John Besh, who also ran the steakhouse at the casino. My fiancée at the time, Christina, was getting fed up with my workaholism. She was starting to make moves to leave me, but I was too distracted to fully notice.

In the midst of this, I got a call from my mother. Safta was summoning us all to come to Israel. She'd been ill and at this point could hardly get out of bed. She wanted to see all of us—her children, her grandchildren—one more time. No one was saying it outright, but I felt we all understood: this was Safta's final wish. Given the disappointment of my current life, I found a trip to visit her in Israel a welcome distraction.

I hadn't seen her in several years, not since the Bar Mitzvah of my cousin Gideon. Though she had been using a wheelchair then, she'd seemed like herself. The safta I saw when I arrived at her house in Jaffa was far more frail. She could barely speak above a whisper. She'd abandoned the art she'd taken up in her old age, painting the port of old Jaffa or drawing flowers with pastels. Now her hands were pretty much useless. She just sat there quietly in her bedroom with the window open, a breeze from the nearby Mediterranean ruffling the curtains. I felt a deflation inside, seeing her this way. And because I've never been very good at confronting sadness, I turned to what I *did* know how to do: cook.

I told my safta I wanted to cook all of my favorite foods that we'd made together when I was young, and this time I would write down the recipes. Her English was poor, and my Hebrew had completely faded at this point. There wasn't a whole lot for us to sit around and chat about. But cooking I could do, and cooking she understood.

For several days, I would leave early in the morning with shekels in my pocket and a grocery list written by Safta herself. I would browse Tel Aviv's markets, inspired by all the produce, meats, nuts, pastries, and halvah lining the alleys in the large open-air stalls. I marveled at the piles of leeks stacked up like firewood, and at the thousands of sweet, ripe cherries displayed in a mound on a wooden tray. The markets gave me a burst of creative energy, and I decided to show off some of my culinary knowledge to my grandmother by making a little something of my own. I came home and whipped up a grilled-peach salad with spinach and feta cheese, which I presented to her with a flourish. "It's good," she said, but instead of further congratulating me, she added, "You should really be focused on the recipes that we need to be cooking together." The message I got was loud and clear: "Why are you wasting time on this? Let's get back to the important work of documenting my recipes." She was taking this project seriously.

Because she was bedridden, we developed a system. I would start cooking in the kitchen and run back and forth between there and her bedroom to ask her the next steps of the recipe, bringing her a taste of how it was progressing. With each bite, she'd tell me what to adjust: "A little more salt," or "Keep cooking that a bit longer." I meticulously wrote down all the ingredients, aware of the value of what she was handing me. We made several of my favorites: leek patties; chopped liver; kebabs; couscous with pomegranates, almonds, and mint. For the first time, I registered with wonder the flavor of za'atar, the ubiquitous Middle Eastern spice of dried hyssop, ground and blended with sumac and sesame seeds. I made lutenitsa, that tomato-sweetened paste of roasted eggplants and bell peppers that I remembered her preparing at our first house in Philadelphia. "Serve in a restaurant with brioche toast points," I wrote in my notebook.

She also taught me some recipes I hadn't recalled so well. One involved grinding walnuts, bread, garlic, olive oil, and vinegar into a sauce with her mortar and pestle. "Eat it with fried fish," she said. We made another sauce, agristada, or, as she called it, "boiled mayonnaise." When she saw the perplexed look on my face, she launched into the technique. You make it by heating chicken broth and flour over low heat with some lemon, salt, and a pinch of sugar, then whisking in egg yolks and cooking it until it thickens. "Macerate some parsley with extra-virgin olive oil, and fold it into the sauce," she dictated to me, and then said I should serve it with rabbit or chicken. I scribbled furiously in my notebook. It produced an incredible sauce that was thick like a sabayon, but savory instead of sweet.

It'd been years since I'd tasted any of these dishes, and I was surprised, shepherding them between her kitchen and her bedroom, at how moving it was to me, not only to eat them but also to make them for my safta. In some small way, it felt as if we were resuming the work we'd done together in the kitchen of my childhood, decades before. This was how we had always spent time together; it was how we'd connected from the very beginning. Now, with Safta so weak and nearing death, the food carried an added emotional power.

At the end of the week in Israel, I'd written down more than a dozen recipes. I bid Safta goodbye with them safely gathered in my notebook. But when I returned to work and my life in New Orleans, I promptly forgot about Israeli food.

•

THE FOLLOWING ARE AMONG the recipes I learned from my safta during that last visit with her, as her health was failing. Years earlier, when she visited us in Philadelphia, these were dishes she'd prepare with us regularly. When she and my saba were visiting, our biggest meal of the day was always lunch—that's when we'd eat many of the hot dishes, the stuffed cabbage, the kebabs. For dinner, we'd have a simple meal of bread, olives, cheese, and a few of these other dishes, like the ikra and chilled yogurt soup. Cooking these recipes now allows me to spend time with my grandmother even after she's gone.

TZATZIKI

Tzatziki was always on my grandmother's table. I could count on it to bring balance to the spice and warmth of all the other dishes we'd eat. It also offered some relief during the heat of summer in her un-air-conditioned apartment in Jaffa. It's so simple—it can be little more than cucumber, fresh dill, and yogurt—but the spices I include go the extra mile, with dill seeds taking the fresh dill flavor to the nth degree. Omit them altogether if you can't find them; it'll still be wonderful and nuanced.

1 cup lightly packed fresh dill fronds
1 large cucumber, preferably seedless, skin on
1 large clove garlic
1 cup Bulgarian yogurt
1 cup sour cream
1 tablespoon extra-virgin olive oil, plus more for serving
  Grated zest of 1 lemon
1 tablespoon lemon juice
½ teaspoon ground caraway seeds
½ teaspoon ground dill seeds
1½ teaspoons Morton kosher salt

1. Chop the dill fronds. Halve the cucumber lengthwise, scoop out any seeds, and cut it into small dice (you should have about 2 cups' worth). Mince or grate the garlic.
2. In a large bowl, combine the yogurt, sour cream, olive oil, lemon zest, lemon juice, spices, and salt. Fold in the dill fronds, cucumber, and garlic. Drizzle more olive oil into the bowl before serving.

CHILLED YOGURT SOUP WITH CRUSHED WALNUTS

Tzatziki morphs easily into this chilled soup, called "tarator." Walnuts give it a lot of body and texture, and the pink peppercorns lend it a lighter peppery flavor that borders on floral. It's everything you'd want to eat on a hot day; sometimes you'll even see it served with an ice cube at the bottom of the bowl, which you're welcome to do if it's a scorcher when you're preparing this.

1 recipe tzatziki (preceding recipe)
⅓ cup ice water, or more as needed
1 cup walnut pieces, toasted
5 or 6 fresh mint leaves
5 or 6 fresh basil leaves
2 tablespoons extra-virgin olive oil, plus more for serving
2 tablespoons lemon juice
1 tablespoon whole pink peppercorns

1. Thin the tzatziki out with ⅓ cup ice water. Roughly chop the walnuts; separately, cut the mint and basil into very thin ribbons.
2. Stir everything into the tzatziki along with the olive oil and lemon juice. Lightly crush the pink peppercorns between your fingertips as you add them to the bowl, and garnish with more olive oil. If you'd like the soup a little thinner, add more ice water, 1 tablespoon at a time.

CHERRY, JALAPEÑO, AND CILANTRO SALAD

YIELD: 4 TO 6 SERVINGS

When you go to markets in Israel, the sheer quantity of cherries that you'll see piled everywhere is out of control. Their abundance is why this salad exists. I first had a version of it at a restaurant inside the market, just steps away from those giant mounds of cherries, as if it were invented to keep them in check. And even though my safta may have been relatively uninterested in the fruit-based salad I whipped up for her during our last visit, I love salads that combine the sweet and the savory as masterfully as this one. The flavors and textures are almost like ceviche: juicy, meaty, tender, so alive, each ingredient the absolute purest and most intense version of itself. If you're not contending with a surplus of cherries, it works just as well with peak-season peaches, plums, or tomatoes. You may even add arugula or another favorite green, to lend heft and absorb all the juices that the fruit will give—though I personally prefer the fruit unadulterated.

- 2 pounds fresh sweet cherries
- 3 tablespoons rice wine vinegar, preferably seasoned
- 3 tablespoons extra-virgin olive oil
- 1 teaspoon Morton kosher salt
  Grated zest of ½ lime
- 1 tablespoon lime juice
- 2 medium shallots, thinly sliced
- 1 jalapeño, seeds and pith removed, thinly sliced
- 1 cup lightly packed fresh cilantro leaves, torn

1. Pit the cherries (you can use your hands to split them into rough halves). You should have about 6 cups' worth.
2. In a large bowl, combine the vinegar, olive oil, salt, lime zest, and lime juice. Add the cherries, and toss to coat. Scatter with the shallots, jalapeño, and cilantro, and serve right away.

ROASTED BEETS WITH TAHINI

Beets are classically paired with goat cheese or Gorgonzola, because their earthy sweetness plays off those bold, tart, and creamy flavors. So it makes a lot of sense to add tahini—another earthy, bold, and distinctive flavor—and lighten it all up with Greek yogurt. What you get tastes familiar but new, and nothing's more beautiful to see on a dinner table. There's plenty of dressing to go around, which I love, but if you want to keep it on the lighter side, make the dressing separately, so people can add only as much as they want.

- 3 pounds red beets, preferably small
- 1 tablespoon extra-virgin olive oil
- 1½ teaspoons Morton kosher salt, divided
- 6 tablespoons raw tahini
- ¼ cup ice water
- 2 tablespoons lemon juice
- 2 tablespoons Greek yogurt
- 1 teaspoon Aleppo pepper
- ½ teaspoon ground coriander
- 8 sprigs fresh dill, chopped

1. Heat the oven to 400°F with a rack in the center of the oven. Scrub the beets well (don't worry about peeling them), and trim their roots and stringy ends. If they're big, cut them in halves or quarters, so they're no more than 3 inches wide at their biggest point.

2. Toss the beets in the olive oil and 1 teaspoon salt. Wrap the beets in foil, two or three to a package, and tightly crimp the edges to make little packets. Lay all the packets side by side on a baking sheet, and roast for 40 to 50 minutes, until you can pierce them with a fork. Let them cool in their packets.

3. When the beets are cool enough to handle, pull them out of the foil and rub off the skins; they should peel off without much resistance. Cut them into 1-inch wedges.

4. In a large bowl, whisk together the tahini, ice water, lemon juice, yogurt, and remaining ½ teaspoon salt. It may seize up at first, but keep whisking and it'll smooth itself out. Season with the Aleppo and coriander, then stir in the beets and dill.

SALMON ROE IKRA

This dip, a staple of my safta's table, was a constant source of fascination for me. It added a salty, rich dimension to her collection of bright salads and pickles, and had a lusciousness that's kind of like the world's most extravagant mayonnaise. Much like salmon itself, salmon roe is delicate, beautifully pink, and only mildly fishy. Once I started dipping pita into it, I couldn't stop until I'd eaten far more than my fair share. If you want to take it to the next level (and impress your friends and family), spoon another tablespoon or two of roe right on top of the finished dip.

¼ cup salmon roe, plus (optional) more for serving
1 tablespoon water
2 egg yolks
1 clove garlic, minced
2 tablespoons lemon juice
½ teaspoon Morton kosher salt
½ cup extra-virgin olive oil
¼ cup canola oil
1 pound raw vegetables, such as carrots, sugar snap peas, radishes, fennel, broccoli, and summer squash

1. In a blender, combine the roe, water, egg yolks, and garlic, followed by the lemon juice and salt, and mix on low until combined.

2. With the machine still running, slowly stream in the oils, then increase the speed to high. Blend until it's smooth and thick.

3. Prepare the vegetables, peeling and/or chopping them as necessary. Serve them with ikra at room temperature. To refrigerate the ikra: press a piece of plastic wrap directly on its surface until you're ready to eat.

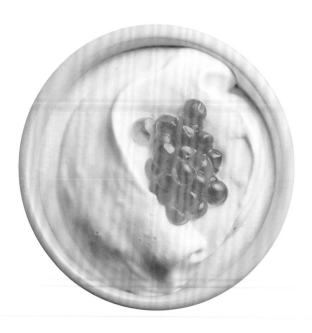

COLLARD SPANAKOPITA

S afta's spanakopita, like most others, included spinach (the name literally means "spinach pie"). During the winter in New Orleans, our markets are inundated with massive amounts of collard and mustard greens, so I prefer to use those, which also carry a lot more of their own flavor. Feel free to use any big leafy type of winter greens, or mix them at will. Though you start with so many greens you'll wonder how they'll fit into one pot—and your arms might get sore from stemming them all—remember that greens shrink. They'll cook down and become a worthy complement to the slew of feta, nuts, and spices.

1½ pounds collard greens or other sturdy greens
1½ pounds mustard greens
½ cup water
1 teaspoon Morton kosher salt
¼ cup extra-virgin olive oil
2 yellow onions, chopped
2 jalapeños, seeds and pith removed, minced
2 cloves garlic, minced
½ cup raw pine nuts or chopped raw walnuts
1 cup lightly packed fresh dill fronds, chopped
1 cup lightly packed fresh mint leaves, chopped
3 cups crumbled feta, preferably Bulgarian
Grated zest of 1 lemon
1 tablespoon lemon juice
1 teaspoon finely grated nutmeg
1 teaspoon freshly ground black pepper
4 eggs, lightly beaten
1 pound phyllo dough, defrosted
½ pound (2 sticks) unsalted butter, melted
¾ cup grated Pecorino Romano cheese

1. Stem, devein, and finely chop the greens. Add them a handful at a time to a pot with the water and salt, and cook over medium heat, stirring occasionally, until they've significantly reduced in size and any moisture has evaporated, 20 to 25 minutes. Drain and allow the greens to cool to room temperature.

2. Meanwhile, heat the oven to 375°F with a rack in the center of the oven. Warm the olive oil in a large skillet over medium heat, and cook the onions, jalapeños, garlic, and pine nuts until the onions and pine nuts have started to brown, 15 to 20 minutes.

3. Add the dill and mint to the cooked greens. Stir in the cooked nuts and vegetables, feta, lemon zest and juice, and spices, and finally add the eggs.

4. Gently unroll the phyllo dough. Put aside half of the sheets for the top crust, and cover them with a dish towel or a loose sheet of plastic wrap so they don't dry out. Brush butter all over one of the remaining sheets; press it into the bottom and up the sides of an approximately 13-by-9-inch baking dish. Repeat with the rest of the phyllo that you've kept for the bottom crust, and spread the filling inside in an even layer.

5. Stack another sheet of phyllo over the filling; brush the top of this one with butter, and sprinkle 1 generous tablespoon Pecorino evenly over it. Repeat with the rest of the phyllo, but don't sprinkle cheese over the very top of the pie. Don't worry about ripping—it's inevitable, and there are so many

(recipe continues)

layers that no one will notice—but be sure you save an intact piece for the very top.

6. Depending on the dimensions of your phyllo dough's sheets, there may be some overhanging crust; if there is, tuck the edge under itself. Use a sharp knife to score five diagonal slits through the top crust (but don't push down past the filling).

7. Bake for 40 to 45 minutes, rotating about halfway through. It's done when it's deeply brown and crisp all over the top. Let cool for a few minutes. To serve: cut diagonally, perpendicular to the scores you made before baking.

STUFFED CABBAGE WITH TOMATOES AND ONIONS

I f any of Safta's dishes is a must-try, it's this one. It doesn't just bring back the flavors of *my* childhood. It also seems to epitomize that feeling of warmth and comfort, so anyone who eats it can feel like they're eating at their own grandmother's house. Although the process may look somewhat long and involved, there's not much to it, and the bulk of your time is completely hands-off as the cabbage putters away on the stove. It's even better the next day, once the flavors have settled.

1 gallon plus 1 cup water, divided
2 large heads green cabbage
4 slices white bread
½ cup milk
1 yellow onion
½ cup extra-virgin olive oil, divided
2 tablespoons Morton kosher salt, divided
2 tablespoons sweet paprika
1 tablespoon ground coriander
½ teaspoon ground allspice
⅓ cup Arborio rice
1¼ pounds ground beef, preferably 80 percent lean
1 cup lightly packed fresh parsley leaves, chopped
4 cloves garlic, crushed
2 sprigs fresh oregano
1 anchovy
½ cup tomato paste
One 28-ounce can peeled whole tomatoes
1 tablespoon pomegranate molasses
5 or 6 fresh mint leaves, torn

1. Bring 1 gallon water to a boil. Remove and discard the cabbages' tough or bruised outer leaves, then make an incision all around the cores and gently peel away one leaf at a time, so they stay as intact as possible. If the leaves keep tearing on you, you can place each head of cabbage, core side up, in a large heatproof bowl, and ladle the boiling water over them so they're completely submerged; top off your pot of boiling water, since you'll need it again in a bit. Let the cabbage sit for 15 minutes, drain the water, and peel the leaves as directed; stop peeling as you near the center, since the leaves need to be at least 7 or 8 inches long (the remainder can be used for shaved cabbage salad, page 118).

2. Working in batches, cook the cabbage leaves in the boiling water for just 1 or 2 minutes, until they're pliable but still have some life in them; if you poured boiling water over the heads of cabbage before peeling, you'll only need to do this parboiling process with the crisper inner leaves. As they finish cooking, pull them out with tongs or a slotted spoon, and lay them flat on a dish towel to cool while you finish the rest.

3. To make the filling: Cube the bread into ½-to-1-inch pieces, and toss it with the milk to soak evenly (don't worry if some of the pieces start to disintegrate). Cut the onion in half; reserve one half for later, and mince the other half. Add it to the filling with ¼ cup olive oil, 1 tablespoon salt, paprika, coriander, and allspice.

4. Rinse the rice thoroughly until the water runs clear; this gets rid of starches that can gum up the filling. Combine it with the rest of the filling. *(recipe continues)*

5. Add the ground beef and parsley to the bowl, and use your hands or a spatula to fold it all together until it's evenly combined. Cover in plastic and refrigerate while you make the sauce.

6. Pull out a large heavy-bottomed pot or Dutch oven, and add the remaining ¼ cup olive oil over medium heat. Thinly slice the other half of the onion, and add it to the oil with the garlic, whole sprigs of oregano, and anchovy; cook, stirring occasionally, for a few minutes, until the onion slices are browned on the edges and the anchovy melts. Add the tomato paste, stirring to break it up, and let toast for a couple minutes.

7. In a large bowl, crush the canned tomatoes between your fingers, and combine them with the last 1 tablespoon salt, pomegranate molasses, and mint. When the tomato paste smells fragrant and caramelized in the pan, stir in the canned-tomato mixture and the last 1 cup water, and bring it all to a simmer.

8. To stuff the cabbage: Mound about ¼ cup filling right near the base of each leaf. Roll them all like burritos, tucking in the sides as you go, taking care not to tear them.

9. Add each parcel of stuffed cabbage, seam side down, to the pot with the sauce, using your spoon to push them to the bottom and snuggle them together wherever they'll fit. You can stack them if necessary. Decrease the heat to low, cover the pot, and cook for 75 to 90 minutes. To check for doneness, partially cut into one of the little packets, and taste a piece of the Arborio rice; it should be intact but creamy. If it needs more time, re-cover, cook for 10 minutes, and taste again; repeat for more 10-minute intervals if needed.

10. Take the pot off the heat, and let the cabbage rest for 30 minutes or so, with the lid still on, to give everything a chance to settle. Discard the sprigs of oregano. Serve the stuffed cabbage warm, taking care not to let the leaves unravel, and spoon some of the remaining sauce over the top.

SAFTA'S STEWED STRAWBERRIES AND ICE CREAM

These strawberries were a staple on Safta's breakfast table, where we'd eat them on toast with butter or cream cheese, or drizzle them onto a baguette and sprinkle feta cheese on top. (Crusty bread is the perfect vehicle for sopping up the sugary red liquid that oozes from berries.) I also liked to spoon them over vanilla ice cream for dessert, and that's how I eat them when I make them today. They're equally good with Greek yogurt. The beauty is that you can do whatever you want with this dish—it's not too thick or jammy, and that lightness makes it really versatile.

1 pound strawberries, roughly chopped
¼ cup sugar
Grated zest of 1 lemon
1½ tablespoons lemon juice
¼ teaspoon Morton kosher salt
1 quart of your favorite vanilla ice cream

1. Combine all the ingredients except the ice cream in a saucepan over medium heat. Stir occasionally; the heat and sugar will pull all the juices out of the berries. Once those juices come to a simmer, decrease the heat to low and leave the pan alone for 12 to 14 minutes, until the strawberries start to slump. You're not looking for this to become jammy; it'll thicken as it cools. Take the pan off the heat, and cool to room temperature.
2. Spoon the strawberries over a big bowl of ice cream—get some berries and some of their syrup.

III

FINDING HOME IN THE SOUTH

14

✦ ✦ ✦

The Lost Crab Cakes of Katrina

On the afternoon when Hurricane Katrina was heading toward New Orleans, I was focused on forming my five hundredth crab cake of the day. I'd ordered dozens of pounds of jumbo lump crab meat and had spent all morning separating pieces of cartilage from the sweet meat. I was scrupulous. I was the relatively new chef de cuisine at Chef John Besh's steakhouse at Harrah's Casino, and I felt a responsibility to lead by example. That morphed into being so perfectionistic that I hoarded the most technically challenging work for myself; I didn't want anyone else to screw it up. But I was also constantly afraid someone would notice *me* screwing up. God forbid one of the cooks would approach to ask me a question and discover a shell I'd missed. While I was picking crabs and barking orders, though, everyone around me was talking about the storm. Piece by piece, the crab pile grew and the news of Katrina's strength intensified.

When I first moved to New Orleans, I didn't know anything about hurricanes. The only one I'd been through, 2004's Hurricane Ivan, hadn't been too dramatic, so I was intent on keeping the kitchen's focus for the busy Saturday night ahead. "We have to be ready for service on time, guys. It's almost five p.m.": this was my favorite mantra every day around 4:45. It reassured me that I was a good boss. But that day, the tension was palpable. A buzz was moving through the restaurant, from guests to servers and from servers to cooks, about what the TV news was reporting of the hurricane. Scores of customers didn't show up for their reservations. Greg, the restaurant's general manager, walked up to me and whispered in my ear, "What's the fucking plan?" I got a call from Octavio Mantilla, John Besh's partner and the former general manager of Antonio's in St. Louis. He was the friend who'd brought me to New Orleans in the first place. Octavio said there was a chance the steakhouse would be closed the next day. That did nothing to answer my staff's growing questions about a "plan."

We uneasily spooned hollandaise onto steaks as the evening wore on and I waited to hear more from Octavio. Information trickled down from the casino's upper management that Harrah's itself might close. The entire city was waiting to hear if there would be a mandatory evacuation, an unprecedented move in New Orleans. Servers and cooks began asking me if they could leave to take care of their families and make plans to evacuate. I began to wonder why *I* was so willing to stay and continue cooking. I looked curiously to the dining room, trying to determine who was still out there. Those who remained seemed content to sip their drinks while waiting for their salads. Didn't they have anywhere to go? Any families to tend to? Weren't they worried about the hurricane—or were they *that* hungry? Or that . . . lonely?

Finally, around 8:00 p.m., Octavio and I came to a joint decision to close the restaurant early. A few die-hard cooks and servers offered to stick around and clean up. As we were wiping down counters, they went over the details of the raging hurricane party they were organizing, which eased the tension somewhat. We packed the freezer with steaks and sauces I didn't want to have to remake on Monday. I personally stacked those five hundred crab cakes on a rack and shut the freezer door, worrying that the customers who ordered them next week would notice that they'd been frozen.

As the last cooks left the kitchen, I was hit with a realization: I had no idea what to do. Everyone else seemed to have a plan, be it partying or evacuating. I didn't know whether to stay or leave. It was a reminder of how much of a lone soldier I'd become in this city. I'd moved here with a fiancée I loved. After two years of my working 16-hour days, 6 to 7 days a week, she'd left. My whole life was centered on cooking. All this came back to me as I stood in that empty kitchen. It was a lonely moment, realizing how fully I'd neglected my life for my work.

The only people I knew to call were Octavio and John. Octavio was like my big brother, after all the time we'd worked together in St. Louis. I didn't know John that well but was eager for his approval. I'd come to New Orleans thinking I was at the top of my game: twenty-three years old, and managing four hundred people as a chef! But, unlike in St. Louis, here I had to answer to someone artistically—it was his restaurant. John would come into the kitchen and let me know if the gumbo wasn't right. I was desperate to avoid that criticism.

It turned out that John and Octavio had hunkered down at Restaurant August with John's gun collection and a plan to sit the storm out and protect the place. They allowed me to join in. I drove home to pick up the cats that my departing fiancée had left with me, Bayou and Mr. Kitty, and headed across town to join them. The restaurant was darkened when I got there, the crystal chandeliers turned off in the dining room. I could barely make out Restaurant August's usual opulence in the low light. The rest of that night involved consuming several bottles of good whiskey, watching the weather forecasts, and daydreaming about how we could turn the contents of the restaurant's walk-in refrigerator—soft-shell crabs, eggs, bacon—into a good breakfast.

The next morning, though, we got news of the city's mandatory evacuation. Katrina was now a Category 5 hurricane, supposedly bigger than the state of Texas, and moving in our direction. All plans of staying at Restaurant August evaporated. Octavio headed west, toward his family in Baton Rouge, and I decided to go east with John, to help his parents in Slidell, Louisiana. We drove out of the city on Claiborne Avenue toward a windswept Lake Pontchartrain. It looked like any other Sunday in the Seventh Ward: people were sitting on their stoops, music blaring, barbecue grills going; everyone was in full celebration mode. John and I both felt a sadness, watching their joy from our car windows, knowing that the eye of the hurricane was headed toward the city.

After helping John's parents in Slidell, we headed 180 miles north to his cousin's house in Butler, Alabama. John's Land Rover was stuffed with the remaining contents of August's walk-in—champagne, truffles, those soft-shell crabs, all the good whiskey—plus my two cats. John's cousin Chris and his wife, Becky, welcomed us in. We dealt with the rising storm the way chefs do: by cooking all day long, watching through the broad picture windows as the pine trees whipped back and forth in the wind. Late that night, fueled by adrenaline and the last of August's champagne, we seized on the news that Katrina was veering east. "It missed New Orleans!" we said to one another. "We should go back!"

John and I headed out of Butler toward New Orleans at 1:00 a.m., aiming to arrive in the city before morning, get the stoves lit, and start cooking. The rush of the storm and our late-night adventure in it had us amped up, the radio blasting. We barely noticed the danger we were in until trees began falling around us in the 60-mile-per-hour winds. We saw power lines sparking in the road, and had to use a chain saw (a fortunate loan from John's cousin) to clear our way on a highway littered with downed trees. As we pressed on, the trip grew more and more ominous. We passed darkened gas stations and realized the whole region was without power. Not long afterward, outside of McComb, Mississippi, we ran out of gas. It was the first moment throughout the storm when I felt afraid. John grabbed my hand and began to pray. I'm not a religious person and, being Jewish, I don't have much experience appealing to Jesus Christ. But if ever there was a time for prayer, that was it. I joined in.

Somehow, we came up with the idea of using a road atlas as a funnel and dumping the gas-and-motor-oil mixture from the chain saw into John's car. Miraculously, the car started back up, and we took the next exit toward a darkened gas station. There were a bunch of us stranded there: a family in a minivan, a young couple in a sedan, and a few pickup trucks. We were all waiting, hoping that the electricity might come back on in the morning. John and I slept restlessly that hot summer night, with pocket-knives drawn, anxious about being robbed.

The next morning, we turned on the car radio and listened in shock to stories of flooding and levee failures throughout New Orleans. The cats in the backseat were woozy from the 90-degree heat and fumes from gasoline that had spilled during the transfer from the chain saw. Finally, a man pulled into the gas station in a pickup truck; he turned out to be a farmer who lived nearby and had some gasoline in a barrel. He moved around the parking lot, stopping to talk to the passengers of each car and negotiate with them on a price for gas. John pulled out a wad of cash and offered him however much he wanted. Our price was two hundred dollars a gallon. At last, we headed out, back toward Butler. It was clear we couldn't attempt a return to New Orleans without more of a plan—and supplies.

On the drive, we stayed glued to the spotty radio signal, trying to piece together the horror stories coming out of New Orleans. Chris and Becky again opened the doors to their house, this time with ghastly looks on their faces. Our imaginations gave way to the footage of our city in complete ruins. We watched the news in total silence. I thought of the staff who'd stayed late at the steakhouse and planned on partying instead of evacuating. I thought of the people we'd seen on Claiborne Avenue less than 48 hours earlier and tried to reconcile that with the sight of people waving from rooftops. We saw videos taken from helicopters of buildings on fire with no one available to put them out. Thick black smoke overshadowed the block that Restaurant August was on, and I wondered what we might have been doing if we'd stayed.

We started putting together a plan to rally supplies from friends and relatives across the country, but John needed to see his family before we attempted a return to New Orleans. His wife, Jenifer, and their children were with his in-laws in North Carolina, so we headed there to regroup for a few nights. My sister, Anit, came from nearby Charlotte to rescue Bayou and Mr. Kitty. She and I decided to cook for John's family, so he and Jenifer could spend time with the kids and craft careful explanations for them about this surprise vacation. My family had never been the kind to console one another emotionally; it wouldn't have even occurred to us that that might be helpful. I was used to being solitary and keeping my feelings to myself. But I was glad for my sister's presence that day. We caught up on years of life spent in different parts of the country. I told her about being left by my fiancée, and she told me about a new job she'd started. She offered to take care of my cats while I figured out my plan post-Katrina.

I only vaguely remember what we cooked that night, which is unusual for me; food is usually the hallmark of my memories. John and his boys went out and caught a bunch of trout. I made Israeli couscous, a salad, and some kind of potato dish. Nobody else remembers the food, either; what we ate didn't matter. What mattered was that we were sitting together and reassuring each other of the future as we passed the potatoes. I had the strong feeling that I was now part of this family, assembled around this table, whether we were blood relatives or not. I was no longer the lone soldier. It was one of most important meals I've cooked in my life.

CRAB CAKES WITH PRESERVED LEMON AIOLI

1 pound jumbo lump crabmeat
4 slices sandwich bread
1 cup mayonnaise
2 tablespoons plus 2 teaspoons chopped fresh chives, divided
1 tablespoon lemon juice
1 teaspoon Zatarain's Crab Boil seasoning
¼ teaspoon Tabasco sauce
1 cup canola oil
1 tablespoon lightly packed fresh tarragon leaves, chopped
3 large fresh basil leaves, chopped
4 teaspoons lightly packed fresh dill fronds, chopped
½ cup preserved lemon aioli (recipe follows)

Crab is practically a recurring character in my Katrina story, from those crab cakes I was obsessing over the day before the storm to the soft-shell crabs we rescued from Restaurant August's cooler, which we later cooked in Alabama as we watched the hurricane blow through.

Crabmeat has such incredible texture that you don't want to mess with it too much. In these crab cakes, it's held together with mayonnaise, while soft sandwich bread adds a little heft and soaks up all the other flavors. Don't get too fancy with your bread choice; it should fade to the background and concede the spotlight to the crab. Zatarain's Crab Boil—Louisiana's answer to Old Bay seasoning—lends the dish a complexity it wouldn't get from crab alone. If you're not lucky enough to be in the Gulf South, you can find it online or substitute ½ teaspoon Old Bay plus ½ teaspoon salt.

1. Pick through the crabmeat to remove any thin, sharp cartilage, taking care not to squeeze the meat; you want it to stay as nearly whole as possible. Put it in a large mixing bowl.

2. Trim the crusts from the bread, and cut the bread into ¼-inch cubes. Combine the crabmeat, bread, mayonnaise, 2 tablespoons chives, lemon juice, crab-boil seasoning, and Tabasco sauce until the bread is coated and everything is incorporated. Use your hands to fold the crabmeat in gently until just combined.

3. Scoop the crab into roughly ½-cup patties (if you want smaller, appetizer-sized cakes, make each one ¼ cup). Pat them to keep them compact, then arrange them on a plate or baking sheet so they're ready to go. Line a separate plate with paper towels, and set it aside.

4. Set a large cast-iron or nonstick skillet over high heat until it's warm, then decrease the heat to medium and add the canola oil; if your skillet is on the smaller side, use only half the oil, and change it halfway through cooking if it gets too foamy and dark. When the oil is smoking, use a thin spatula to transfer the cakes gently into the skillet, leaving plenty

(recipe continues)

of space between them; you'll probably need to do this in batches. They should just barely be holding together, and that's what makes them so tender.

5. Leave the crab cakes alone for 3 minutes before checking the bottoms for a nice golden crust. Flip, and cook for another 2 to 3 minutes, then transfer the cakes to the lined plate while you cook the rest. Fold the remaining 2 teaspoons chives with the rest of the herbs into the aioli, and serve it with the warm crab cakes.

PRESERVED LEMON AIOLI

YIELD: ABOUT 1½ CUPS

Preserved lemons—whole lemons that are packed in salt—give this aioli some subtle brininess and funk. It really holds its own. At first, preserved lemons seem a little foreign, with a sharp smell and new texture (the rind is so softened that you can use the entire fruit), but ever since I started cooking with them, I look to them for bright complexity. If you can't track them down in the store, substitute the grated zest of 1 lemon or try making your own; recipes are widely available online and the process is straightforward. This recipe makes a fair amount—and leftovers are great with raw vegetables, roasted vegetables, or sandwiches.

¼ cup lemon juice
1 tablespoon minced preserved lemon
2 cloves garlic, roughly chopped
½ teaspoon Morton kosher salt
2 egg yolks
½ cup extra-virgin olive oil
½ cup canola oil

1. Put the lemon juice, preserved lemon, garlic, and salt in a blender or small food processor before adding the egg yolks; blend until completely combined.

2. Combine the oils in a cup and, with the blender on (let it run for a few seconds before you carefully remove the top), pour the oils in a slow, steady stream as you continue to blend. The aioli will thicken; it's done when it looks like pudding. Use it right away, or store it in the refrigerator for up to a few days.

ROASTED SPECKLED TROUT WITH TAHINI AND PINE NUTS

YIELD: 4 TO 6 SERVINGS

This is an Israeli interpretation of the dish I may have served the night of that post-Katrina meal I cooked with my sister in North Carolina. That time was such a blur that I can't completely recall the actual dish, but the homey flavors of this one would've been just the thing we all wanted (and needed) to eat. It takes no time at all to prepare, and is a fantastic example of the marriage of seafood and tahini, which may be completely unexpected if you haven't tried it before. (And, if you've got a batch of ready-made prepared tahini [page 392], you're halfway there: add ½ cup to the stock, and skip steps 1 and 2 altogether.) It's not too far off from the classic New Orleans pairing of fish and brown butter. Any delicate white fish will work beautifully.

1 tablespoon lemon juice
½ clove garlic, crushed
¼ cup raw tahini
1¼ teaspoons Morton kosher salt, divided
3 tablespoons ice water, plus more as needed
¼ cup extra-virgin olive oil, divided
1½ to 2 pounds skinless trout fillets
2 teaspoons sesame seeds
1 teaspoon ground coriander
¼ cup seafood stock or lobster stock (page 132)
¼ cup pine nuts, toasted
5 or 6 fresh mint leaves, chopped
1 tablespoon lightly packed fresh cilantro leaves, chopped
1 tablespoon lightly packed fresh parsley leaves, chopped

1. Heat the oven to 400°F. Combine the lemon juice and garlic in a nonreactive bowl, and allow to steep for at least 20 minutes, until the juice is thoroughly infused.

2. Strain the lemon juice, add it to the tahini with ¼ teaspoon salt, and beat on medium speed. It will seize up at first, but then it will be incorporated. Once it's got a uniformly fudgy consistency, slowly add the ice water and beat on high; again, it may seize up or look curdled, but it should smooth itself out into a thick mousse. If it doesn't, add more water, ½ tablespoon at a time. Set aside.

3. Spread 2 tablespoons olive oil over a rimmed baking sheet. Arrange the fillets side by side on the sheet, and drizzle the remaining 2 tablespoons olive oil over them, along with the sesame seeds, coriander, and remaining 1 teaspoon salt.

4. Roast the fish for 8 to 10 minutes, until it's opaque and easily yields to your fork. Gently transfer the fillets to a serving plate.

5. While the fish bakes, combine the tahini and seafood stock in a small saucepan, and whisk over low heat just until the sauce is warm. To serve: pour the sauce all over the fish, then top it with the pine nuts and fresh herbs.

ISRAELI COUSCOUS WITH SUMMER VEGETABLES AND CARAMELIZED TOMATO

YIELD: 4 TO 6 SERVINGS

Hurricane Katrina happened at the end of August, a moment when a bounty of summer vegetables was available as we landed in North Carolina. This dish capitalizes on them with all the nourishment of comfort food, the kind of thing we sorely needed after evacuating New Orleans. Toasting the tomato paste, as Safta taught me, adds a complex sweet-savory flavor—that one little technique is a trusted friend that I've relied upon through the years. Ingrained in my muscle memory and etched into my cooking, it made me feel she was with us in the kitchen during that crazy time.

1. Heat the broiler. Combine 1 gallon water and 1 tablespoon salt in a large pot, and bring to a boil.
2. Meanwhile, cut the eggplant and zucchini into roughly 1-inch pieces, then combine them with the chopped onion, ¼ cup olive oil, and remaining 1 tablespoon salt. Spread everything in an even layer on a rimmed baking sheet, and roast for 10 to 15 minutes, stirring the pieces every 5 minutes or so, until they are evenly golden and the eggplant is very tender.
3. When the water comes to a boil, add the couscous, and cook for about 6 minutes, until it's tender and still has a little bite. Drain it, and set aside.
4. Strip the leaves from the thyme, and finely chop them with the parsley. Warm the remaining ¼ cup olive oil in a large skillet over medium heat, then add the garlic and herbs. Cook for just 30 seconds to 1 minute, before the garlic has a chance to brown.
5. Stir in the tomato paste, and continue to cook, breaking it up with your spoon, for 5 to 10 minutes, until it's fragrant and deeply caramelized. Remove the skillet from the heat, and fold in the roasted vegetables, couscous, and remaining ½ cup water, followed by the olives and basil. Serve warm; leftovers keep well for a few days.

1 gallon plus ½ cup water, divided
2 tablespoons Morton kosher salt, divided
1 large eggplant
1 large zucchini
1 yellow onion, chopped
½ cup extra-virgin olive oil, divided
1 cup Israeli couscous
4 sprigs fresh thyme
1 cup lightly packed fresh parsley leaves
3 cloves garlic, thinly sliced
¾ cup tomato paste
½ cup assorted olives, black or green, pitted and halved
8 fresh basil leaves, torn

15

✦✦✦

Red Beans to the Rescue

John and I prepared for our first trip back to New Orleans after Katrina as if we were heading into a war zone. We didn't know exactly what we were going to do there, but we knew that people were hungry and we could cook. We figured we needed a stockpile of gasoline, butane burners, propane tanks, gallons of water, and canned food, all the essentials to sustain ourselves and others in a city that was in chaos.

We didn't go into New Orleans our first night back, though. Instead, we headed to John's house in Slidell, a little more than 30 miles from New Orleans, to assemble our team. As we headed south from North Carolina, John's Land Rover had become command central for rallying supplies and help. A call to Chef Kelly English in Memphis yielded hundreds and hundreds of pounds of food. John's brother, a doctor, let us know he was coming from Memphis to help out with medical needs. John's

brother-in-law was on the road from Houston with a truckload of gasoline.

Our 9-hour drive was spent on the phone, fielding offers like these. Only my cell phone worked, because I'd kept my St. Louis number, a 314 area code. No one with a 504 area code—the one from New Orleans—would be able to make calls for a long time. My little Sprint Treo phone was working overtime as we started hearing from employees scattered around the region. Everyone was desperate, crying, pleading. Myra, a cook from the steakhouse, was frantic on the phone, not sure what she was going to do. She was in Texas and needed clothes for her kids, toilet paper, just the basics. Other people called about their last paycheck: when would they be able to get it? We wrote down their addresses on the pages of the atlas that had served as our miracle funnel when we ran out of gas a few days before in Mississippi.

We made it through a checkpoint on the dubious strength of the fact that we were hauling a trailer and looked official. Driving through the suburbs of Slidell was surreal. We saw burnt-out homes and fallen trees on crushed cars. Debris was everywhere. People had nailed signs up on their houses that read, "We will shoot you if you come onto our property."

Luckily, John's house was in an area that hadn't flooded. When we rendezvoused there with the rest of our team, we were immediately hit with the smell. He had a huge ice-chest freezer in his garage that was full of wild boar and venison he'd shot on a hunting trip; it had now been sitting there for a week in 95-degree weather. It was stomach-churning, that smell. We dumped the freezer and the refrigerator on the curb, and I set about trying to figure out something for us to cook for dinner. What could I make from what was left in John's cabinets, or from the snacks we'd bought on our trip? How about seared Spam braised in Campbell's tomato soup with a Doritos chip crust? After driving all day and suffering the emotional toll of passing through flood-ravaged neighborhoods, we found it pretty tasty.

Everyone was exhausted. We set up makeshift beds on the tile floor of John's kitchen. In the heat and humidity, with no electricity or air-conditioning, that floor was the coolest place in the house. We took turns sleeping and cooking. The plan was to prepare a massive load of hot food so we could take it somewhere in the morning and serve it to whomever we could find. We'd thought, *What's something we could make that would be simple and portable?* The answer was clear: red beans and rice.

In normal times, red beans and rice are a staple of New Orleanian life, traditionally served on Mondays. They're rich and deceptively simple: a big pot of beans that have been stewed slowly with smoked ham hock until the beans are creamy and infused with the flavor of the meat. You start with what's known in New Orleans as "the holy trinity," onions, green bell peppers, and celery. The vegetables are sautéed until just soft and aromatic, with some bay leaf and Creole spices—paprika, garlic, a little celery salt, and the all-important cayenne pepper. Add some stock and the ham hock, then do something else for 5 or 6 hours, letting the beans slowly meld with the meaty broth. When the beans are nearly finished cooking, you add smoked sausage so that it retains its moisture and has a texture that snaps when you bite through the casing. I love the many textures of a good pot of red beans: shreds of smoked ham hock, the rounds of sausage, and the beans themselves, which just barely hold their shape.

We had a problem, though: We didn't have any unspoiled meat. No sausage, no smoked pork. No bell peppers or celery or onions, either—none of the things you traditionally put in red beans. These were going to have to be simple vegetarian beans. But with enough Tabasco, Worcestershire sauce, and the right amount of Zatarain's Creole Seasoning, we could make them good enough. "Get those beans creamy," John said as we stirred them with a large metal paddle.

We cooked all night. By 7:00 a.m., the beans were ready. Somebody had brought a flat-bottomed boat for us, the kind covered in camouflage that you take out duck hunting. We loaded up the boat with coolers full of red beans and rice, and hauled it on its trailer to a hospital in Slidell. At this point, a few days after the storm, FEMA hadn't shown up yet. No one had made it to this hospital. Though it wasn't flooded, they'd been without power for a week. Doctors, nurses, and patients had all been there that whole time, the staff working with just the bare minimum, running out of supplies, using generators to keep going. I'd never seen people so happy to see us. Doctors came outside in their scrubs, and patients in their hospital gowns with oxygen tanks and tubes in their noses, to get their bowls of red beans. We set up a 6-foot table and ladled the food into foam containers. People were truly hungry. We served them the entire boatful of food in a matter of hours.

The next day had us serving a similar boatload of red beans

and rice in the New Orleans area. We had to drive 3 hours to get from Slidell to New Orleans, a trip that normally takes 45 minutes. Sections of the bridge across Lake Pontchartrain had been damaged in the storm surge, so we had to drive all the way around the lake on land. To figure out where we should set up next, we'd gone to Harrah's Casino, where I'd been working the day before the storm hit, and which was serving as command central for the city. Governor Kathleen Blanco, Mayor Ray Nagin, and officials from the National Guard were all stationed there, trying to figure out what to do. "Go to the Walmart on Tchoupitoulas Avenue," we were told. "That's where all the cops and people doing search and rescue are based."

The streets of New Orleans were so filled with trash and debris, we couldn't recognize where we were. All the street signs were gone, all the familiar landmarks. The parking lot of the Walmart was a sea of people. Policemen, yes, but also citizens with boats and trucks. They'd been rescuing people who'd been stranded on their rooftops for nearly a week in the heat, pulling dead bodies out of homes and out of the water, walking or boating through the toxic sludge to pick up whatever was left of our city. These were the people we were going to feed.

John and Octavio dropped me off with the food and headed back to Harrah's to help with the operation to remove the casino's thirty million dollars in cash from the building (a process that required six or seven armored trucks, flanked by Hummers with machine guns). It was going to be me, the red beans, some very hungry people, and a Walmart that had been thoroughly looted. I asked to venture into the store in search of Tabasco for my red beans. Everyone ignored me, so I headed inside. I couldn't walk down any of the aisles, the place was so badly trashed. I had to step over things to make my way through the store. The electronics section was barren—all the cell phones and televisions, gone. But the grocery section was still stocked. Plenty of Chef Boyardee and ramen noodles that no one had bothered to take. I found my Tabasco and got out of there.

With my steaming pot of red beans, I was the most popular guy in the parking lot. Everyone gathered around my table and talked to me while they ate. The police officers were wearing yellow bands on their uniforms to differentiate them from any of the folks who'd supposedly looted a police station and stolen uniforms, weapons, and ammunition. It was hard to know which of the rumors floating around were true and which weren't. I was shocked when I heard a police officer refer to shooting looters as "target practice," insinuating that he could go out there and shoot black people as long as he didn't shoot "the wrong ones." Katrina's aftermath was bringing out the worst in people. But: it was also bringing out the best. Another man came up for a helping of food and mentioned that he'd been out in his boat for the last 14 hours, pulling people out of houses.

I served red beans to these folks who were doing search and rescue for the next 3 days, more red beans and rice than I'd previously made in my whole life. During that week, the way I thought about food changed. How important is arugula coulis? So what if there wasn't smoked sausage in the beans; these beans *were* making a difference. I could see the gratitude in people's eyes, and it made me tear up. Here I was, offering food and comfort, inducing memories of better days, and giving each person a small piece of myself with every bowl. I felt as if I was contributing something greater than myself—and as if this city really needed me.

THE HOLY TRINITY

EMILY'S FAMOUS RED BEANS AND RICE

During Katrina, red beans and rice reminded me of what I love about cooking: a simple, hearty plate of food can bring someone comfort under any circumstance. I matured as a chef as I handed out those Styrofoam bowls of beans, cobbled together with not much more than salt and the spices we could scrounge up.

Now red beans are a part of my weekly routine, but my wife, Emily, makes them very creamy and rich, deeply flavored with smoked ham hock and sausage and spiked with Tabasco. Every Monday, she starts them on the stove by noon, and they cook for hours, until our friends arrive. It's a come-one, come-all kind of ritual, so naturally, she makes a huge batch. Leftovers taste wonderful all week.

I use red-bean nights to celebrate our life and friends, remembering a time when the future was less sure. That's part of why we don't hold back on the rice, which is loaded with butter, olive oil, and soft onions. If you're taking the time and effort to make beans this good, the rice should match (though, of course, you can make rice with only water, or with half the fat, if nutrition is a pressing concern). Red beans are a nourishing meal anytime, but they're best when you go all out.

2 pounds dried red beans, soaked overnight
¼ cup extra-virgin olive oil
6 ounces bacon, chopped
2 yellow onions, divided
2 stalks celery, chopped
1 green bell pepper, chopped
2 dried bay leaves, divided
1 tablespoon sweet paprika
½ teaspoon cayenne pepper
1 large smoked ham hock or shank
1½ quarts chicken stock
1 pound smoked pork sausage
4 teaspoons Morton kosher salt, divided
4 teaspoons Tabasco sauce, plus more for serving
2 teaspoons sugar
½ cup canola oil
4 tablespoons (½ stick) unsalted butter
1 pound jasmine rice
3 cups water, or more as needed
1 bunch scallions, sliced

1. Drain the beans, and set them aside.
2. Warm the olive oil in a large heavy-bottomed pot over medium heat. Add the bacon, and cook, stirring occasionally to break it up, for 6 to 8 minutes, until it's golden.
3. Meanwhile, chop one of the onions. When most of the bacon's fat has rendered, add the onion to the pot, along with the celery, bell pepper, and one of the bay leaves, stirring well to coat everything with the fat.
4. Continue to cook, stirring occasionally, until the onion is translucent and the celery and bell pepper just start to soften. Stir in the paprika and cayenne, allowing the spices to toast for a minute or so.
5. Add the beans, ham hock, and stock. Increase the heat to high to bring everything up to a boil, then skim any foam from the top of the pot, reduce the heat to low, and cover

(recipe continues)

with the lid. Let it cook, low and slow, for at least 3 hours, until the beans are falling apart. It's not a soup, but there should be enough broth so that you see some movement in the pot; top it off with more stock if you need to.

6. Fish the ham hock out of the pot, pull all the meat off the bone, give it a rough chop, and add it back to the pot; slice the sausage about ¼ inch thick and add that, too. Season with 2 teaspoons salt, Tabasco, and sugar. (Yes, sugar—it might seem odd, but it gets all the ingredients to play together nicely.) Continue to cook, covered, over low heat, for at least another ½ hour, until it all starts to pull together. At this point, if you prefer, you can leave it alone for a couple of hours, returning just to stir occasionally.

7. While that happens, make the rice: First, chop the other onion. Combine the canola oil and butter with the other bay leaf in a separate pot over medium heat. Once the butter melts, add the onion and remaining 2 teaspoons salt.

8. As soon as the onion is translucent, stir in the rice. Defer to the package instructions for a water ratio; for 1 pound (about 2 cups) of jasmine rice, I add 3 cups of water. Increase the heat to high, and bring to a simmer; then decrease the heat to low, cover, and cook for another 15 minutes or so, until it's tender.

9. Remove the rice from heat and let it rest for 10 minutes with the lid on, then fluff it with a fork. Remove and discard the bay leaves from both pots. Serve red beans over a scoop of rice, and sprinkle with scallions.

OUR MONDAY-NIGHT
RED BEAN TABLE
AT HOME

GREEN SALAD WITH GREEN DRESSING

Salad isn't the traditional New Orleanian accompaniment to red beans, but it's become a tradition in my home. I usually get home on Mondays to a kitchen counter strewn with whatever looked good at the market, and while Emily takes care of the beans, the produce is my domain; I love to put together salads that are unfussy and unbuttoned. It's a great opportunity to be off the cuff, since you can take the lead from whatever's available to you. Add some nuts or spices, a little oil and acidity, and you're good to go.

If "green salad" makes you think of the puny bowls of greens that come on the side at restaurants, this recipe will be a 180 for you. It's anything but puny, capturing the very essence of green: vivid, fresh, and vegetal. When raw produce tastes this good, I love just to let it do its thing. The feta and sunflower seeds are worthy accompaniments, adding depth without competing.

Cut the stem off the lettuce, but keep the leaves whole. Thinly slice the zucchini and avocado. In a salad bowl, toss the vegetables with the dressing until they're evenly coated. Add the feta, fresh dill, and sunflower seeds to finish.

½ pound salad greens, such as Bibb lettuce or Romaine hearts
2 small zucchini
1 avocado
½ cup green dressing (recipe follows)
¾ cup crumbled sheep's-milk feta, preferably Bulgarian
¼ cup lightly packed fresh dill fronds
2 tablespoons roasted sunflower seeds

GREEN DRESSING

Packed with herbs and creamy with yogurt, this is sort of like a variation on Green Goddess dressing, though it's thick and rich enough that you could also serve it as a dip with good crusty bread. I love the avocado oil, because it magnifies all those green flavors, but olive oil works, too; and you can play around with any soft herbs—use all parsley and cilantro if you can't get enough dill, or try adding some mint if you have a surplus—as long as there are about 6 cups total.

1. Put 2 quarts water and the baking soda in a pot, and bring it to a boil. While you wait, prepare an ice bath.
2. Get a strainer ready to go in your sink, or keep a slotted spoon on hand to fish out the herbs. Cook the dill, parsley, and cilantro in the boiling water for just 5 seconds—about as

2 quarts plus 2 tablespoons water, divided
¼ teaspoon baking soda
  Ice water for an ice bath
2 cups lightly packed fresh dill fronds
2 cups lightly packed fresh parsley leaves
2 cups lightly packed fresh cilantro leaves
½ cup Greek yogurt
¼ cup avocado oil
2 tablespoons white-wine vinegar
1½ teaspoons Morton kosher salt
½ teaspoon ground dill seeds, optional
1 clove garlic, minced

long as it takes for you to add it all. Drain, and immediately plunge the herbs into the ice bath to stop the cooking; then squeeze them dry in a clean dish towel.

3. Add the yogurt, avocado oil, vinegar, salt, dill seeds, and 2 tablespoons water to a blender, then pile the herbs and garlic on top. Blitz for 30 seconds to a minute, until the herbs are puréed into the dressing.

ARUGULA WITH CITRUS, OLIVES, AND ZA'ATAR

Bright fresh citrus and oily black olives are perfect complements to each other—you barely need to do anything at all, and they come together beautifully—and tart but earthy za'atar makes them both pop. Use the best citrus you can get your hands on, any kind you like. We have a satsuma tree in front of our house, so I usually use that variety of orange. If it weren't for the pungent garlic, the dressing would be something you might want to drink on its own!

- 1 pound mixed oranges and/or grapefruit
- 1 small clove garlic
- 1½ tablespoons lemon juice
- 1 tablespoon honey
- ½ teaspoon minced fresh ginger
- ¼ teaspoon Morton kosher salt
- 2 tablespoons extra-virgin olive oil
- 4 ounces arugula
- ¼ cup salt-cured Kalamata olives, pitted and halved
- 1 teaspoon za'atar

1. Peel and halve all the citrus, then lay the halves flat and use a serrated knife to cut them very gently into ½-inch slices. Set them aside.

2. To make the dressing: Grate the garlic into a bowl, then add the lemon juice, honey, ginger, and salt. Whisking all the while, stream in the olive oil so that the dressing emulsifies.

3. Toss the arugula and olives in the dressing until they're coated. Pile in the citrus, and sprinkle the za'atar all over as a garnish.

TOMATO AND PEACH PANZANELLA

YIELD: 4 TO 6 SERVINGS

This is a deep-summer no-brainer, making the most of those two fruits, which hit peak juiciness and sweetness simultaneously. (It's also the perfect salad for Emily, since tomatoes and peaches are two of her absolute favorite things.) With the toast, it's got such a good balance of temperature and texture—the warm bread softens with all those juices but is crispy enough to hold its own.

5 thick slices ciabatta or crusty country loaf
1½ pounds heirloom tomatoes, divided
1 clove garlic
¼ cup sherry vinegar
1 teaspoon Morton kosher salt
¼ cup extra-virgin olive oil
1½ pounds peaches
½ red onion
6 sprigs fresh tarragon
6 sprigs fresh mint
1 teaspoon ground sumac

1. Heat the oven to 350°F. Tear the bread by hand into coarse ½-to-1-inch pieces. Spread them over a rimmed baking sheet, and bake for 15 to 25 minutes (fresh bread takes more time), rotating after the first 15 minutes and checking every 5 minutes after that, until the bread is hard and very dry.

2. While the bread toasts, take ½ pound of the tomatoes, halve them along their equators, and drag the flat parts on the coarsest side of a box grater so the pulp falls into a salad bowl. (Throw away the skin when it gets too close to keep grating.) Finely grate the garlic into the same bowl, making sure you scrape away any tiny pieces that are stubbornly clinging to the underbelly of your grater. To that bowl, add the vinegar and salt, then gradually whisk in the olive oil.

3. Core and cut the remaining 1 pound tomatoes into 1-inch pieces; halve and pit the peaches and do the same with them. Thinly slice the onion, then strip the leaves from the tarragon and mint, give them a chop, and add them all to the dressing. Tumble in the croutons while they're still warm from the oven.

4. Gently toss the salad by hand so you don't scuff up the bread, and sprinkle the sumac over the top of everything. This salad is best served fresh, when the warmth of the bread contrasts with the vibrant raw fruit.

FARRO AND KALE WITH
SAFFRON VINAIGRETTE

There are so many vegetables packed into this one bowl—with just as many textures—that the sweet, nutty farro is more of a finisher than the foundation. Saffron is expensive but adds a real depth of flavor. Skip it if you need to, but don't miss the chilies. All these flavors improve and marry together with a little time, so you can make this ahead for a party or eat it all week (but don't add the nuts until right before you eat). It's just as good alongside the red beans as it is a stand-alone for a light but filling meal. And you should absolutely feel free to substitute whatever's on hand and convenient for each component, as we do at home: cook up some dried beans separately, and use them instead of fresh; use Swiss chard instead of kale, turnips or beets instead of radishes, celery or even apples instead of cucumbers.

1. Combine the farro and water, and refrigerate overnight. Not only will this cut down your cooking time, but it also retains more nutrients and jump-starts the grains' sprouting process, giving you a sweeter flavor. This step isn't mandatory, though; if you're short on time, you can skip ahead to step 3.

2. Transfer the soaked farro (water and all) to a pot along with the beans, 1½ teaspoons salt, and the árbol chili. Bring to a boil over high heat, then skim away any foam. Decrease the heat to medium-low, and simmer for 7 to 10 minutes, until the farro is tender but still has some bite. Drain and let cool completely.

3. If you have not precooked the farro, combine it with just the water and salt; bring to a boil, then decrease the heat to medium-low and cook for 20 minutes, until it's softened but still very chewy, before adding the fresh beans and árbol chili. Cook for another 7 to 10 minutes, until the beans and farro are both tender but still intact, before draining and cooling.

4. Meanwhile, mince the shallot, garlic, and rosemary leaves. Add them to your salad bowl with the orange zest, and set aside.

5. Combine the vinegar, orange juice, and saffron in a small saucepan. Bring the mixture up to a simmer, then

1 cup farro
3 cups water
1 cup shelled fresh butter beans, lima beans, or peas
1 tablespoon Morton kosher salt, divided
1 dried árbol chili pepper
1 small shallot
1 small clove garlic
1 sprig fresh rosemary
Grated zest of ½ orange
¼ cup rice wine vinegar, preferably seasoned
2 tablespoons orange juice
⅛ teaspoon saffron threads
¼ cup extra-virgin olive oil
½ pound curly kale, stemmed and deribbed
½ pound radishes
1 large cucumber, preferably English
1 cup walnut pieces, toasted

(recipe continues)

immediately remove it from the heat and let cool to room temperature. Strain the mixture into the bottom of your salad bowl.

6. Fish the árbol chili out of the pot, split it lengthwise, and carefully remove its seeds (they're incredibly spicy). Mince it, and add it to the salad bowl, along with the olive oil and remaining 1½ teaspoons salt. Whisk to combine.

7. Finely chop the kale, and thinly slice the radishes. Quarter the cucumber lengthwise (if it has seeds, scoop them out), and thinly slice it. Add the vegetables, farro, and beans to the salad bowl, and toss everything to combine. At this point, you can add the nuts and serve it right away, or keep the salad in the refrigerator for a day or two and add the nuts right before serving.

APPLE AND FENNEL SALAD WITH CANDIED PECANS

YIELD: 4 TO 6 SERVINGS

This salad is fun to eat, so crisp and fresh, especially in the fall and winter. As simple as it is to throw together, the flavor combinations are really striking. Candied pecans are, hands down, better than pretty much anything else (make a huge batch, and hoard some for snacking or gifting), but if you don't have the time to make them, they can be replaced with simple toasted nuts—the dressing's got enough flavor to pull its own weight, helped along by the scallions and pink pepper.

1. Heat the oven to 325°F, and line a baking sheet with parchment paper.

2. In a large glass or metal bowl, beat the egg white until it's frothy enough to hold soft peaks. Mix in the sugar, ½ teaspoon salt, and Aleppo pepper, then fold in the pecans until they're evenly coated. Spread this mixture over the prepared baking sheet, and bake on the center rack for 20 to 25 minutes, rotating halfway through. You'll know the nuts are done when they smell great and the coating has completely dried. Keep in mind that if you taste one while it's still hot it will be a little soft; the nuts become crunchy as they cool, so go by sight and smell rather than texture.

1 egg white
2 tablespoons sugar
1½ teaspoons Morton kosher salt, divided
½ teaspoon Aleppo pepper
1 cup pecan halves
3 tablespoons orange juice
1 tablespoon apple-cider vinegar
1 tablespoon honey
¼ cup extra-virgin olive oil
2 large apples, preferably Pink Lady or another sweet-tart variety
1 large fennel bulb, with its fronds
4 scallions, thinly sliced
2 tablespoons whole pink peppercorns

3. Combine the orange juice, vinegar, honey, and remaining 1 teaspoon salt. Whisk vigorously while you stream in the olive oil, mixing until it emulsifies into a smooth dressing. Set aside.

4. Core the apples, and thinly slice them into half-moons. Pull the fronds from the fennel, remove its stems, and halve the bulb; thinly slice the bulb, and chop or tear the fronds. Toss the fennel and fronds together with the scallions in a large bowl. Lightly crush the peppercorns between your fingertips as you add them.

5. Pour in all the dressing, and delicately toss to combine. Add the nuts just before serving.

16

✦✦✦

Manischewitz for Willie Mae

In New Orleans, several months post-Katrina, with nobody to cook for, I was plagued by questions: *Who am I now? Do I really belong here, in the South?*

I was still on staff at Harrah's Casino, but it would be months before the slot machines would be dinging there again, months before there would be customers in the steakhouse. We had a massive cleanup job ahead of us. The first day I walked down the hallway toward the kitchen, I turned a corner to find a thick coating of dried blood all over the floor, with footprints in it that went in every direction. It looked like a crime scene or something out of a horror movie. Then I realized what it was: before the storm, we'd put a lot of steaks and burger meat in the freezer. After several weeks, all the blood had oozed out of that meat and

seeped out onto the floor. The casino had hired some guys in hazmat suits to come in and clear the rotting food out of the refrigerators, and it was their footsteps we could see.

The blood was just the start of the dramatic scenes we encountered in the casino. Wild animals had found their way inside during or after the storm, and we had frequent encounters with snakes, raccoons, nutrias, cats, and squirrels. Some of them hid out for an astonishingly long time, too. One day, months later, after we had reopened the steakhouse, a cook came running out of our dry-storage area—he'd lifted up a box and found a giant snake living under it. The restaurant was packed full of customers, and the kitchen was open to the dining room. I had to deal with it. "Nobody make a noise!" I whispered. "I'm going to get the snake, and I'm coming out with it. I don't want anybody to say a word. *Don't* scare the customers." I snuck into dry storage and managed to get the snake into a box. I put a lid on it and started heading out. As I was walking, the snake started poking its head out one side. Once I saw that, I screamed like a little child and dropped the box! Fortunately, the casino's maintenance guys were able to recapture it and get rid of it.

Animals and blood included, it took us weeks of cleanup to get the kitchen back in working order. It was heavy, heart-sinking labor: 16-hour days of scrubbing. Cleaning, gutting, crying—that was the routine.

Then, one day in January, John called to say that a group of people from Oxford, Mississippi, were in town to help rebuild a fried-chicken restaurant that had been flooded with several feet of water. He wanted me to bring them lunch while they worked. "Just pack up a bunch of food," he said. "This might be a good time to test some of the new menu items you've been working on."

In all honesty, I was still trying to figure out the whole mystique around Southern food. I'd learned the methods for making grits and grillades and jambalaya; I knew these dishes *tasted* good. But it seemed that there was something more to the food of this region—something that inspired passionate dedication from the people who lived here. What was it about this one fried-chicken restaurant that would make people travel from around the South to work on repairing it?

The stench of rot and death wafted over us as we opened the doors to get out of our Harrah's van outside the restaurant in the Seventh Ward. We stepped over debris humming with flies to set ourselves up. I'd decided we would go all out for these generous volunteers: 8-foot tables, white tablecloths, butane burners, metal chafing dishes. The crisp white tablecloths stood in stark contrast to the mess. We served prime rib and jambalaya. We got sauté pans going, and fried beer-battered onion rings, all on a street in the middle of destruction.

I was introduced to a frail, older African American woman named Willie Mae Seaton. This was her restaurant, Willie Mae's Scotch House. I'd never eaten there before the storm. I brought her a plate of food and knelt beside her wheelchair to speak with her. She went on about how thankful she was for everyone who had come there, but she didn't seem hopeful that she would ever serve another customer. "You seem like you might need a drink," I joked with her, and she told me her beverage of choice was Manischewitz. Manischewitz?! The kosher wine? Yes, that was Willie Mae's favorite. I made a mental note of it.

The way the volunteers working on Willie Mae's restaurant received us registered deep in me. The jambalaya might not have had much sentimental value for me, but it meant something to *them*. This must be some kind of church group, I initially thought. But it turned out the gospel they were preaching was one of Southern food. They were from a nonprofit called the Southern Foodways Alliance, which was dedicated to the study of the region's food and culture. When I was there at the job site, serving them lunch, I had that feeling again, the one I'd had with the red beans: that what I was doing mattered. I started thinking about how the fried chicken, pork chops, and butter beans Willie Mae had served in her restaurant had caused us all to be there now, like one little culinary anthill in the middle of a landfill. There must have been magic in that food.

The next time I brought lunch to the volunteers, I considered my dishes differently. I again made jambalaya but found a new reverence for the dish as I cooked it, rendering bacon and adding the "holy trinity" of diced bell peppers, onion, and celery. I browned chicken thighs and sausage with a healthy dose of Creole seasoning, allowing the meat to caramelize in hot butter and bacon fat before folding in the rice and bathing it all in chicken broth. I also made them barbecue shrimp, which, despite its name, includes no "barbecue" sauce. Instead, the stock is made by combining shrimp heads and shells with oyster liquor, that juice that seeps from oysters when you're shucking them. To that, a lot of black peppercorns are added, along with lemon halves and an unreasonable amount of Worcestershire sauce; you cook it down until it's a rich, pungent, almost acidic sauce with a peppery bite. Then it's enriched by adding heavy cream and butter, tossing in the shrimp, and cooking it all down so that the sauce turns a milk-chocolate color, thick enough to coat the shrimp. With some crusty French bread, it's the kind of dish that will inspire people to travel hundreds of miles to labor for free, rebuilding a storm-fallen restaurant.

I cooked for the Southern Foodways Alliance volunteers many times during the next few months, always bringing with me a bottle of Manischewitz for Willie Mae. When the steakhouse at the casino reopened, its new menu was a reflection of the time I'd spent cooking in the streets. Everything felt more personal to me. We served redfish rubbed with Creole spices, crispy potatoes, and plump crawfish tails crowned with the creamy, sweet fat from their heads. I would revel in the aroma of thinly pounded veal loins that we'd tenderize by simmering with celery, onions, bell peppers, and stock. Those grillades would sink into a mound of creamy white grits when you plunged your fork in. This was food that resonated with this place, this city, and the people who cared for it, among whom I now included myself.

INGREDIENTS FOR STEWED OKRA

BUTTERMILK BISCUITS

T his is the product of years spent in pursuit of the perfect biscuit, a goal I chased through conversations and cooking with various biscuit pros throughout the South. A lady named Miss Katrina, who worked for me when I was a chef at Harrah's Casino in New Orleans, taught me Biscuits 101. I remember being astonished by the amount of buttermilk she used in one batch of dough—it felt like more than I'd used in my life—but the biscuits had such rich flavor as a result.

Later, at a large communal dinner put on by the Southern Foodways Alliance, I deliberately grabbed a seat beside a woman I'd heard was an expert in the realm of biscuits. She's the one who taught me that one simple change in technique—pushing the biscuit cutter straight down, rather than twisting it into the dough—helps you achieve loftier biscuits, because the dough rises evenly as it cooks. I was making progress.

Years after that, a chef friend, Ashley Christensen, clued me in to another tip she'd learned: grate the butter, and then freeze it. This strategy was a little more off the rails, but it's brilliant, because it enables you to incorporate the butter quickly, before it has a chance to get too warm. It stays in distinct pieces that you don't need to manipulate, and it translates to flakier, taller biscuits.

The crowning achievement, though, has always been layers that you can actually see and peel back. Mike Carmody, who was a baker at Domenica, taught me a way of rolling and folding the dough almost as you would boreka dough (page 22). That clinched it. Impossibly light yet unbelievably rich, this, in my mind, is the best biscuit you can bake. It needs nothing at all but gets along well with stewed strawberries (page 174) at breakfast, or, at dinnertime, with any of the other recipes in this chapter.

1. Grate the butter on the coarsest side of a grater, and spread it in a layer on a parchment-lined baking sheet. Freeze until all the pieces are very cold.

2. Before you make the dough, be sure you've measured your ingredients and lined up all your tools—rolling pin, bench scraper, flour for dusting—since it's crucial that the butter stay as cold as possible while you work. Once you get

½ pound (2 sticks) unsalted butter, very cold
4 cups (480 grams) all-purpose flour, plus more for dusting
2 tablespoons sugar
2 teaspoons Morton kosher salt
1½ teaspoons baking powder
⅛ teaspoon baking soda
1¾ cups buttermilk, chilled, plus more for baking

SHREDDED BUTTER
FOR BISCUITS

started, you have to move quickly, and every second counts.

3. In a large bowl, whisk together the flour, sugar, salt, baking powder, and baking soda. Scrape the butter into the bowl, and use a spatula to toss it as you would a salad, until every piece of butter is coated. Pour in the buttermilk, and stir the dough until it forms a scraggly mess. It will still be incredibly crumbly, but you want to get all the flour moistened.

4. Flour a work surface and your hands. Tip out the dough, and press it into a 12-by-9-inch rectangle; it will be crumbly and unruly, but a bench scraper helps to pull it all together. As best as you can, swoop the scraper or a spatula under the dough to lift it up, fold it in thirds, as you would fold a letter, and push in the sides to reinforce and keep them straight. It'll be so crumbly you'll think it's impossible that it could come together. Trust that it will, and keep working quickly.

5. Flip the dough upside down, and rotate it a quarter-turn. Flour your rolling pin and the top of the dough and, with firm, even strokes, roll it back out into a 12-by-9-inch rectangle. Fold it again into thirds, then flip and rotate it. Dust with a bit of flour if the butter ever wants to stick, and make sure your rolling pin stays clean.

6. Repeat this process of rolling and folding one last time. Each time, it will cohere a bit more.

7. Finally, rotate the dough and roll it into a slightly smaller rectangle, about 10 by 8 inches, and square off the edges so they're neat and firm. Cut it evenly, either into six hefty biscuits or twelve smaller biscuits, pressing straight down with your bench scraper or knife—and not in a sawing motion, so you don't damage the layers of butter and flour. Refrigerate the biscuits on a baking sheet for at least 30 minutes.

8. Heat the oven to 450°F with a rack in the upper-middle position. Brush or spoon a bit of buttermilk on the tops of the biscuits, and bake for 25 to 30 minutes, rotating the pan after 15 minutes. Wrap them in a clean dish towel to keep them warm, and serve fresh from the oven if you can. If that's not possible, split and toast them before eating. Save leftover biscuits in a ziplock bag for up to 3 days.

STEWED OKRA AND
BACON OVER GRITS

YIELD: 6 SERVINGS

Ever since I met the crew from the Southern Foodways Alliance, I've attended their annual symposia, which bring together food lovers—writers, chefs, and farmers—from around the South and beyond. Each multiple-day gathering is a big, fun production dedicated to documenting and honoring Southern food and culture; at one symposium, there was a *ballet of dancing okras.* I've never thought about humble okra the same way since.

I like to think of this dish as many aspects of the South all wrapped up into one tasty package. You can hibernate, curled up with a bowl of it, but it's also fit to serve to company, and the leftovers can't be beat. Look for good stone-milled corn grits; all that time on the stove goes a long way to making them creamy, and the stewed okra nestles on top.

Water, for the okra and the grits
1½ pounds fresh okra
¼ cup extra-virgin olive oil
¾ pound bacon, roughly chopped
1 yellow onion, chopped
2 cloves garlic, minced
2 dried bay leaves
¼ cup tomato paste
4 tomatoes, cored and roughly chopped
2 cups chicken stock
1 tablespoon Worcestershire sauce
4 teaspoons Morton kosher salt, divided
1 teaspoon Tabasco sauce, plus more for serving
1½ cups coarse white grits (not instant)
4 tablespoons (½ stick) unsalted butter

1. Bring a big pot of unsalted water to a boil. Cut the tops off the okra, and chop it into 1-inch pieces. Cook it for about 90 seconds, until it's a very vivid green, then drain and set aside. This parboiling isn't totally necessary, since it cooks for a while later, but this keeps it from getting too slimy.

2. Warm the olive oil in a heavy-bottomed pot or Dutch oven over medium heat. Add the bacon, and cook for a few minutes, stirring a few times to break it apart and render most of its fat. When the first pieces are browning on the edges and your kitchen smells like Sunday morning, stir in the onion, garlic, and bay leaves, and cook for 8 to 10 minutes, until the onion pieces start getting some color along the edges. Add the tomato paste, breaking it apart with your spatula, and let it toast for a few minutes to build flavor, until the oil is orange and smells like tomatoey caramel.

3. Add the reserved okra to the pot, along with the tomatoes and chicken stock. Season with the Worcestershire, 2 teaspoons salt, and Tabasco. Let it come back up to a simmer, and burble away, stirring occasionally, for 50 minutes to 1 hour, until the liquid has significantly reduced but is still bubbling. This will thicken as it sits, so leave a little time before you eat.

4. While the stew cooks, make the grits. Put some water in a large saucepan, following the package instructions on your grits for the right ratio; I use 6 cups water for 1½ cups grits. Add the remaining 2 teaspoons salt, and bring it to a boil over high heat, then whisk in the grits. As soon as it comes back up to a boil, cover and reduce the heat to low, so there's just a bit of gentle movement in the pot. Cook, stirring occasionally, until the grits have absorbed all the water and are a creamy texture, 45 minutes to 1 hour. Take the pan off the heat, and stir in the butter until it melts. Remove and discard the bay leaves, and cover the pot if you're not eating right away.

5. To serve: Scoop some grits in the bottom of a bowl and add a big ladleful of the okra. Pass around more Tabasco at the table.

ZA'ATAR FRIED CHICKEN

This is my Israeli-style tip of a hat to Willie Mae and her spectacular fried chicken, renowned across America. With extra-crispy skin encasing juicy, tender meat, it's truly among the best culinary creations ever invented. You'll love how the za'atar nestles into the hot crust. If you're a fried-chicken aficionado, you know how much flavor and tenderness a brine contributes, and you might make yours with milk or buttermilk—a classic. I prefer to use water as a base, because milk's sugars caramelize unevenly during frying, whereas water gives you a nice, even golden brown.

1 whole chicken, or 10 pieces bone-in chicken (see page 220)
1 quart plus 1 cup water, divided
½ cup plus ½ teaspoon Morton kosher salt, divided
½ cup sugar
5 cups ice water
2 to 3 quarts canola oil
½ cup all-purpose flour
½ cup cornstarch
1 teaspoon baking powder
1 teaspoon sweet paprika
1 teaspoon ground cayenne pepper
½ teaspoon ground allspice
⅓ cup za'atar

1. If you're using a whole chicken, break it down according to the directions on page 220 so that the rib bones and first wing joint stay attached to the breast. Cut each breast in half crosswise, leaving you with two drumsticks, two thighs, four breast halves, and two wings. Place all the pieces in an airtight container or ziplock bag.

2. Combine 1 quart water, ½ cup salt, and the sugar in a saucepan, and cook over high heat until everything dissolves. Remove from the heat, stir in the ice water, and pour it into the ziplock bag to submerge the chicken. Refrigerate overnight.

3. Pull the chicken out of the brine, and set it on plates or a rimmed sheet to warm up slightly while you heat the oil and prepare the batter.

4. Fill a large heavy-bottomed pot about halfway with canola oil (for a 5-quart Dutch oven, you'll want about 2½ quarts). Clip a candy thermometer to the side of the pot, and bring the oil to 375°F over medium-high heat. The oil's temperature is important not just for cooking but also for safety, so keep an eye on it. Meanwhile, heat the oven to 175°F and line an ovenproof plate or cooling rack with paper towels, to keep the chicken warm as it comes out of the fryer.

5. Make the batter: In a large bowl, whisk together the flour, cornstarch, baking powder, remaining ½ teaspoon

(recipe continues)

salt, paprika, cayenne, and allspice. Add 1 cup water and thoroughly combine.

6. Use tongs to coat the chicken thoroughly with batter, one piece at a time, and let any excess drip off. Carefully lower it into the oil, making sure you don't overcrowd the pot. (I like to cook the dark meat all at once, so it cooks evenly, then do the same with the white meat.)

7. Flip each piece after a minute or two—make sure you don't beat up the crust—and periodically check the oil's temperature to make sure it doesn't dip below 350°F; adjust the heat on your stove as needed. Fry the chicken until its skin is a deep, even golden brown and its internal temperature is 160°F. Depending on the size, this will take 10 to 15 minutes.

8. With your tongs, move the chicken to the prepared plate or rack. Generously sprinkle it all over with the za'atar, roughly ½ tablespoon per piece.

9. Let the oil come back up to 350°F, then continue to fry the rest of the chicken. Serve it right away, or keep it warm in the oven until you're ready to eat.

HOW TO BREAK DOWN A CHICKEN

You can, of course, buy bone-in chicken pieces at the supermarket, but breaking down a chicken is a rite of passage for any cook, and a great, elemental way to build confidence and skills in the kitchen. (For larger animals, unless you know what you're doing, I suggest leaving the butchering to the professionals.) My way of doing it leaves the rib bones attached to the breast, so that the meat holds its shape and gets a little extra flavor. Here's how I do it:

- Start with a heavy, sharp chef's knife. You'll be cutting through bone and joints, and wrestling with a dull knife can mangle the meat.

- Remove the neck and any giblets, then use your knife or kitchen scissors to cut out the backbone. Cut close to the spine, so you don't waste too much meat, and save it for stock. This takes a little elbow grease, and if you've never done it before the sound of the bones might scare you, but that's part of it!

- Lay the chicken with its breast side down, and gently spread it out to expose the cavity. Find the breast plate—a long, narrow triangle that's made of hard, thin bone on its wide end and tapers into cartilage toward the legs—and, with a sharp paring knife, cut shallow incisions along the sides. Loosen it and pull it out.

- Flip the chicken so the breast is facing up, and pull the legs away from the body so the skin is taut. With the heel of your hand, press down to pop the hip joint. Use your chef's knife to cut through the seam of skin that runs along the thigh and cut straight through the joint. Rather than saw away at it, use long, firm strokes to help ease the knife through the chicken. Repeat with the other leg.

- Cut through the ball joints that separate the thighs and drumsticks. At first, it can be a challenge to know the exact angle to follow, so don't sweat it if you have to try a few times and your cuts aren't the most beautiful or precise.

- Locate the joint that attaches the wing to the breast; you'll want to leave it intact. Cut through the "elbow" joint to separate the wing in half, and, if you'd like, remove and discard the wing tips. Repeat with the other wing.

- Separate the chicken breasts, and cut each breast piece in half, pressing firmly on your knife through the rib bones so that they stay attached to the meat.

ZA'ATAR

JIM CORE'S KALE AND ANDOUILLE JAMBALAYA

D on't be fooled by the kale in the name: with this much schmaltz, bacon, *and* butter, it's far from virtuous. Jim Core, a farmer in the New Orleans area, came up with it long before kale was trendy, as a way of putting his unwanted bumper crop to use. He found some surefire ways to make kale more appealing, such as this one: fold it into brown rice with spicy Cajun sausage, top it with buttery toasted breadcrumbs, and serve it hot on a chilly winter day. Sure enough, when he started offering it at the farmers' market, he wouldn't just sell out of the jambalaya—he'd also sell out of the kale itself. The weekend after he passed away, in 2012, I made a big batch and gave it away at the market in celebration of his life.

Jim was ahead of his time in lots of ways; he was also the first farmer to give me heirloom tomatoes. I learned a lot through him about the importance of a chef-farmer relationship. I used to bring my cooks to help with the kale harvest at his farm, showing them just how much labor went into producing the vegetables that landed on their cutting boards.

True to Jim's spirit, I make this in a huge batch. That's the way it makes sense: serving a crowd, perfect for entertaining. (If you've got a surplus of kale, too, so much the better.) The smell alone will lure everyone into your kitchen, and the schmaltz-infused panko topping is super-good, something you've probably never encountered in other jambalayas but will not regret. Feel free to substitute olive oil or ghee if you have trouble tracking down schmaltz and don't have time to make it.

- 2 tablespoons plus ¼ cup schmaltz (page 394) or extra-virgin olive oil, divided
- ½ pound bacon, chopped
- 2 pounds smoked andouille sausage, sliced
- 2 yellow onions, chopped
- 3 cloves garlic, minced
- 1 tablespoon Morton kosher salt
- 1 dried bay leaf
- 2 teaspoons sweet paprika
- 1 teaspoon celery salt
- ½ teaspoon freshly ground black pepper
- ½ teaspoon cayenne pepper
- 2 bunches curly kale, stemmed and roughly chopped
- 7 cups chicken stock
- 4 cups brown rice
- 4 tablespoons (½ stick) unsalted butter
- 1 cup panko breadcrumbs

1. Combine 2 tablespoons schmaltz and the bacon in a large Dutch oven or ovenproof pot over medium heat, stirring occasionally. After 8 or 10 minutes, when the bacon is brown around the edges and most of its fat has rendered, add the sausage and cook until the edges start to brown, another 6 to 8 minutes. With a slotted spoon, remove the meat and reserve it, leaving the fat in the pot.

2. Add the onions, garlic, salt, and bay leaf to the pot. Cook until the onions are soft with browned edges, 5 to 6 minutes. Stir in all the spices, and let them toast and become fragrant for a minute.

3. Fold in the kale. Add it gradually if you need to; it will really shrink down as it cooks. Give it a good stir to coat it with the fat and seasoning, and once it's started to soften, add the stock, rice, and reserved sausage and bacon.

4. Increase the heat to high to bring everything up to a simmer, then stir in the butter and reduce the heat to low. Cover the pot and let the rice cook until it's tender and has absorbed all the stock, about 1 hour. If there's still a lot of liquid by the time the rice has cooked through, bump the heat up to medium and cook for a few more minutes without the lid. Remove and discard the bay leaf, cover the pot once again, and set it aside off the heat while you make the topping.

5. Heat the oven to 500°F with a rack toward the top, set as close as you can get the pot to the heating element. Melt the remaining ¼ cup schmaltz, and stir in the panko. Sprinkle this in a thin, even layer over the top of the jambalaya, and bake for 8 to 10 minutes, until the crust is deeply golden.

17

✦✦✦

Day Off for Dates

I was exhausted. I needed a day off from carving cowboy steaks and tasting spoonfuls of crab-and-corn bisque. Since Hurricane Katrina, I'd worked more than 150 days in a row; my whole life was the steakhouse, the steakhouse, the steakhouse. When I got an invitation to a party from some well-to-do customers, I thought it might be a good idea for me to take an evening off and go.

Given the grandeur of their neighborhood, I figured I should look civilized for their party. I hadn't worn anything other than jeans since Katrina, but I put on a pair of slacks and a button-down shirt. I arrived to discover that it was basically a mixer for Jewish newcomers to the city, a place for folks to meet and—just *maybe*—fall in love, so they could eventually make Jewish babies. Of course, I immediately felt awkward. What would I have to talk about? I'd been through what felt like a war

post-Katrina, and all I'd been up to more recently had to do with truffle butter and beef tenderloin. Not exactly small-talk material.

I was downing my fourth finger sandwich, talking only to the workers who'd been hired to set out the food, when I saw a girl walk into the room. She was beautiful and blonde with cute dimples, and she was wearing a brightly patterned dress. Though she was surrounded by other attractive women, I noticed her—something about her radiated happiness, a confidence that was magnetic. *I have to figure out how to talk to her,* I thought.

I put down my glass of kosher red wine and headed over to introduce myself. This was a bold move for me. I'd never been particularly good at hitting on girls and usually only went out with the ladies who asked *me* out first. But I managed to make my move, awkwardly, after someone near us mistook her for someone else. "That's not me," she said. "Well, who *are* you?" I asked. And she laughed. Her name was Emily, and she was working in real-estate development for a huge construction company in town. I sent her an e-mail a few days later inviting her to dinner at the steakhouse. "Come with some of your friends," I wrote. "I want to cook for you and show you what I do."

To my surprise, she actually came in for dinner, bringing a whole group of her friends. I wanted to make this a meal she'd remember. I sent out all the highlights of our menu: ribeye with smoked marrow butter, butter-poached lobster tails, a corn-and-crab risotto served in the corn's husk (also containing a significant amount of butter). For dessert, I pulled out all the stops and made them sorbet tableside, using liquid nitrogen. These were early days for such culinary techniques; I'd only recently started experimenting with them myself. I had to wear big rubber gloves and a welder's mask—that was my outfit as I stood by Emily's table, carefully pouring liquid nitrogen into a bowl and whisking vigorously as the vapors rose from it. It

ROSEBUDS AND SPICES
FOR ROSE TAHINI
SYRUP

was a champagne sorbet, which is particularly fun because it freezes so fast that the sorbet stays carbonated. Amid the wisps of liquid-nitrogen vapor, I could see Emily's smile. *She likes it,* I thought.

An e-mail I sent her after this dinner went unanswered for weeks. But the next time I ran into her, out at a bar, I was struck again by her kindness and, well, how *normal* she seemed. This was a moment, post-Katrina in New Orleans, when so many of us were still unnerved from the storm. We couldn't talk about anything "normal." And Emily seemed to move through life with an attitude of easy welcome.

A few days later, my culinary school friend Keven was in town visiting, and we were about to head to Restaurant August for dinner. Out of nowhere, I thought, *I should call Emily and see if she wants to join us.* We were already en route to dinner when this occurred to me.

She answered my call, and said that, sure, she'd like to come. "When?" she asked.

"Um, well, we're going . . . right now."

"Awesome," she said. "I'll be right over."

This is how smooth I was romantically: I invited the girl I liked to be a third wheel with me and my best college friend and gave her less than 10 minutes' notice. But we had a wonderful dinner. I asked her if she knew what foie gras was and, without so much as waiting for a response, launched into a 15-minute explanation of it—how buttery and amazing fattened goose liver was, how you could sear and caramelize it and make a terrine from it, how well it went with sweet things like cherries or honey. She seemed very interested and heartily enjoyed the food. It was only months later that I found out she had already known exactly what foie gras was, and already loved it, but she had seen how excited I was to describe it to her that night at August and didn't want to interrupt me. It became a running joke with us: I was always trying to teach her about foods that she already knew.

The truth is, Emily ended up teaching *me* about so many things—first and foremost, about loving life in New Orleans. About the round king-cakes of the Mardi Gras season, painted in purple, green, and gold icing, with a tiny plastic baby hidden within the pastry for someone to find. About bringing a few pounds of boiled crawfish to the edge of the bayou and peeling and eating their sweet meat outdoors. About dancing in the street to the music of a brass band at a Sunday second-line parade.

About the amazing piano playing of the New Orleans icon Professor Longhair. Before I started listening to New Orleans music, Emily and I had met a dog in the dog park named Professor Long Ears. When she introduced me to the legendary pianist, I exclaimed, *"Just like the dog!"* I realized, dating Emily, that I was falling in love twice: with her, and with the music-and-fun-filled life she led in New Orleans. That was now starting to be my life, too.

I did my best to add to her life as she was adding to mine. The first time I cooked for her at her house, I was still trying to impress her. I made dates wrapped with bacon, stuffed with Gorgonzola cheese, and cooked, just briefly, on the grill. It's a dish that's cheating, a little bit—there's no way it can be bad. The dates are honeyed and sweet with a near-creamy texture, which balances nicely with the salty funk of the cheese. The outside, wrapped in smoky bacon and grilled, crisps, while the cheese on the inside melts, and the date softens up. It's a bite that hits all the senses. I made that in her tiny galley kitchen in the French Quarter, leaning out onto the back porch to use her little grill. It was the first course of a feast: the dates, then lobster risotto, and pumpkin crème brûlée that I took care to serve in miniature pumpkins. I took the whole day off from work to cook for her. The date—and the dates—were worth it.

DATE PANCAKES WITH ROSE TAHINI YIELD: 4 TO 6 SERVINGS

This goes out to all the workaholics out there. Get off the clock, grab your partner, and take some time for dates. I swear, it'll pay off more than a paycheck ever could.

When Emily and I were first dating, I made heart-shaped pancakes for Valentine's Day. In that spirit, the rose tahini adds a romance to the recipe. It's magical and delicious on nearly anything sweet; if you haven't tried it, I hope this recipe will spur you to action. However, if you're cooking these on a Sunday morning and feeling lazy, you can simply add ¼ teaspoon ground cardamom to the pancake batter and serve them with dark maple syrup instead.

1. Beat the egg whites until they hold soft peaks when you lift the beater. Set them aside.

2. Melt 4 tablespoons butter and let it cool slightly. In a large bowl, whisk it together with the egg yolks, milk, cider vinegar, and orange juice; then stir in the dates. Separately, combine the flour, salt, and baking soda.

3. Fold the dry ingredients in with the milk mixture; a few small lumps are okay, and better than overworking the batter, which will already be pretty thick. Finally, just as it's coming together, fold in the egg white, using gentle strokes so you don't deflate it.

4. Set a nonstick pan over medium-low heat, and add about 1 teaspoon butter. Once the butter stops foaming, ladle the batter into the pan in roughly ⅓-cup scoops, making sure you don't overcrowd them in the pan. Cook without disturbing for 2 to 3 minutes, until the edges are deeply golden brown; you might also see some bubbles along the edges. Flip, and cook for another minute or so, until the other side has a good crust, too.

5. Give the batter a good stir before adding each new batch, since the dates will settle at the bottom. Top the warm pancakes with a drizzle of rose tahini and a small pat of butter.

3 eggs, separated
4 tablespoons (½ stick) unsalted butter, plus more for cooking and serving
1½ cups milk
2 tablespoons apple-cider vinegar
2 tablespoons orange juice
16 dates, preferably Medjool, pitted and thinly sliced
2 cups all-purpose flour
1 teaspoon Morton kosher salt
1 teaspoon baking soda
½ cup rose tahini (page 393)

RICOTTA WITH DATE AND PECAN PESTO

YIELD: 6 TO 8 SERVINGS

We kept this on the menu at my Italian restaurant, Domenica, for years; it was a favorite and is sure to make a comeback someday. You'll want to make sure to use the best and freshest ricotta you can find, which usually requires a trip to your local farmers' market or cheese shop, or at least the cheese counter in your supermarket—the dairy aisle just can't supply a product as fresh as you want for a dish this simple. Since the cheese is so creamy and the dates are so sweet, I love to offset it with a really great, peppery olive oil and crusty, full-flavored bread.

1. Cut the baguette on a bias into ½-inch slices, and arrange them on a baking sheet. Toast at 425°F for 6 to 8 minutes, until they're browning along the edges. Remove, and cool slightly.

2. Combine the parsley, pecans, Parmesan, ½ teaspoon salt, and dates; then stir in the olive oil and vinegar.

3. Drain the ricotta of any excess water, and season with the remaining ½ teaspoon salt. Spread it in a rimmed serving dish or bowl, with a wide, shallow well in the center for the pesto. Don't be shy—each bite should get a little of the creamy ricotta, bright pesto, and oil. Double-dipping is encouraged.

A crusty baguette

2 cups lightly packed fresh parsley leaves, chopped

1 cup chopped pecans, toasted

⅓ cup finely grated Parmesan cheese

1 teaspoon Morton kosher salt, divided

4 dates, preferably Medjool, pitted and finely chopped

1 cup extra-virgin olive oil

2 tablespoons best-quality balsamic vinegar

1 pound ricotta

CHICKEN LIVER PÂTÉ WITH CELERY AND DATES

I'm still fond of the chopped liver that my mom made when I was a child, but, as I've grown older, it's sort of evolved into this pâté: richer, creamier, with a pretty pink color. Chicken livers are sometimes misunderstood, often unwanted, so they're cheap and easy to get with any butcher, but this preparation truly feels like fine dining. With the crisp, fresh celery and sweet roundness of the dates, it's just damn good. If you're making this in advance, you can prep the butter and chicken livers, or even make the whole recipe through. Most important is that all the ingredients in the pâté itself are kept very cold—temperature is just as important as any of the ingredients. It'll help yield an airy texture to the finished pâté.

½ pound chicken livers, drained
3 teaspoons Morton kosher salt, divided
6 tablespoons unsalted butter
¼ yellow onion, thinly sliced
1 clove garlic, crushed
2 sprigs fresh thyme
½ teaspoon whole black peppercorns
½ teaspoon whole allspice berries
2 tablespoons brandy
½ teaspoon sugar
⅓ cup heavy cream, very cold
1 egg, very cold
2 cups water, plus more for a water bath
1 stalk celery, finely chopped
6 Medjool dates, pitted and chopped
1 tablespoon extra-virgin olive oil
1 tablespoon lemon juice
A crusty baguette

1. Rinse the chicken livers under the tap, and pull or trim off any large pieces of white fat. Pat them dry and combine with 2 teaspoons of the salt, then freeze in a ziplock bag or on a plate for 1 or 2 hours, or until they're semi-frozen but not rock-hard.

2. While the livers chill, combine the butter, onion, garlic, thyme, black pepper, and allspice in a large skillet over low heat, stirring occasionally for 20 to 30 minutes until the onions are very soft. You're not looking to build color here; you just want to pull all those flavors out to infuse the fat.

3. When the onions are so soft they're almost melting, take the pan off the heat. Carefully add the brandy and sugar and return it to the stove for 30 seconds or so for the alcohol to cook out. Strain the butter into a small heatproof bowl, cover, and refrigerate for at least 30 minutes, or until the chicken livers are ready. (As long as you don't chomp down on a peppercorn or allspice berry, the onions make an awesome snack.)

4. Heat the oven to 250°F. Set an ovenproof bowl or small casserole dish—it should hold 2 to 3 cups—inside a roasting pan or other deeper, larger pan.

5. Add the cream and very cold livers to a blender and mix on high for 30 seconds, or until the mixture is smooth. With the blender going, pour in the egg and then scrape in the chilled butter. Blend until very smooth and custardy.

(recipe continues)

6. Pour the pâté into the bowl and fill the roasting pan with hot tap water that's roughly level with the pâté (it's helpful to put the roasting pan in the oven before adding the water so it doesn't splash). Bake for 60 to 70 minutes, until the center is barely set and no longer wobbly, with a little rosy color; if you have a thermometer, it should read 135°F to 140°F throughout. Carefully remove the dish from the water bath and let the pâté come to room temperature, then refrigerate until well chilled, at least 4 hours.

7. To make the celery and date salad, bring the water and remaining 1 teaspoon salt to a boil in a small saucepan; get a colander or sieve ready to go, since the next step happens quickly. Cook the celery in the boiling water just until its color perks up a bit, 20 seconds or so; drain. Combine with the dates, olive oil, and lemon juice, and set aside.

8. Slice the baguette diagonally and arrange the slices on a baking sheet. Toast at 425°F for 6 to 8 minutes, until they've built some nice color along the edges. To serve, top the chilled pâté with the celery and dates spread evenly over the top.

DATES, TURNIPS, AND BACON WITH GORGONZOLA DRESSING

Every winter, I find myself surrounded by more turnips than I know what to do with. When Emily and I first started dating, I'd bring her along on trips to pick them up from our farmers and cart them back to the restaurant. We would load up the car with over 100 pounds of the root vegetables, still covered in the dirt they came from. I was—and still am—always trying to figure out new and delicious ways to make the most of that abundance, a welcome thing in the coldest months of the year.

This is kind of a remix of the classic appetizer, bacon-wrapped dates stuffed with Gorgonzola, that I made for Emily during those days. It's equally impressive, and equally simple, but you can eat much more of this than you can stuffed dates. All that time in the oven makes the bacon crisp up and the dates get nicely chewy. Everything drapes itself around the turnips, so you can polish off a big bowl before you know it.

1. Heat the oven to 425°F with a rack in the center of the oven, and line a rimmed baking sheet with foil or parchment.

2. Trim the roots and tips off the turnips, and cut them into ½-to-1-inch pieces. Chop the bacon into roughly 1-inch pieces, break it apart to disperse it with the turnips, and toss to coat with the salt and 2 tablespoons olive oil. Spread the mix over the baking sheet, tuck the rosemary in the middle, and roast for 20 minutes.

3. Scatter the dates among the bacon and turnips, and give it all a good stir so the bacon fat is shared around. Roast for another 15 to 20 minutes, until the turnips are tender but not mushy.

4. Meanwhile, use a fork to mash the Gorgonzola and mix it with the yogurt, orange juice, and remaining 2 tablespoons olive oil until you have a thick, relatively smooth dressing.

5. Once you've finished roasting, remove and discard the rosemary and move the rest to a bowl. Gently toss it with the dressing and serve warm, scattered with parsley.

2½ pounds turnips, peeled
½ pound thickly sliced bacon
1 teaspoon Morton kosher salt
4 tablespoons extra-virgin olive oil, divided
1 large sprig fresh rosemary
12 Medjool dates, pitted and quartered
2 ounces Gorgonzola Dolce
3 tablespoons Greek yogurt
2 tablespoons orange juice
¼ cup lightly packed fresh parsley leaves, chopped

18

✦✦✦

Not So Semplice

My life had turned into the kind that I'd always admired from the outside: friends, a beautiful girlfriend, a dog named Henry, regularly eating crawfish and dancing in the streets of New Orleans. And then I decided to leave it all to move to Italy.

During the six months I spent with Emily, I'd been honing an idea. I wanted to cook Italian food. Ever since my early days at Sonoma, through my time in the kitchens of Antonio's in Las Vegas and St. Louis, I'd had an affection for the cuisine. I also suspected that what I considered Italian food likely paled in comparison to what was actually being cooked and eaten in Italy. I daydreamed of opening a restaurant called Semplice—"simple" in Italian—that would serve traditional Italian food. I had visions of home-cured soppressata, hand-rolled cavatelli, and pots of polenta, the sorts of dishes I imagined grandmothers cooked. While I was working at the steakhouse, I started writing up a business plan. I was determined to make it a reality, and pre- sented the plan to John and Octavio. "This is my dream," I told them. "As much as I love the steakhouse, I think the casino isn't for me. I've been thinking about this concept for years."

Over the course of our meeting, another idea emerged: I could move to Italy for a while. It made per- fect sense: if I wanted to open a true Italian restaurant, I should go learn from Italians themselves! "Well," John said, "I could call Marc Vetri and see if he could help set you up."

Marc Vetri was a chef from Philadelphia who'd become known for his Italian cooking, especially the delicacy of his pastas. Within days, he'd offered to connect me with restaurants he knew in Italy. I would quit my job at the steakhouse and live off all the savings I'd been accumulating over the years of doing nothing but work. *I'll go, and work, and stay until I run out of money*, I decided. It was a big risk. In an industry as fickle as this one, there was no guarantee that I'd come back from Italy, broke but full of ideas, and actually be able to open my restaurant. But I knew I needed to try. The only problem: I had to tell Emily.

She knew that I'd been daydreaming about opening an Italian restaurant, but she certainly didn't expect me to say, "I'm off to Italy! Bye!" When I told her, though, her response was unequivocal: "That's amazing," she said.

"Oh, and I've sublet my apartment," I added. "Can I move in with you for a few weeks before I leave?"

"Okay!" she said, as cheerfully as she could muster.

It was really happening; I was really going. For the last few weeks before I left, I cooked for Emily. Her little back porch—overlooking a bunch of banana trees tucked into a French Quarter courtyard—became the epicenter for grilling parties, abundant with barbecued chicken and cornbread. I'd learned that Emily adored fresh tomatoes and set about preparing them in every fashion I could think of. I cut thick rounds, layered them with mozzarella, and dotted them with basil pesto. We made New Orleans classics, too, such as gumbo and boiled shrimp.

Meanwhile, I practiced my feeble Italian by reciting, over and over again, the lessons provided by Rosetta Stone: "Bee-chee-cletta roh-sah," I would say. "Be-chee-cletta jah-low." Even amid all my excited preparations, I could tell Emily was sad, but she never guilt-tripped me for leaving. She encouraged me to pursue my dreams, not once asking me to stay. It made me realize how much I loved her. She gave me the confidence to follow the pull I felt to Italy and to trust that choice. *She deserves someone better than me,* I thought, *someone who wouldn't put a perfectly roasted porchetta above her.* As I boarded my first flight, I thought that surely this would be the time she would realize that.

HEIRLOOM TOMATO AND
BURRATA CAPRESE

When I was first falling for Emily, I knew how much she loved tomatoes, so I did what any sensible person in my situation would do: made Caprese salad. My version had perfectly ripe heirloom tomatoes and velvety burrata, which is like extra-fresh mozzarella with a soft and creamy center. When you have those things, you don't need much else, and, in fact, you shouldn't steal their thunder with anything too crazy. The only way to improve upon it is with fresh basil, which I make into a pesto (recipe follows) that drapes over every bite.

- 2 pounds good heirloom tomatoes, cored and sliced
- ½ pound burrata
- 2 tablespoons extra-virgin olive oil
- 1 tablespoon best-quality aged balsamic vinegar
- ¼ cup pesto (recipe follows)
- ½ cup chopped walnuts, toasted
- ½ teaspoon Maldon or other flaky sea salt

1. Arrange the tomatoes on your serving platter; tear large shreds (about bite-sized) of the burrata by hand, and scatter them throughout, being sure not to lose any of its creamy goodness en route.
2. Drizzle the olive oil and vinegar all over, dollop the pesto on it, and sprinkle the nuts and some flaky sea salt over the top. Serve right away.

PESTO

So much of the Italian food we know here in America has been lost in translation by the time it becomes well known, and pesto is a perfect example. Many of us have made pesto dozens of times, but when you go to its source—Liguria—you realize why it's become world-renowned. There, when you drive through the villages, the air is heavily scented with basil.

This method will change what you think you know about this simplest of sauces. The nuts and cheeses give it body but aren't the focus, and I skip the garlic altogether, so the basil can shine. That's why I blanch it: this wakes up the herb without making it taste cooked. Make sure you grate the cheese on the finest side of your grater to keep your pesto smooth and silky.

- 2 quarts water
- ¼ teaspoon baking soda
  Ice water for an ice bath
- 1 quart lightly packed fresh basil leaves
- ½ cup raw walnut pieces
- ½ cup finely grated Pecorino Romano
- ½ cup finely grated Parmesan cheese
- ½ cup extra-virgin olive oil
- 1 teaspoon Morton kosher salt

1. Combine the water and baking soda, and bring the pot to a boil. Separately, add ice to a medium bowl and top it off with water. Get a colander ready in your sink.

(recipe continues)

2. Drop the basil into the boiling water and blanch for 5 seconds, then immediately drain it and shock it in the ice bath to stop the cooking. Lay a clean dish towel flat, and spread the basil on it to dry thoroughly (leave the ice cubes in the bowl).

3. Move the basil to a food processor, and add the walnuts, cheeses, olive oil, and salt. Whiz until it's incorporated but not completely puréed.

SMOKED CHICKEN WITH HARISSA

YIELD: 1 CHICKEN
(ABOUT 4 SERVINGS)

1 whole chicken (4 to 5 pounds)
1½ tablespoons herb salt (page 391)
1 cup water, plus more for the wood chips
1 quart wood chips, like applewood or pecan
3 tablespoons harissa (page 389)
Charcoal for the smoker
1 can beer
1 lime

The chicken I grilled for Emily was very simple; if only I could have wooed her with this one. The combination of herb salt and harissa is all you need to make this one of the most unforgettable chickens you've ever eaten, much less cooked yourself. Smoking the bird goes above and beyond—my favorite preparation, worth the extra time if you've got a smoker. (Or find someone who does: they'll be happy to make the trade if you share your dinner.) Feel free to smoke 2 or 3 while you're at it; the method remains the same. But if you prefer to just pop it in the oven, I have a roasted version that's also awesome (see the following recipe).

1. Pat the chicken dry inside and out, then pat the herb salt evenly over the skin and inside the cavity. Place it on a plate with the breast side up and refrigerate, uncovered, for at least a couple of hours and preferably overnight. Leaving it uncovered helps the skin fully dry out, which translates to a much crispier skin when it cooks.

2. Fill a bowl with water, and add the wood chips so they're completely submerged. Let them soak for 1 hour. Meanwhile, rub the harissa all over the chicken and let it come to room temperature as you get the smoker ready.

3. Close your smoker's dampers halfway and fill it one-third to halfway with charcoals. Light them and, once they're white-hot along the edges, stir them to disperse the heat evenly. Scatter the soaked wood chips among the coals; top with a heat deflector (if you have one) and the grill rack.

4. Close the lid and let the smoker start to warm up. Play with the dampers—cracking them open in ⅛-inch increments makes it warmer by increasing the airflow, whereas closing them more dulls the oxygen and cools it down—and be patient between adjustments since the changes aren't instantaneous. Give it time.

5. Once the smoker hits 250°F, open the can of beer (feel free to take a few sips first) and, leaving the can right side up, sit the chicken over it to stuff the cavity. Place the chicken in a roasting pan, leaving the can upright with the chicken perched on top, and pour the water inside.

(recipe continues)

6. Put the roasting pan on the grill and close the lid. Close the dampers, too, so that they're only slightly cracked open; this will help regulate the heat, which should stay right around 250°F throughout the cooking process. At first, the temperature may fluctuate, so you'll need to check the temperature every 15 or 20 minutes, adjusting the dampers as needed, until it hits equilibrium.

7. At this point, you can basically kick back and just check every hour or so. The temperature may continue to fluctuate, but it's such a low, slow process that you've got leeway. The chicken is ready when the internal temperature at the thickest part of its thigh reads 160°F on an instant-read thermometer; this should take approximately 5 hours, but start checking after 4 hours.

8. Allow the chicken to rest for 10 minutes before carving it. Cut the lime into wedges and serve them on the side.

 ## ROASTED CHICKEN WITH HARISSA

YIELD: 1 CHICKEN
(ABOUT 4 SERVINGS)

If you don't have a smoker (or if you don't have all day to hang out while it cooks), roasting a whole bird is a surefire way to deliver the same unbeatable flavor. There are a lot of very straightforward roasted chicken recipes out there, and a lot of mediocre roasted chicken recipes. This recipe asks a little more of you—you'll season the bird overnight, truss it, roast it over a bit of water to add moisture, then finish it at a super-high temperature for crispy skin—but it's so good it'll instantly earn its keep.

1 whole chicken (4 to 5 pounds)
2 tablespoons herb salt (page 391)
1 cup water
2 tablespoons harissa (page 389), plus more for serving
1 lime

1. Pat the chicken dry inside and out, then pat the herb salt evenly all over the bird. Place it on a plate with the breast side up and refrigerate, uncovered, for at least a couple of hours and preferably overnight.

2. Heat the oven to 325°F with a rack in the lower-middle portion of your oven. Set a roasting rack inside a roasting pan, and pour the water into the bottom. If you don't have a roasting rack, any slotted rack that keeps the bird elevated from the roasting pan will work.

3. Truss the chicken (if you've never done this, there are plenty

of easy tutorials online, and doing so will ensure that it cooks evenly), and rub the harissa all over the skin. Set it in the rack, again with the breast facing up, and roast it for about 1½ hours, until you can easily pierce the leg meat with a knife.

4. Take the pan out of the oven, and bump the heat up to 450°F. Once it's come to temperature, roast the chicken for another 15 to 20 minutes, until the internal temperature of the chicken breast is 160°F. The skin will be nicely crisped up with good color, the harissa almost blackened in some areas.

5. Let the chicken rest for 10 minutes before carving it on a rimmed platter or cutting board (it may give off a *lot* of juice). Cut the lime into wedges, and serve them on the side along with more harissa.

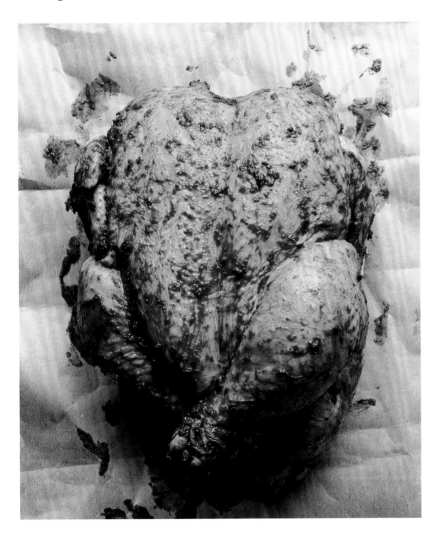

SCHMALTZY CORNBREAD WITH GRIBENES

1 cup milk
4 tablespoons (½ stick) unsalted butter, softened
1 egg
1¼ cups medium- or coarse-grind cornmeal
1 cup all-purpose flour
½ cup sugar
1 teaspoon baking powder
½ teaspoon Morton kosher salt
¼ cup schmaltz (page 394)
¼ cup cane syrup or honey
½ cup gribenes (page 394)

Here's a little tip: bake your cornbread in a layer of rendered chicken fat and it'll get a thick, incredible, and deeply flavored crust. I love to play that up with a topping of gribenes, the addictive, crackling-like chicken skins that are a natural by-product when you render the schmaltz yourself (see page 394). No need for butter—the cane syrup soaks right in. Bring this to any party or dinner table and you'll hit it out of the park.

If you don't want to make your own schmaltz and gribenes, you can ask for schmaltz or duck fat at your butcher counter. Otherwise, use ghee, or clarified butter, which is sold in the international section of most supermarkets. There's no substitute for fresh, crispy gribenes, but the cornbread is so good that it won't feel incomplete if you leave them out.

1. Heat the oven to 400°F. Use a fork to beat the milk, butter, and egg in a large bowl; the mixture will be a bit lumpy, which is fine.
2. Separately, combine the cornmeal, flour, sugar, baking powder, and salt. Stir them into the wet ingredients; the batter will be pretty thick.
3. Melt the schmaltz in a 9-inch cast-iron or ovenproof nonstick skillet over high heat. It'll start to bubble, then sizzle, then smoke. Scrape the batter into the smoking-hot skillet, and smooth it into an even layer. Transfer immediately to the oven.
4. Bake for 20 to 25 minutes, until it's very golden along the edges and completely set in the center when you shake the pan. Invert the bread onto a plate, drizzle the cane syrup over it, and top with the gribenes.

BANANA BREAD WITH CAROB MOLASSES BUTTER

Emily had a bunch of banana trees in the backyard of her apartment, and it always felt like vacation when we were back there, because it was so lush and tropical. We'd harvest the bananas and make this quick bread together.

Taking the time to let your bananas get overripe—brown, to the point where you wouldn't want to eat them whole—gives you a noticeably better bread, and labneh makes for a more tender crumb (don't worry if you can't find it; Greek yogurt is a

great substitute). Poppy seeds give an understated earthy crunch while keeping the delicate flavors of baharat and orange blossom water in check. As always, if you don't have baharat on hand, pumpkin-pie spice is the next best thing. This bread is good enough to need no accompaniment, but butter whipped with carob molasses—with its full, chocolaty tones—is a spectacular finishing touch.

1. Heat the oven to 350°F, and line a 9-by-5-inch loaf pan with buttered parchment paper.
2. Whisk together the flour, baharat, 1 tablespoon poppy seeds, baking soda, and salt. Set the mixture aside.
3. In a large bowl, cream 1 stick of butter with the brown sugar with a mixer on medium-high speed, scraping the sides occasionally. When the mixture is smooth and light and no longer appears grainy, beat in the eggs one at a time, followed by the labneh, vanilla, and orange blossom water. Stir in the bananas by hand. Don't worry if the batter looks curdled; that can happen with this kind of loose mixing, and it sorts itself out in the oven. Now fold in the dry ingredients just until combined.
4. Pour the batter into the prepared loaf pan and sprinkle the remaining 1½ teaspoons poppy seeds evenly over the top. Bake for about 1 hour, rotating the pan after 30 minutes, until a knife comes out clean. Let it cool completely in the pan before you cut into it.
5. Whip the remaining stick of butter with the carob molasses until it's light and airy. Smear the butter on the bread to serve. If it's wrapped well, you can keep banana bread for a few days and, if you like, reheat each slice in the toaster or a 350°F oven. Refrigerate any leftover carob-molasses butter, and let it soften completely before using.

½ pound (2 sticks) unsalted butter, softened, divided, plus more for the pan
1⅔ cups all-purpose flour
1½ tablespoons baharat (page 385)
1½ tablespoons poppy seeds, divided
1 teaspoon baking soda
½ teaspoon Morton kosher salt
1 cup light-brown sugar
2 eggs
¼ cup labneh (page 38) or Greek yogurt
1½ teaspoons vanilla extract
¼ teaspoon orange blossom water
4 overripe bananas, roughly mashed
1 tablespoon carob molasses or blackstrap molasses

IV

AN

ITALIAN

SOJOURN

✦ ✦ ✦

19

A Bed by the Dough Mixer

I wanted out of this restaurant. How could that be? I was in Italy, living the daydream I'd had for years. Almost nothing was the way I'd thought it would be.

My journey to Italy began with the kind of coincidence that affirmed my decision to go on this trip. I arrived in Philadelphia for my layover en route to Milan, and up walked Chef Marc Vetri with his wife, Megan, and their one-year-old son, Maurice, in a stroller. Not only was Marc one of my culinary icons, a Jewish chef from Philly with a specialty in Italian food, but he was also the person who'd connected me with the restaurant near Bergamo where I was headed at that very moment. I owed this whole adventure to him and his chef partner, Jeff Michaud. By chance, he was also flying to Milan that day and then driving to Bergamo. He offered to give me a ride to the restaurant when we all arrived, so I wouldn't have to navigate the Italian train system. I couldn't believe my good luck.

Bergamo is at the foot of the Italian Alps, which gorgeously dominate the landscape. As Marc drove us out into the countryside, I admired beautiful old villas with their backdrop of snowcapped mountains, and a medieval city sitting on top of a

hill that seemed as if it'd been untouched for centuries. When we arrived in Trescore Balneario, the little town that was home to Ristorante LoRo, Marc parked at the bottom of a huge hill. At that moment, I began to regret my three suitcases, only one of which contained clothes. One suitcase weighed approximately 75 pounds because I'd packed it full of books I thought I might need on my trip, including a cultural history of Italian cuisine and the deluxe thousand-page edition of an Italian-English dictionary. Marc was nice enough to help me drag that suitcase up the hill, and polite enough not to make fun of me for it until years later.

Ristorante LoRo was housed in an aging villa with curved brick ceilings and a little cave off one of the dining rooms in which wine was stored. Far from the scene in my fantasies of a little Italian grandmother, or nonna, rolling pasta, the kitchen was very modern and filled with sleek equipment. Antonio and Francesco, the owners of the restaurant, were *certainly* not nonnas. Antonio was a short, stocky guy who looked as though he'd been very dedicated to lifting weights at some point. Francesco was his physical opposite, tall and lanky, freckled and red-haired. He drove a Ducati, a fast Italian sports motorcycle, and liked to walk around with the helmet, as if it made him look cool.

Marc and I sat down with Antonio and Francesco when we arrived, and they began to catch up in rapid Italian. I had no idea what they were saying. When we first walked in the kitchen, though, I'd noticed that they were making rolls for bread service and filling them with culatello, a cured meat that's like prosciutto but aged longer, so it has a deeper, richer flavor. They were brushing the stuffed rolls with egg yolk and sprinkling them with poppy seeds before baking them. That got me excited.

After Marc and his family left, Antonio and Francesco took me upstairs to show me the small apartment above the restaurant that I'd be sharing with two servers and another cook. My bed should have been a warning sign of what was to come: a wire cot with a thin, uncovered mattress, about 4 inches from an industrial-sized dough mixer. Visions of myself receiving a dusting of flour as I slept floated through my head. But I refused to be worried. I threw down my suitcases, put on an apron, and hustled back down to the kitchen to start working.

On my first night working at Ristorante LoRo, one of the other cooks got sick, leaving just Antonio and me in the kitchen. I was thrown into the mix out of necessity; there were customers in the dining room, and Antonio couldn't cook everything on his own. He shouted at me in Italian all night long—he didn't speak English—and I did my best to piece together what he needed. At one point, he yelled what I thought was *"sale,"* which means salt. So I handed him a box of salt. Furious, he screamed it again: "Insalata!" Which, of course, meant "salad." The only method of communication that worked for us that night was my watching him put together a dish, and then doing my best to replicate it, relying on the international language of cooking. At the end of service, I swept and mopped the floors and did my best to write the evening off as an anomaly. Then I got upstairs and realized that there were no sheets or pillows for me, just a bare mattress. I pulled a couple of T-shirts out of my suitcase, folded them up to form a pillow, and fell into an exhausted sleep.

The next day, I got started promptly at 8:00 a.m. Things seemed better with Antonio. He walked into the kitchen carrying a sack full of bright-red shrimp called gamberi rossi and smiled a bit as I began to peel them. They were gorgeous shrimp—a brilliant ruby color even when they're raw, and sweet with a soft, almost creamy texture. The next few days brought a number of positive moments like that. One of the servers at the restaurant, Enzo, drove me to his family's house to provide me with a bed-sheet, a pillowcase, and a colorful Spider-Man comforter that had been his as a kid. Antonio promised to take me to meet a cheese maker in the Alps and go shopping for ingredients in the market together.

On Easter Sunday, he had me over for dinner with his family. When we walked in, his wife and mother-in-law were in the middle of cooking, and food was everywhere. A grill was covered with slender zucchini, rounds of onions, and fat cotechino sausages. They were making crostini by rubbing olive oil and garlic on ciabatta, placing it over coals next to the vegetables, and topping it with marinated tomatoes and olives. Antonio's wife, Francesca, had made a lasagna with silky green pasta, béchamel, Fontina, and layers of prosciutto throughout. The pinnacle of the meal was a whole roasted capretto, or baby goat. Francesca's mother had braised it with olives, raisins, and red wine, and was serving it with a coarsely ground whole-grain polenta that was typical of that part of Italy. In his most innovative cooking move yet, Antonio put a little polenta down on a plate, sliced a fat chunk of Taleggio cheese on top of it, then spooned more polenta over that. As we carved the capretto, the cheese melted within the mound of polenta. I was beside myself with happiness. In addition to the glorious food, it also helped that Francesca spoke a little English, so I had someone to talk to. Antonio and I had not progressed beyond trading a few stiff words.

After a honeymoon that lasted a few days in the wake of Easter dinner, things got worse for me at Ristorante LoRo. No matter how hard I tried, studying my Italian dictionary at night, my attempts to engage in conversation with Antonio were stymied. After a certain point, he would just ignore me altogether, as if I weren't standing there talking to him. Francesco's behavior also began to strike me as odd. During the midday break between lunch and dinner service, I'd walk into the dining room of the restaurant and find him asleep on the reception desk. At family meal, he would make fun of me for not understanding what he was saying. They were even worse with one another. Francesco would come into the kitchen in the middle of dinner service and have an argument with Antonio, verging on a temper tantrum, as they slammed doors and shrieked at one another at the top of their lungs. I'd been in kitchens where the chefs yelled (I'd been one of those chefs myself, in fact), but I'd never seen anything like this. At times, it felt like I was five years old again, listening to my parents fight before they divorced. I would just back into one corner of the kitchen and polish the already sparkling stainless-steel equipment.

Each day, I was given the same tasks: peeling potatoes, peeling shrimp, pushing all the shrimp heads through a food mill to get the juices from them, mopping and sweeping the floors. They wouldn't let me do anything else. I *was* learning by watching what Antonio and the other cook did in the kitchen, though. I'd pay close attention as Antonio made a dish for family meal of linguine with shellfish, crushed tomatoes, chilies, and plenty of garlic. He'd undercook the linguine, add it directly to the sauce with a little bit of the pasta water, and toss and baste it with extra-virgin olive oil. It came out beautifully creamy, peppered with tender mussels, clams, and lobster. But any effort I made to ask questions was met with silence from Antonio. On my one day off, Sunday, I'd jump on the first bus out of town and explore, eating as many meals in other restaurants as I could, enjoying my brief freedom from the gloom of the LoRo kitchen. It didn't help that I missed Emily horribly. I treasured every e-mail I got from her and stole away to a wireless café in town to read them whenever I could. We made plans for her to come visit a few months later, and that time seemed like a beacon to me, something I could look forward to.

I gradually realized that I needed to figure out how to get away from LoRo, where it was clear that they just wanted my free labor. I needed to find another restaurant in Italy where I had a better chance of learning and growing. I threw out hints to Antonio and Francesco: "I've been thinking I'd really like to go to Tuscany at some point and learn about the cuisine of that region," or "What about Le Marche? I've heard they make an amazing black-truffle-and-sweetbread lasagna there." Francesco would tell me, "Oh yeah, sure, I have a friend at a place, I'll give him a call." And then he'd blow me off, acting as if we'd never discussed it. I was going to be on my own in formulating an escape plan.

One evening, Antonio and Francesco were catering a party for a wealthy woman who had one of the most stunning homes I'd ever seen. It was in La Città Alta, an ancient city that was surrounded by a wall the Venetians built in the sixteenth century. In the kitchen was a brick bread oven built into one wall and a gorgeous copper six-burner range on another. I wanted to see more of the house, but Antonio kept me confined to the kitchen. At one point, when I went out into the dining area to admire the food, he quickly rushed me out of the room.

When no one was looking, I found solace in some salami I was cutting for the affettati misti, an impressive platter of sliced meats. I snuck a quick taste of it and stopped short. It tasted unlike any other cured meat I'd had before—sweet and creamy, with the flavors of nutmeg, red wine, and garlic mingling together. I needed to know more about this meat. Quickly, I stole the tag off the salami, knowing that if I was caught either eating it or putting a piece in my pocket I would likely be thrown into the Po River to float away. *Maybe that wouldn't be so bad,* I thought to myself. *Maybe I'd end up being rescued by a nonna in a muumuu who'd use her rolling pin to pull me in.* When we got back to LoRo that night, I recruited Enzo, the server who'd loaned me his Spider-Man comforter, to help me read the stolen salami label and Google the name of its producer, Podere Cadassa. With Enzo's help, I typed out a letter to the e-mail address we found.

Hello, my name is Alon Shaya, and I am an apprentice from New Orleans here to learn how to cook Italian food. I tasted your salame gentile at a party we were catering, and it was the best salami I have ever had in my life. I would love to come and learn how to make it. I will work very hard and as much as you need me to. I ask only for a place to sleep and food to eat in return. Please let me know if I could come and interview at some point.

A couple of days later, I received an e-mail in Italian. Excited, I got Enzo to read it for me. Podere Cadassa agreed! They didn't even need to interview me. They just wanted to set a date for me to come and work! Emily was due to come for her visit in just a few weeks, and I told Antonio that when she did I would be leaving too and not coming back.

I'll remember the day she arrived as one of the happiest of my life. I picked her up in Milan, and we drove back to Ristorante LoRo in a little rented Fiat. To me, it was as if she were a female knight in shining armor, rescuing me from my misery. I hastily gave her a tour of the restaurant and my tiny sleeping quarters. "I can't believe you've been sleeping in this thing," she said, looking at my cot next to the dough mixer. "You're using a *towel* for a pillow?" It didn't matter anymore, though. We jumped in the Fiat and drove off. I was free.

 ## SLOW-ROASTED LAMB SHOULDER

YIELD: 8 TO 10 SERVINGS

When I think of the best meal I had while living in Italy, I think of the roasted capretto (or baby goat) that Antonio's mother-in-law made for Easter dinner. It was arrestingly delicious. Inspired by that legendary feast, I make it with lamb, which is easier to find, a little bigger, and even more impressive. (If you can find goat, or if you prefer pork, feel free to use either, as long as the weight is roughly the same.)

This dish is a true centerpiece—a mic drop. A contented silence always falls over the table when everyone starts eating, as if they're all paying respect to the lamb. This is a good weekend project: the lamb sits overnight, then spends hours in the oven, and every minute is worth it. As it roasts, it mainlines its flavors into everything else in the pan, creating its own rich gravy, which melds perfectly with polenta (recipe follows) but can also be soaked up with a good, crusty bread.

1. Pat the lamb dry, and rub 2 tablespoons salt all over it. With the smooth, fatty side of the shoulder facing up, cut 6 slits into the top of the meat, spaced evenly apart, and deep enough to serve as little pockets. Tuck a clove of garlic and a 1-to-2-inch piece of rosemary in each one, ensuring that they're hidden away and not exposed, then wrap the whole shoulder tightly in plastic and refrigerate overnight.

2. Heat the oven to 400°F with a rack in the lower-middle position. Scatter the onions, carrots, and celery at the bottom of a deep roasting pan, then pour in the water. Set a rack inside, and add the lamb shoulder, fatty side up. Roast for 50 minutes to 1 hour, rotating the pan after 30 minutes, until it's starting to smell great and browning well on the edges. Lamb shoulders do vary in size, so check on it periodically, particularly if yours is on the smaller side.

3. Pull out the rack with the lamb, and set it off to the side on a baking sheet. Stir the tomato paste into the chopped vegetables on the bottom of the roasting pan, using your spoon to break it apart gently, and roast for 8 to 10 minutes, until it's just starting to caramelize. Pour in the wine, and return it to the oven for another 6 to 8 minutes, until the sauce is reduced by about half.

4. Cut off the tops and bottoms of the oranges, then halve them horizontally and add them to the roasting pan, along with the olives, raisins, chicken stock, bay leaves, cinnamon stick, red-pepper flakes, and remaining 1 teaspoon salt. Set the rack with the lamb on top and press a sheet of parchment over the lamb, tucking the edges under. As best you can, since it'll be hot, wrap the whole pan tightly with overlapping sheets of foil. The parchment and foil will work together to keep the moisture inside.

5. Decrease the heat to 300°F and roast for 5 to 6 hours, until the meat is extremely tender all over, and pulling off the bone. Again, lamb shoulder varies in size, so start carefully checking under the foil and parchment after 5 hours to ensure that it doesn't dry out. If you can't easily pierce it with a fork, re-cover and continue to cook for 30-minute intervals.

6. When it is done, move the lamb to a rimmed baking sheet or cutting board to rest; remove and discard the sprigs of rosemary and the garlic, and fish out the bay leaves and cinnamon stick from the pan. With a ladle, skim and discard

(recipe continues)

1 lamb shoulder (5 to 8 pounds), bone-in
2 tablespoons plus 1 teaspoon Morton kosher salt, divided
6 cloves garlic
2 to 3 sprigs fresh rosemary
2 yellow onions, coarsely chopped
2 large carrots, peeled and coarsely chopped
3 stalks celery, coarsely chopped
½ cup water
3 tablespoons tomato paste
¾ cup red wine
2 oranges
1 cup Castelvetrano olives, pitted and halved
1 cup golden raisins
3 cups chicken stock
2 dried bay leaves
1 cinnamon stick
½ teaspoon red-pepper flakes

as much fat as you can from the juices in the pan, but try not to carry along too many of the spices or aromatics. Pour all that remains into a large tureen for serving.

7. Carve the lamb shoulder near the table, so everyone gets the full effect. To do this, first trim and discard the thick yellow tendon on its side. Make a diagonal cut into the meat, following the little ridge on the shoulder blade and using the tip of your knife to loosen the meat gently along the bones, especially when you get to the ball joint. Do the same thing along the bottom, following the rib bones. Serve with pan juices ladled over the top, and preferably a side of creamy polenta (recipe follows).

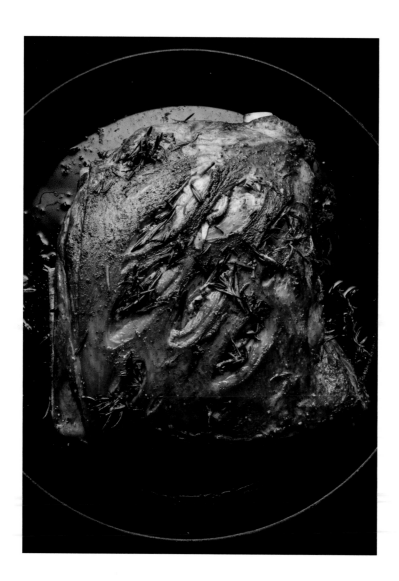

CREApy POLENTA WITH TALEGGIO

Just as we had it in Italy, this polenta has a trick up its sleeve: a buried mound of Taleggio cheese. The perfect partner for a showstopping lamb shoulder, it's also a simple, rich, and impressive dish to serve on its own. If you're serving it with the lamb, you'll want to start it about an hour before the meat is done roasting—this gives the lamb a bit of time to rest before they're served together. And if you can, use a freshly milled, stone-ground polenta, which takes on a creamier texture and allows the corn's flavor to shine through. I buy mine from a local miller in New Orleans, but Anson Mills in South Carolina has a great product; you can find it on their website.

- 2 quarts water
- 2 teaspoons Morton kosher salt
- 2 cups polenta
- 4 tablespoons (½ stick) unsalted butter, very cold
- ½ pound Taleggio cheese

1. Combine the water and salt in a pot, and bring it to a rolling boil over high heat. Slowly whisk in the polenta, and as soon as it starts to thicken, decrease the heat to the lowest setting and cover the pan.

2. Continue to cook for 45 minutes to 1 hour, returning every 15 minutes or so to stir and check on it. It's ready when every single grain is tender and full; take it off the heat, stir in the butter until it melts, and keep it covered until it's time to eat.

3. Trim the rind from the Taleggio, and add the cheese to a serving platter. Immediately before serving, ladle the polenta over the cheese and around it, so it melts. Serve this communally, preferably alongside the tureen of pan juices from slow-roasted lamb (preceding recipe)—when guests serve themselves, they will get a ladleful of polenta and find the cheese hidden inside.

20

✦✦✦

A Real Live Nonna!

I don't know whether it was the Alpine setting, the speck we'd been devouring, my being there with Emily, or the fact that Céline Dion was singing her heart out on the stereo, but I got a little choked up. Our travels around Italy included moments of unbelievable beauty and pleasure that solidified my love for this country and its food—and for my girlfriend.

After Emily aided in my escape from Ristorante LoRo, we set off on a rambling route around the country, Bergamo to Bolzano, Lucca to Livorno, Colonnata to Chianti. We started inauspiciously in Milan, where I booked us a hotel near the train station that rented rooms by the hour. I thought that was perfect: we weren't going to be in our hotel room very much, so we could just pay for the hours we needed to sleep! Emily looked at me pointedly.

"What do you think people *do* in this place *by the hour*?" she asked.

"Um," I responded.

Now that I'd lost all credibility on that front, Emily booked our accommodations for the rest of the trip. All I thought about was the food.

When it came to eating, I was happily in charge and had everything organized. I'd made us a grand food itinerary, mapping out all the little pastry shops, gelaterie, trattorie, and osterie, all the fancier ristoranti that we needed to try. Our two-week trip was going to be filled to the brim with transcendent eating experiences.

One of our first stops was in a small town on Lago di Garda, a lake in northern Italy. There, in a Michelin-starred restaurant called Il Volto, we had one of the most simple and perfect dishes I'd ever tasted. When it arrived at the table, it looked fairly basic:

a fillet of pike from the nearby lake with nothing but tomato sauce and some fried zucchini on the plate. Then I tried it. The sauce was bright and fresh, with an intense tomato flavor, and it was dotted with small pools of a rich, grassy olive oil. Atop the sauce, the pike was tender, white, with crispy skin and flesh that fell from your fork in delicate flakes. The zucchini was shaved very thin, fried until crispy, and speckled with sea salt. It was a revelation in simplicity and ultra-fresh ingredients prepared well. There was nothing flashy about it. *This, truly, is what I came to Italy for,* I thought to myself.

Most of our journey was built around specific foods that were the culinary hallmarks of specific places. We went to Colonnata for lardo, those thick, white slabs of pork fat that are cured in marble tubs for months with spices like cinnamon, star anise, coriander, orange zest, and white wine. We went to Venice for squid-ink pasta with sepia. At every restaurant we visited, if I got a chance, I'd peek into the kitchen, looking for what I'd decided was the hallmark of the best food: an elderly woman cooking. It became a running joke with Emily, how often I'd say to her, excitedly, "Look! There's a real live nonna in there!"

In Bolzano, we were on the hunt for speck. It's a smoked pro-sciutto, spiced with pepper, juniper, and laurel. We asked the owner of our little bed-and-breakfast for directions to a restau-rant on our list. He handed us a postcard with a drawing of trees and hills and mountains, and one winding road that curved around them all. "The road is like a piece of spaghetti," he told us. He was right. At some moments, we questioned whether we would ever arrive, especially since our little Fiat stalled out on the steepest of the hills. Finally, though, we pulled in at a tiny restaurant with a small herd of cows grazing behind it. An old woman was in the kitchen (cue my line to Emily), and her daughter ran the dining room. They served us bresaola—cured beef eye round—shaved thin, under a heap of arugula, with some extra-virgin olive oil, cracked black pepper, and one of the local hard cheeses grated over the top. The bresaola was the rosy-pink color of a sunset and had a beautiful softness to it. Then they brought out the speck. The meat came from the pigs rooting around in the mountain soil behind the restaurant. I tasted it, just as Céline Dion was singing "My Heart Will Go On" from the *Titanic* sound track, and something welled up inside me. This food *spoke* so powerfully of this place.

When we arrived in Livorno, on one of the last days of our trip, we weren't sure what food to seek out. It's a port city on the Ligurian Sea, on the western coast of Tuscany, so we knew the seafood would be good. We decided to wander the sprawl-ing indoor market and admire its wares. "Why don't we buy a bunch of things and make a lunch, picnic-style?" Emily sug-gested. The bounty of the market was overwhelming. Hundreds of vendors sold fresh, cooked, and pickled seafood; rows of cured meats hung above our heads. There were stalls with fresh porcini mushrooms and purple, green, and yellow artichokes called "spinosi," which had spikes sharp enough to draw blood from inexperienced cooks. One man sold a cold salad of tender white octopus tentacles sliced into rounds and tossed with leeks, extra-virgin olive oil, and sprigs of fresh thyme. I bought slices of an Italian headcheese seasoned with orange and rosemary, and a Gorgonzola so soft it seeped from the corners of the butcher's paper it was wrapped in. We selected several different pestos, one made with dried tomatoes and another the more traditional variety of basil and pine nuts.

We carried our haul to a bridge overlooking Livorno Harbor, which was filled with the vessels that supplied the market with its seafood bounty. The bridge's stone wall became our table, and we set about ripping off hunks of bread, dipping, topping, and slathering it with dozens of combinations. My favorite was a layer of mortadella that had been studded with black truffles on a crusty semolina loaf and a layer of roasted bell peppers that'd been marinating in a spicy chili oil. Emily and I would make bites for one another, passing our concoctions back and forth. I was grateful to her for being my partner in the culinary adventure of the past few weeks. She didn't flinch at the prospect of six meals a day, with an itinerary designed to bypass every museum and historical site in favor of a trattoria or pasticceria. Though I did allot one afternoon for us to sit on the beach and relax, the rest of the time she was down for the ride. *She's the one,* I thought to myself. She was about to return to New Orleans, and she'd hinted to me that she wasn't ready to settle down yet. And I had months more ahead of me in Italy.

FRESH LOUISIANA SHRIMP

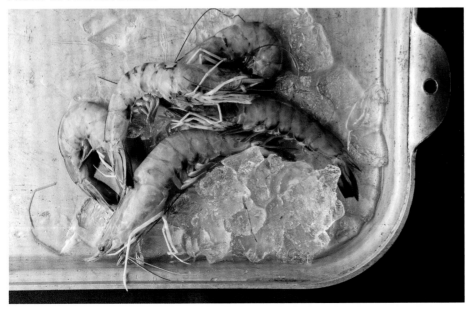

MARINATED SOFT CHEESE WITH HERBS AND SPICES

This dish was a revelation when Emily and I ate it in Milan: when you start with great ingredients, you're wise not to mess with them. It's a moment of perfect simplicity; at the right temperature, olive oil and cheese can be as flawless as anything that costs you far more time, money, or energy. Any brand of soft aged cheese will do—I like La Tur, a mixed-milk cheese that's as creamy as goat, with just a little sheepy funk, softened by the cow's milk. Mt Tam, a domestic triple-cream cheese, is a great alternative. Have fun with the spices: throw in a couple cloves instead of the star anise, add a sprig of rosemary instead of the bay, or use lemon instead of orange.

8-ounce wheel of soft goat or mixed-milk cheese, such as La Tur
3 cloves garlic, unpeeled
1 teaspoon whole allspice berries
½ teaspoon whole coriander seeds
½ cup extra-virgin olive oil
2 dried bay leaves
1 dried árbol chili pepper, or ¼ teaspoon red-pepper flakes
1 star anise pod
Two 2-inch strips of orange peel, orange part only, divided
A crusty baguette
Maldon or other flaky sea salt, to finish

1. Heat the oven to 325°F. Put the cheese in the bowl or rimmed plate from which it'll be served, to let it soften.
2. Use the side of a knife or a rolling pin to crush the garlic lightly, just so it starts to open up in its skin. Lightly crush or roughly chop the allspice and coriander, and add them, with the garlic, to a small ovenproof saucepan, along with the olive oil, bay leaves, árbol chili, star anise, and one strip of orange peel. Cover with a lid, and bake for 40 to 45 minutes; the garlic will be very golden and the orange rind will have darkened quite a bit.
3. Once the sauce has come together, remove the saucepan from the oven and increase the heat to 425°F. Take the second strip of orange peel and give it a little twist over the pan to release the oil, then drop it into the pan and let the oil cool down.
4. Cut the baguette on a bias into ½-inch slices, and arrange them on a baking sheet. Toast at 425°F for 6 to 8 minutes, until they've built some nice color along the edges.
5. Pour the seasoned oil over and around the softened cheese, letting the spices run free, and sprinkle on the salt just before serving. Slather the toasts with the cheese, and encourage your friends to dab up every last drop of the infused oil.

Seeing all the chilled and marinated seafood in the markets of Livorno made me think of Louisiana mainstays like pickled shrimp and crab ravigote. As I ate the cold octopus salad, I kept thinking that you could substitute shrimp.

There's something very humbling and hospitable about gathering round to peel your own seafood. You'll see a lot of ingredients in the list, but the vast majority are spices, meant to be customized (added or omitted) according to your whims and pantry contents. As long as you season the broth and pickling juice boldly, you can use whatever you want, and the spices will mature as they sit. Note that if you buy shrimp that *don't* have their heads on, you'll need only 2 pounds.

- 2 teaspoons whole allspice berries
- 2 teaspoons whole coriander seeds
- 2 teaspoons whole black peppercorns
- 12 cardamom pods
- 4 star anise pods
- 1 lemon
- 2 quarts water
- 3 tablespoons Morton kosher salt, divided
- 1 teaspoon red-pepper flakes
- 1¼ cups rice wine vinegar, preferably seasoned
- 1¼ cups extra-virgin olive oil
- 2 tablespoons whole-grain mustard
- 1 cup caperberries, halved and stemmed
- ¼ red onion, thinly sliced
- 1 jalapeño, seeds and pith removed, thinly sliced
- 1-inch knob fresh ginger, thinly sliced
- 1 clove garlic, thinly sliced
- 2½ pounds shrimp, shells and heads on (see headnote)

1. Roughly crush the allspice, coriander, black peppercorns, cardamom, and star anise with a mortar and pestle or by pounding them in a large ziplock bag. No need to pulverize them—you just want to loosen up the flavor. Divide the mixture in half.

2. Grate and reserve the zest of a lemon. Slice the lemon, and combine it in a large saucepan with half of the crushed spices along with the water, 2 tablespoons salt, and red-pepper flakes; bring it all to a boil. Decrease the heat to medium, and keep the water at a low simmer for at least 10 minutes to season the broth.

3. While that is happening, make the pickling liquid: combine the vinegar, olive oil, mustard, lemon zest, and remaining 1 tablespoon salt in a large sealable container (you'll be adding all the shrimp to it later, so make sure it has enough room), then mix in the other half of the spice blend, along with the caperberries, onion, jalapeño, ginger, and garlic.

4. Cook the shrimp in the simmering broth until they're pink and firm; depending on the size, this will take only 1 to 3 minutes. Drain, and let cool completely before peeling the shrimp and discarding the rest.

5. Stir the peeled shrimp into the pickling liquid, making sure they're submerged. Cover and refrigerate for at least 2 hours, and preferably overnight, before serving.

WHITE ASPARAGUS WITH EGGS AND SPECK

YIELD: 4 TO 6 SERVINGS

This salad is inspired by that tearfully wonderful speck dish I had in Bolzano. White asparagus tastes crisp and clean, serving as a backdrop for great ham and a creamy dressing. It's the perfect dish for springtime, when asparagus is at its absolute best and herby, eggy sauces just feel right. Blanching white asparagus in a little sugar helps magnify its mild sweetness, making it taste like the best version of itself. If you can only find green asparagus, which has more of a vegetal flavor, skip the sugar.

- 2 quarts water, plus more for the eggs
  Ice water for an ice bath
- 3 eggs
- 3 tablespoons sugar
- 1 tablespoon plus ¼ teaspoon Morton kosher salt, divided
- 1 pound white asparagus
- 3 tablespoons extra-virgin olive oil, divided
- 2 tablespoons Bulgarian yogurt
- 2 tablespoons mayonnaise
- 1 tablespoon capers, chopped
- 2 teaspoons chopped fresh tarragon
- 4 dashes Tabasco sauce
- 2 ounces speck, thinly sliced
- ½ teaspoon Aleppo pepper

1. Fill a pot with water and bring it to a boil; prepare an ice bath on the side. Decrease the heat to medium, gently lower in the eggs, and boil for 10 minutes. Plunge the cooked eggs into the ice water, and cool completely before peeling the shells.

2. In the same pot you used for the eggs, combine 2 quarts water, sugar, and 1 tablespoon salt in a pot, and bring it all to a boil. If most of the ice melted in the ice bath, top it off with some more.

3. Wash the asparagus, and trim its woody stems; if the spears are thick, run a vegetable peeler along the sides to make them more tender. Drop them into the boiling water, and cook for 1 or 2 minutes, just until they're tender but still have some snap. Drain, and immediately transfer to the ice bath to stop the cooking.

4. To make the dressing: stir together 2 tablespoons olive oil with the yogurt, mayo, capers, tarragon, Tabasco, and remaining ¼ teaspoon salt.

5. Arrange the asparagus spears side by side on a serving platter, and pour the dressing all over them, leaving the delicate tips undressed so people can see them. Roughly tear the speck, and tuck it throughout; then chop or thinly slice the eggs, and scatter them all over the top. Finish with a drizzle of the remaining 1 tablespoon olive oil and sprinkled Aleppo pepper.

SEA BASS IN CARTOCCIO WITH TOMATOES AND OLIVES

YIELD: 4 SERVINGS

I made numerous versions of fish baked in parchment in culinary school and in Las Vegas, but none could come close to the one that I ate ("in cartoccio," as the Italians say) at Ristorante Lorenzo, in the posh town of Forti dei Marmi, on the Tuscan coast. It was so beautiful and delicate.

This is one of the most efficient and clever ways to cook a fish; it traps all the moisture, gently cooking the fish in its own steam, and packs in a ton of flavor. Not to mention it cuts down on dishes, and everyone has a lot of fun tearing into his or her own little packet. Something like this stands on its own, but it really feels like a meal worth celebrating when it's accompanied by buttery, warmly spiced couscous (recipe follows), which soaks up the juices from the fish. Don't sweat it if you can't track down sea bass—any firm white fish will be perfect.

1 lemon
¼ cup extra-virgin olive oil, plus more for sealing
2 tablespoons za'atar
1 tablespoon capers
2 teaspoons Morton kosher salt, divided
1 teaspoon red-pepper flakes
One 2-inch knob fresh ginger, peeled and minced
1 large heirloom tomato
½ red onion, thinly sliced
¾ cup olives, such as Castelvetrano, pitted and halved
Four 7-to-8-ounce black sea bass fillets, skin on

1. Heat the oven to 400°F. Cut four pieces of parchment, each about 18 inches long. Fold each piece in half crosswise, and, starting at the bottom of the crease, cut diagonally and then circle around at the top so that when you unfold the parchment, it's a giant heart shape. This isn't for sentimental reasons! It's to make your life easier when you crimp the parchment around the fish.

2. Grate the lemon's zest into a bowl with the olive oil, za'atar, capers, 1 teaspoon salt, red-pepper flakes, and minced ginger. Squeeze the juice from the lemon into the same bowl. Cut the core from the tomato, and slice it into thin wedges. Toss them with the onion and olives into the oil mixture.

3. Lay the parchment hearts flat, and place a fillet, skin side up, on one side of each piece, in the wide part at the top. Brush a light smear of olive oil around the borders of the paper. Sprinkle the remaining 1 teaspoon salt on the fish, then evenly distribute the tomato mixture over all four fillets, and pour any leftover dressing on top.

4. Fold each sheet of parchment in half to enclose the fish in a neat packet, and tightly crimp the paper's edges, starting at the point where the rounded edge stops and working your way toward the narrower side. For the best and tidiest seal,

(recipe continues)

fold long, overlapping triangles, pinching them flat before
making the next one.

5. Lay the enclosed packets on a baking sheet, and bake for
   15 to 20 minutes. Check for doneness by carefully opening
   one packet; the fish should be firm and completely opaque.
   To serve: Place each packet on a plate, and let people cut it
   open on their own.

SPICED COUSCOUS

When you need a simple, light grain dish to round out any meal, there's nothing better than couscous. It's as neutral as pasta but has a delicate, totally unique texture that feels special. This version is deeply aromatic, a perfect sidekick for the bold flavors of the fish in cartoccio.

1. In a cold saucepan, combine the butter, onion, garlic, thyme, zests, spices, and salt. Set it over low heat and cook, stirring occasionally, 5 minutes or so, just until the scents start melding together; you don't want any color to develop.

2. Add the water to the pan, and increase the heat to high. Once the water boils, stir in the couscous and immediately remove the pan from the heat. Cover with a clean dish towel, hold it in place with the pan's lid, and let the pan sit for 5 minutes; this traps all the steam that the couscous gives off, which would otherwise weigh it down. Remove and discard the anise pod and cinnamon stick, and fluff the couscous with a fork before you serve it.

3 tablespoons unsalted butter
¼ yellow onion, minced
½ clove garlic, minced
½ teaspoon fresh thyme leaves, minced
Grated zest of ½ lemon
Grated zest of ½ orange
1 star anise pod
One 3-inch cinnamon stick
1 teaspoon Morton kosher salt
2 cups water (or amount called for in couscous package instructions)
1½ cups (about 10 ounces) couscous

21

✦ ✦ ✦

My Italian Guardian Angel

Here she was: the answer to my prayers. The one I'd been hoping for. The person I'd dreamed about while eating cold penne pasta on the plane ride to Italy. Her name was Eddy, and what had brought me to her was the theft of that salami tag back when I was at Ristorante LoRo. It felt like a lucky twist of fate, guided by my fondness for cured meats.

I'd not communicated with the Bergonzi family, who owned the salumificio Podere Cadassa, since I'd written to them out of the blue after tasting their salami and asked if I could come work for them. Months after they'd said yes, I arrived in the little town of Vedole, in the province of Parma, after dropping Emily off at the airport to fly back to New Orleans. What I found when I pulled up at the address they'd given me was like something out of a daydream about Italy. The salumificio and a restaurant the family also owned, Al Vedel, were both housed in a lovely Italian villa, several large buildings of pink stucco covered in fragrant jasmine vines. The family lived there, too. Each morning, I learned, they would sit in the villa's courtyard, sipping cappuccini and eating buttery pastries that were like an Italian version of croissants, while their large black dog ran around with dried chrysanthemum blossoms stuck in her fur. The salumi were aging in a basement cantina that had been built of brick more than a century before; over a thousand culatelli, teardrop-shaped and dusted with white mold, hung there like ripe fruit. The fermented aroma would permeate the air vents and scent the soft bath towels I would use while I stayed in the villa's third-floor apartment. If at Ristorante LoRo I was living like a servant, sleeping curled up by the dough mixer, at Podere Cadassa I was in a fairy tale, one perfumed by culatello, in which all the hero's dreams come true.

Everyone in the family was responsible for a different aspect of the business. Enrico was in charge of the restaurant, Al Vedel, while his sister, Monica, oversaw the waitstaff in the front of the house. Her husband, Marco, took care of the salumificio. And Eddy, Enrico's wife, ran the dessert and bread programs and cooked meals for the whole family, including her and Enrico's children, Carlo and Julia.

On my first day, I was nervous that they wouldn't accept me, that I'd find myself in another situation in which I'd have to force information from people instead of being given the fundamentals of Italian cooking I was longing to learn. I hurried down to the kitchen in Al Vedel, ready to prove to them that I was skilled and dedicated. I was put on the garde-manger station and told I'd be in charge of making a horse tartare dish. Raw horse. I had never eaten horse before, and certainly never even considered consuming it raw. I was taken with the uniqueness of the flavor—a little gamey, somewhere between venison and beef. The Bergonzi family made sure I tasted everything, handing me little cuts of culatello and salami and coppa, as they sliced it for their affettati misti platter. They were generous from my first minutes in their company.

Al Vedel is a typical Parmigiano restaurant. Those cured meats were the star of the show, but the Bergonzis would also make the iconic pasta dishes of the region: tortelli d'erbetta, a pasta stuffed with ricotta and spinach, bathed in butter, and served with a cloud of freshly grated Parmigiano-Reggiano on top. They made a lovely anolini in brodo, tiny little ravioli floating in a special broth. Their brodo in terza, which literally means "broth in thirds," was made from one part pork shank, one part beef shoulder, and one part old hen, deliberately chosen at that stage of its life for the rich flavor of its meat. I made it my mission to learn everything I could about what they were cooking.

I'd come down to the kitchen early in the morning and ask questions about what we'd cooked the day before.

"Why do you start the brodo in terza for the anolini in a pot full of ice?" I would ask.

"Because you want to draw the blood out of the meat slowly,

so it can season and clarify the broth as it gradually heats up to a simmer," they'd say. Brilliant.

I took notes as they spoke, writing every detail of every meal in my journal. While others took a break between the lunch and dinner services, I'd hang around the kitchen to help cook family meal with Eddy.

Eddy was a short, matronly woman with a crop of brown hair, who always had a warm smile at the ready. She'd noticed how committed I was to learning everything I could. And so, over the course of our afternoons cooking together, she gradually took me under her wing. She would walk me through the various steps of whatever she was doing, transforming my understanding even of dishes I thought I knew how to cook. I'd always made risotto the way I'd learned to do it in culinary school: sweating onions in olive oil, adding Arborio rice, and then adding broth, slowly, to that. Instead, Eddy taught me a technique for toasting the rice in a dry pan before adding any broth or vegetables. There are natural oils in the rice, she'd tell me, and gently toasting it will bring out those flavors instead of diluting them. We made a fresh salami-and-porcini risotto, using meat that had been caught at the bottom of the restaurant's machine for filling the casings. We'd cook that together with onions and chicken broth until it was almost like a salami soup. Then we'd pour some into the toasted rice, watching it sizzle and absorb the liquid, as the perfume of the salami's red wine, garlic, and juniper mingled with the nutty scent of the rice.

More than *talking* about food, she'd *show* me about it—and not just in the kitchen. I mentioned to Eddy that I liked nocino, a walnut liqueur that they had on Al Vedel's cordial list. The next week, we'd go to her parents' backyard to pick green, unripe walnuts from their tree, and then make nocino from scratch. I'd tell her I liked a certain honey she was using, and she'd respond, "Next Tuesday, we'll go to my cousin's beehives and harvest honey." There I'd be, a week later, draped in netted protective gear, highly conscious of my bee-sting allergy, lifting up the lid of the hive to reveal row upon row of sweet gold.

Everyone around the Bergonzi family was assimilated, somehow, into their food. Even the crossing guard at the children's school was a limoncello maker. "The best in town," Eddy assured me. She took me to make pasta with her nonna, who was in her early eighties, a fragile, tiny little woman in a muumuu. Like many Italian nonnas who knew what was what, she kept a long piece of wood behind her couch for pasta making. It looked like a huge cutting board, though it was only ½ inch thick. Eddy's nonna and I pulled that out and put it on her dining-room table. We mixed the flour and eggs by hand, making a little well in the flour and cracking the eggs into its center, whisking it around with our fingers until a golden dough formed. Then we rolled out our pasta dough on that plank of wood with a long wooden mattarello, or rolling pin. I watched her hands, pushing the mattarello down the length of dough and then folding the dough back over it, using it to stretch out the long, silky strands of pasta.

It felt as though Eddy and her family had entrusted me with the culinary knowledge that was their heritage, as well as their business. What truly sank in for me, working with Eddy day after day, was that this restaurant wasn't just their work, it was their vocation. You could taste that in the excellent food, yes, but you could also see it in the way they cared for their customers. Feeding people seemed almost like sacred work for them. It was an attitude I intended to adopt myself.

WILD MUSHROOMS FOR RISOTTO

TORTELLI D'ERBETTA

When I lived in Parma, Eddy took me to a *caseificio* to watch the cheese makers at work. Starting with milk from the region's prized cows, they skimmed the cream to make butter, transformed the skimmed milk into Parmigiano-Reggiano, then used the whey (a natural by-product) to make ricotta. Those three ingredients come together to become tortelli d'erbetta, one of the most iconic dishes of the Parma region and a signature at Al Vedel. To me, it exemplifies the beautiful logic of Italian cuisine—when nothing goes to waste, everything comes full circle. The greens for which this dish is named are a product of Italian resourcefulness, too: Italians get most of their sugar from beets, and with beets come leafy tops. Those are typically used in the filling, though I prefer spinach for its milder flavor. Use any fresh greens you'd like; just make sure you remove all the tough stems before you weigh it out.

Ravioli by any other name, "tortelli" is a regional term for this stuffed pasta. It's common nowadays to see pasta dressed in brown butter, but to do that here would be to miss the point: you don't want to disguise the beauty of these simple ingredients (or the boatloads of Parmesan that you'll add before serving).

- 1 pound ricotta
- 1 teaspoon plus 4 tablespoons Morton kosher salt, divided
- 2 gallons water, divided
- ½ pound fresh spinach
- 1½ cups finely grated Parmesan cheese, divided
- 1 egg
- ½ teaspoon finely grated nutmeg
- Grated zest of 1 lemon
- All-purpose flour, for dusting
- 1 recipe fresh pasta (recipe follows)
- 4 tablespoons (½ stick) unsalted butter

1. Unless your ricotta is especially thick, without any extra water, combine it with 1 teaspoon salt for at least a few hours before you plan to make the pasta. Set it in a fine-mesh sieve over a bowl, cover, and let drain in the refrigerator. This step does require a bit of planning ahead, but you'll be surprised how much water escapes. It's not worth going to the trouble of making fresh pasta if the filling will be soggy.

2. Bring 1 gallon water to a boil with 2 tablespoons salt. Pile in the spinach (it will quickly shrink in size), and cook for 1 minute. Drain, and when it's cool enough to handle, wrap it in a clean dish towel and wring the life out of it. Your goal is to squeeze out every last drop of the water. Finely chop it, and combine it in a bowl with the drained ricotta, 1 cup grated Parmesan, egg, nutmeg, and lemon zest.

3. Fill the same pot, once again, with 1 gallon water and 2 tablespoons salt. Bring it to a boil, this time for the pasta.

(recipe continues)

4. Lightly flour your work surface. Work with the rolled-out pasta one sheet at a time; each sheet should be about 5 inches wide and 12 to 16 inches long. Trim away any jagged edges and either brush water over the dough or pat it all over with a damp paper towel. Drop the filling along the center of the sheet in tablespoon-sized mounds, spaced about 2 inches apart.

5. With clean, dry hands, pull the pasta up over the filling to fold the whole sheet in half lengthwise. Gently press the pasta around the filling to smooth out any air pockets, then trim along all the edges and between the tortelli to seal and separate them. As you work, set them aside in a single layer on a baking sheet or large plate.

6. In a wide, deep skillet, melt the butter and then remove it from the heat. Cook half the tortelli by boiling for 1½ to 2 minutes, until the pasta is cooked through and silky. Fish out the tortelli, and cook the second batch in the same water.

7. Add all the cooked tortelli to the skillet, and toss to coat with all the melted butter; if necessary, turn the heat back to medium-low to reheat gently. Shower with the remaining ½ cup Parmesan before serving.

FRESH PASTA

YIELD: 4 SERVINGS
(ABOUT ½ POUND)

I appreciate all pasta—and there are some great dried pastas out there—but I pretty much approach dried and fresh versions as entirely different things. Bow ties with butter and Parmesan might be on the kids' menu at most restaurants, but fresh pasta with the same basic ingredients is something to celebrate. You'll need a pasta roller to get it thin and pliable, but it's well worth the investment. (If you don't have one, though, hand-rolled cavatelli, page 313, is an excellent crash course.) As with most doughs, there isn't much to it beyond patience and muscle memory, and the more you make it, the more naturally it will come. Shape the rolled pasta around a filling for tortelli d'erbetta (page 277) or cut it into linguine and sauce it any way you like.

1¼ cups all-purpose flour, plus more if needed and for dusting
½ cup semolina
2 eggs
2 egg yolks
2 teaspoons extra-virgin olive oil

1. Combine the flour and semolina on a clean work surface. Make a wide, deep well in the center, and add the eggs, yolks, and olive oil. Use a fork to whisk in shallow circular movements, working your way from the center outward, to incorporate the surrounding flour gradually. You don't want to break the "walls" of the well, so keep your strokes short.

2. Once the mixture is as thick as pancake batter in the center, use your fork or a bench scraper to pull all the remaining flour into the center, and work it in by hand. It'll be incredibly firm and dry now but will gradually hydrate.

3. When the dough is cohesive enough to knead, begin to use the heels of your hands to push the dough down, then fold it over itself. Put your weight into this, as if you're giving someone a back rub—you can't possibly overwork it—and press down rather than outward, so you don't rip it. The dough will become relatively smooth but stiff, like clay. Depending on your flour and the humidity where you are, the dough may be so dry and stiff that you'll worry you're doing it wrong, or it may be a little stickier. If it's sticky, add flour 1 tablespoon at a time; if it's too dry, flick a little water over the dough or wet your hands and keep at it. This whole process takes about 10 minutes of elbow grease, but then you're done with your arm workout for the day. Wrap the dough tightly in plastic, and let it rest at room temperature

for 30 minutes to 1 hour, or refrigerate for up to a couple days.

4. Cut the pasta dough in half, and keep one half wrapped so it doesn't dry out. Use a rolling pin to roll the other half into a rectangle that's just narrow enough to fit through your pasta roller, about 5 inches. Lightly dust the dough with flour if necessary; it should be dry and matte.

5. With the pasta roller on the widest setting, feed the dough through once, catching it with one hand as it exits so it doesn't break. Fold the dough in half horizontally (so that it's half as long), flatten it slightly with the rolling pin, and

(recipe continues)

feed it through again. Repeat this process for a total of
8 to 10 times so it becomes gradually smoother and more
pliable but still matte and never sticky; after the final roll,
don't fold the dough in half, but cover it with a dish towel
while you repeat with the other half. If at any point it's too
wide to fit through the roller, fold it in half vertically (so it's
half as wide) and continue. You can also cut it in half and
work with one piece at a time if it becomes so long as to be
unmanageable.

6. Working with one piece of dough at a time and leaving the
rest covered, dial down the roller by one setting, making it
a little narrower, and carefully feed the pasta through once.
(Don't fold it in half.) Continue to dial down the width of
the roller one notch at a time, passing the dough through
once each time, until the pasta is barely translucent, 5 or
6 inches wide and about 2 feet long. For most rollers, this
will be the third- or fourth-to-last setting.

7. Cut the dough into 12-to-16-inch sheets so they're easier
to work with. If you're using this dough to make noodles,
cut them to size with a knife or pasta cutter and either
cook right away or transfer to a ziplock bag and freeze. For
tortelli, lay the sheets flat on a countertop, covered with a
towel until you're ready to fill them; if it's humid or your
house is hot, it can't hurt to separate the sheets with a piece
of parchment paper.

PORK AND MUSHROOM RISOTTO

This is the risotto that Eddy and I made together one day, the one that changed the way I'd make risotto forever. Toasting nuts and spices draws out their natural oils and subtle aromas; why not show the same love to your grains? By toasting the Arborio in a dry pot, she invited its inherent flavor to become a part of the whole dish.

Another thing she taught me, which you often learn when you share a kitchen with a good cook, was economy. To make her legendary cured salami, she would grind and season fresh pork with red wine, garlic, and juniper, then stuff it into casings to hang and age. The process left behind savory bits—call it fresh salami—that, rather than be wasted, became the star of this dish. Caramelized with onions and a slew of mushrooms, it built so many layers of flavor; feel free to use your favorite variety or combination of fresh mushrooms.

- 3 tablespoons red wine
- 2 cloves garlic, minced
- 1 sprig fresh thyme
- 1 tablespoon Morton kosher salt
- 1 teaspoon honey
- ¼ teaspoon ground juniper berries
- 1 pound ground pork shoulder
- 2 quarts chicken stock or pork stock
- ¼ cup extra-virgin olive oil
- ¼ pound fresh shiitake mushrooms, stemmed and chopped
- ¼ pound fresh oyster mushrooms, chopped
- ½ ounce dried porcini mushrooms, chopped
- 1 yellow onion, chopped
- 2 cups Arborio rice
- 3 ounces Parmesan cheese, finely grated, plus more for serving
- 4 tablespoons (½ stick) unsalted butter
- 1 cup lightly packed fresh parsley leaves, chopped

1. Combine the wine and garlic, let them steep at room temperature for 30 minutes, then strain out and discard the garlic.

2. While the garlic steeps, strip the leaves from the thyme and mince them, then combine them in a large bowl with the salt, honey, and juniper. Once the wine is ready, add it along with the pork, and gently but thoroughly combine.

3. Add the stock to a saucepan over low heat, and cover with a lid to keep it warm. Separately, heat the olive oil in a large skillet or Dutch oven over high heat. Once it's shimmering, pinch the pork into tablespoon-sized pieces, and carefully (the oil may spatter) drop these into the pan in a single even layer. Leave them alone for 1 to 2 minutes while they build a flavorful crust, then give them a stir and let them cook for another minute or two, until they're evenly browned on the outside (the centers may still be pink, but they'll cook more later).

4. Decrease the heat to medium, and use a slotted spoon to transfer the pork to a large bowl, leaving its rendered fat in the pan. Add all the mushrooms (both fresh and dried). As they cook, stir to scrape up all the brown bits that the pork left behind, and keep sautéing until the mushrooms become golden; they'll absorb a lot of the flavorful fat.

(recipe continues)

5. Stir in the onion, and increase the heat to high, cooking until the onion browns, around 5 minutes. Take the heat back down to low, and add a splash of the hot stock to deglaze the pan. Have all this join the pork on the sidelines, then wipe out the pan.

6. Add the Arborio rice to the freshly wiped pan, and toast it over medium-high heat, stirring constantly, for 5 to 8 minutes; dry-roasting it this way pulls out all its natural flavors. To do this, you need to cook it long enough to release that familiar rice aroma, but not so long that it starts to darken in color. Let your nose be your guide.

7. Reduce the heat to medium-low, and fold in the reserved pork, mushrooms, and onion along with 1 cup of warm stock; stir until all the liquid absorbs. Continue to cook, stirring occasionally, and add the stock ½ cup at a time, letting the rice drink it up before adding more. By the time it's done, it should look thick and creamy, and when you drag your spoon across the bottom of the pot, it will stay dry for a couple seconds before the rice pools back in. A good risotto is loose and yielding, but the individual grains of rice should still have just a bit of bite.

8. Remove the pot from the heat, and stir in the Parmesan, butter, and parsley. Serve right away, with more Parmesan passed at the table.

BLACKBERRY TORTA DELLA NONNA

The fact that I know the secret to this torta makes me feel like a part of Eddy's family. She taught me how to make it, and she learned it from her mother, who'd learned it from *her* mother. The first time I saw it, I thought it must have been technically very challenging to shape the top crust into such perfect mounds. What kind of crazy, molecularly inclined nonna had been the one to figure that out? The secret—a pile of amaretti cookies, dipped in rum for good measure—is so simple, a nonna's sleight of hand. They're available at Italian specialty stores or online. If you can't get your hands on fresh, sweet blackberries (or are looking for a shortcut), ¾ cup of your favorite jam is a fine replacement for making your own. Just spread it directly over the bottom crust.

12 tablespoons (1½ sticks) unsalted butter, softened, plus more for the pan
1½ cups confectioners' sugar, sifted
Grated zest of 1 lemon
¾ teaspoon Morton kosher salt, divided
3 egg yolks, divided
2 tablespoons water
1½ cups almond flour
1 cup all-purpose flour, plus more for dusting
Canola oil, for brushing
1 pound blackberries
¼ cup granulated sugar
1 teaspoon cornstarch
1 tablespoon lemon juice
14 to 16 amaretti cookies
¼ cup spiced rum
2 teaspoons milk
1 tablespoon turbinado sugar

1. Start creaming the butter, confectioners' sugar, lemon zest, and ½ teaspoon salt in your mixer on low speed, gradually bumping it up to medium and then high, until the mixture is very creamy and fluffy; pause regularly to scrape the sides of the bowl.

2. Add two egg yolks along with the water; continue to beat until it's light and airy. Add the almond flour and all-purpose flours separately, then turn the mixer back to low speed and beat them in until they're fully incorporated.

3. Tear four sheets of parchment paper, about 14 inches each, and lightly brush the top of each with canola oil. Set them aside.

4. Lightly flour a work surface, dump the dough directly onto it, and press it into a mound. Divide it in half and shape each half into a roughly 6-inch disc. Sandwich each one between two sheets of the oiled parchment (with the oiled sides touching the dough) and roll them both into 11-inch circles. Refrigerate for at least 30 minutes or overnight.

5. Meanwhile, for the blackberry jam, combine the blackberries with the granulated sugar and remaining ¼ teaspoon salt in a saucepan over medium heat. As the berries start to soften and give off liquid, use a fork to mash them roughly. Once the juices come to an active simmer, reduce the heat to medium-low, and cook for another 25

(recipe continues)

to 30 minutes, stirring occasionally, until the berries are thick and jammy with just enough liquid so there are some bubbles in the pan.

6. Dilute the cornstarch in the lemon juice, and stir it into the berries. Cook for another minute or two to take out any starchy flavor, then remove from the heat. Once the jam has cooled, you can proceed right away or refrigerate it for a day or two.

7. When you're ready to bake, heat the oven to 350°F with a rack in the center of the oven, and generously butter the bottom and sides of a 9-inch tart pan.

8. Peel one layer of parchment from one round of dough and use the other layer to lift and invert it into the bottom of your tart pan. Peel away that piece of parchment and press the dough into the bottom and up the sides of the pan. Patch any thin spots or holes with tiny scraps of excess dough.

9. Spread the blackberry jam evenly over the crust, all the way to the sides. One by one, dip the amaretti cookies into the rum, and arrange them concentrically over the jam, ¼ to ½ inch apart, with their round tops facing up.

10. Peel a layer of parchment off the other piece of dough, and invert it over your pan as you did for the bottom crust. Remove the last piece of parchment, trim away any overhanging crust, and very gently push the edges together to seal. Prick the top crust a few times with a fork. Any tears can be gently smoothed over with a wet fingertip.

11. Make an egg wash by beating the milk with the remaining egg yolk, then brush it all over the top crust, and sprinkle the turbinado sugar evenly over it. Place the pan on a baking sheet, and bake it for 35 to 40 minutes, rotating the pan after 20 minutes. You're looking for the crust to be firm and deeply golden, with a fine crumb similar to shortbread. Serve this tart warm or at room temperature, on its own or with a scoop of good ice cream.

CHOCOLATE-HAZELNUT SEMIFREDDO

1 cup hazelnuts, toasted

9 egg yolks

2 tablespoons plus ½ cup sugar, divided

¼ cup water

5 ounces dark chocolate, chopped

2 tablespoons spiced rum

½ teaspoon Morton kosher salt

2 cups heavy cream, very cold, divided

1½ teaspoons baharat (page 387) or pumpkin-pie spice

1 recipe chocolate-candied hazelnuts (recipe follows), optional

I worked the dessert station at Al Vedel for a while, cranking out semifreddo, zabaglione, and tiramisù to the kitchen's sound track of Michael Bublé and Frank Sinatra. Those desserts inspired this nutty custard, which is a lot like ice cream or gelato but made without any special appliances beyond a candy thermometer (super-affordable, and the key to a good consistency).

I love this method, because whipping the egg yolks with hot sugar creates a consistency that's at once more velvety and more stable. Spiced rum adds a nice little kick (and keeps the texture soft) but can be omitted; likewise, if you don't have baharat on hand, you can replace it with pumpkin-pie spice or ground cinnamon. And don't sweat it if you don't have (or don't want to make) the candied hazelnuts—just skip them altogether. Like any good frozen dessert, this semifreddo is yours for the adapting.

1. If the hazelnuts still have their papery, dark-brown skins, wrap the nuts in a clean dish towel or hand towel and rub them vigorously to help remove them. No need to be obsessive about this, but it'll keep them from tasting too bitter. Finely chop the nuts, and set aside.

2. In a stand mixer with the whisk attachment, or with an electric mixer and heatproof bowl, whip the egg yolks and 2 tablespoons sugar on high speed until they're pale, thick, and fall in ribbons rather than drips when you lift the beater. Pause occasionally to scrape down the sides of the bowl. Set the bowl aside.

3. Clip a candy thermometer inside a small saucepan, and add the remaining ½ cup sugar. Pour the water evenly over the sugar to moisten it, then cook over medium heat without stirring until the syrup reaches 235°F; it shouldn't yet have any color. Keep an eye on it, since the temperature can increase in leaps.

4. Working very slowly and carefully, with the mixer on medium speed, drizzle the hot sugar syrup into the egg mixture, and whip continuously to combine. Once you've added all of it, increase the mixer speed to high, and beat for a couple minutes, until the outside of the bowl is cool to the touch and the mixture is glossy. *(recipe continues)*

5. Melt the chocolate in a double boiler or in a microwave in 30-second intervals; when it's mostly but not completely melted, stir it by hand until it's smooth. Add it to the mixing bowl along with the rum and salt, and beat everything until incorporated.

6. In a separate bowl, whip 1½ cups cream until it holds stiff peaks when you lift the beater. Stir in the baharat and the finely chopped hazelnuts. Fold about half of this mixture into the chocolate mixture to lighten everything up, then fold in the rest until it's incorporated. Scrape into a 9- or 10-inch deep dish pie plate or round casserole dish, cover with plastic wrap, and freeze until set, at least 4 hours.

7. Let the semifreddo sit at a cool room temperature for at least 10 minutes before eating, so it can soften a bit. Meanwhile, whip the remaining ½ cup cream and dollop small spoonfuls over the semifreddo's surface along with a scattering of the candied hazelnuts, then scoop big, messy scoops into bowls for serving.

CHOCOLATE-CANDIED HAZELNUTS

YIELD: 1½ CUPS

This is another recipe I picked up from Eddy, and another one that's exponentially more impressive than you'd expect, based on the minimal effort and skills it takes to make. You do need a candy thermometer to help you get the candy coating right, but the whole process, from start to finish, is pretty seamless. Chocolaty and crisp, these add perfect textural contrast to the semifreddo but are just as easily enjoyed on their own or given as a gift—they'll disappear before your eyes. Feel free to double the recipe.

1½ cups hazelnuts, toasted
1 cup sugar
¼ cup water
½ cup cocoa powder

1. Rub the skins off the hazelnuts as in step 1 of the semifreddo recipe, removing as much as you can but not obsessing over it. Cut a large sheet of parchment or foil, about 16 inches long, and set it aside.

2. Clip a candy thermometer to the side of a small saucepan. Combine the sugar and water inside and gently stir just to combine, making sure you're not letting the sugar climb up the sides of the pan, since it can burn. Without stirring it at all, cook over medium heat until it reaches 250°F.

3. Stir in the cocoa powder and let the mixture reach 275°F; it will look like molten lava. Fold in the nuts and keep stirring vigorously, allowing the mixture to reduce until, almost like magic, it becomes a dry, crumbly mix with cocoa clinging to the nuts like a candy shell (it should register around 300°F on your thermometer).

4. Immediately remove the pan from the heat and spread the nuts in a single layer over the parchment. Using a clean dish towel or paper towel to protect your hands from the heat, gently break apart any large clumps and allow the nuts to cool completely. These (along with the little chocolate crumbs) will stay crisp for about a week in an airtight container.

✦ ✦ ✦

22

Enzo the Pizzaiolo

'd been in Italy for more than 4 months and was surprised at the lack of good pizza I'd encountered during my stay. Only once had I eaten one I considered truly great, and it was in the oddest of circumstances. I'd missed my bus back to Ristorante LoRo and was wandering down a country road in Trescore Balneario, where I decided to stop at a Chinese restaurant to use the bathroom. Once inside, I saw a wood-burning oven. It was such a surprising juxtaposition—Chinese food in Italy, with a pizza menu to boot—that I decided to try one. I ordered a pizza with crispy salami, creamy Taleggio cheese, and raw arugula. It came out beautifully charred and crisp, with a sourdough tang in the dough. None of the dozen or so wood-fired pizzas I'd tried since I arrived in Italy came close to it.

I told that to Eddy one day as we were rolling out bread dough in Al Vedel's kitchen. "Well, I have a friend who makes the best pizza in Parma," she said. "We'll go on Sunday for dinner and bring the whole family." That is how the whole gang of us ended up one evening at Pizzeria Il Gabbiano, or the Seagull Pizzeria.

The first thing I noticed as we walked in was more than a dozen shiny new Berkel meat slicers distributed around the dining room. Those machines could cut a perfectly thin slice of prosciutto without damaging the meat. (I later learned that the restaurant doubled as a dealership for the slicers, which explained why there were so many. They weren't just showing off.) Then I saw the deck ovens in the kitchen. What? *Deck* ovens? Like the kind they use to reheat slices in New York City pizzerias? Where were the wood-burning ovens? My hopes for the quality of the pizza were quickly deteriorating.

I was looking at the open kitchen, thinking that there must be some kind of mistake, when I saw a guy dressed all in white, with a white bandanna wrapped around his head, who was slapping dough around and yelling something across the dining room. It was as if there were a spotlight on him: he lit up the room with his energy. This was my introduction to Vincenzo De Santis, the pizzaiolo. In some ways, Enzo embodied a certain kind of Italian man: He had a bravado, a force of personality, and a Ferrari parked in his garage. He lived in an apartment above the pizzeria along with his adult brother, Antonio, his adult sister, Fili, and their mother. They all ran the restaurant together, but Enzo was the star. He commanded the room with his presence, a stark contrast to a side of him I learned about later, which seemed more teenage boy than chef. He had his bedroom walls covered with posters of fast cars and hot girls, his bureau topped with model Ferraris and decades-old sports trophies.

As soon as we sat down, Enzo came over with two monster bottles of his favorite beer, Super Baladin. He was clearly good friends with Eddy and her family. He began telling us about the beer in rapid, mumbling Italian, pausing every few minutes to shout something so loud that all the people eating would turn their heads. After getting to know him, I learned that those exclamations were likely one of two things: he was either graciously welcoming a friend into the restaurant or giving a complaining guest detailed directions to another pizzeria in town. He was a man whose passions could not be hidden, the sort of guy who could convince you of the coming of the Messiah in the form of pizza. According to him, his pizza was on this earth to save you from all the other, evil pizza out there. But I had yet to try it myself, and I was skeptical about those deck ovens.

When the pizzas we'd ordered arrived, I analyzed their structure, height, shape, smell, look—every aspect of them. They didn't look like the pizzas I was used to seeing. There were none of those little charred black spots, like you'd see on a traditional Neapolitan pizza. His was a little more golden, with rolling hills and valleys of bubbles in the crust. I took a bite and was blown away. The crispness, the way the pizza held its shape, the balanced flavor of the dough, the quality of the toppings—one with a marinara spiked with white anchovies, oregano, and spicy chilies, and another covered in black truffles and stracciatella cheese, which is creamier than mozzarella or even burrata. As I took another bite, I watched him flipping pizza dough in the air, showboating, laughing with whoever was nearby. I leaned over to Eddy. "I want to come work for him," I said.

Several months later, I was in my chef's whites in his kitchen, ready to start tossing some dough myself. That was met with a hoarse "Aspetta, aspetta"—*Wait, wait.* Enzo made it clear that I wasn't ready to touch the dough yet. My first day, I grated mozzarella cheese for hours. The following days, I sliced mushrooms, chopped cherry tomatoes, picked basil, cleaned artichokes, prepped every pizza topping known to man. Everything but the dough. Disappointed, I gravitated toward Enzo's sister, Fili, who was in charge of the non-pizza items in the restaurant. When everyone else took a midday break, I stayed in the kitchen with Fili, helping her roll cavatelli and make a skillet apple cake that she served with a cookies-and-cream gelato. When Enzo saw me eyeing the cake batter she was mixing up, though, he would grab my arm and pull me back to the pizza station to keep prepping toppings.

For the first few weeks, he called me Alex. I didn't care. I followed him around like an annoying six-foot-one little brother. For the first few days, when I watched him making pizza dough, every time he went to add the yeast in he'd turn his back on me—he'd sprinkle in a couple of things that I couldn't see. I knew he was doing it on purpose. But at night, after service, things would change. As I scrubbed the marble counters and swept the floor, I'd watch him make pizzas for the staff. Then we'd sit and eat, drink grappa, and talk. I'd use my same little arsenal of words that I knew in Italian. "Molto buono!"—*Oh my God, that's so good!* "Come fa così?"—*How do you make this?* He'd smile, and his eyes would get wide and sparkling. He was soaking it up, the praise.

The more grappa we drank, night after night, the more he noticed my enthusiasm and dedication, and the more he'd share with me about ingredients. We talked about sauce, flour, water, mixing, anchovies, basil—nearly every single detail that goes into making pizzas. He'd take me back into the kitchen and stick his hand into the bin of flour, lifting some of it up, rubbing it between his fingers, and admiring it for almost a full minute. Neither of us would say a word. We'd just stand there in silent reverence for the quality of his flour. Then he'd look over at me and say, "Vedo. Questo farina e buona. È buonissima."—*See here. This is a good flour. The best.* Eventually, Enzo let me help him portion out the dough and roll it into balls to be ready for service. It's not easy to get them to be perfectly shaped without a seam in the middle, but I was doing it. "There're two kinds of people in the world," he told me in Italian. "People that have hands for dough, and those that don't. You have hands made for dough." As we grew closer, he started calling me Alan. I was touched.

But after a few weeks, I still hadn't been allowed to roll out a pizza. And I was getting frustrated. I had only several weeks left to learn from him. One day, at the end of lunch service, I was the only one left in the kitchen. Everyone else was in the back, and a ticket for the last customer in the dining room came through. I said to myself: "*I'm* going to make this pizza. I've watched Enzo do it dozens of times. I'm just going to go for it. The worst they can do is yell at me." So I pulled out a ball of dough and started rolling it out. Then Antonio, Enzo's brother, came in and saw what I was doing. I could tell he didn't know what to say. His eyes got really big, and he ran into the back. I knew he was going to tell on me. I didn't stop. A minute later, Enzo and Antonio ran back through the door like a tornado. I could feel Enzo watching me, and Antonio watching him. By that point, I already had the dough rolled out. "Va bene," Enzo said. "Lui è pronto."—*It's okay. He's ready.* It felt as if he'd decided that I was worthy. From that moment on, I made pizzas every day.

My favorite pizza that Enzo made was never offered to paying customers. He saved it for family meal, after service, always saying it was too good to serve to just anybody. I looked forward to waking up every morning so that it would eventually be

1:00 a.m. and I could eat what I came to call the Pizza Enzo. It had the creaminess of mozzarella, the bite of anchovies, the freshness of basil, complemented by the spiciness of good olive oil. I'd daydream throughout the day about the silky slices of mortadella creating valleys that would fill with pools of sweet cherry-tomato juice. All those delicate flavors were brought together with a gentle sprinkle of Sicilian oregano that had been dried on the vine.

More than that pizza, though, the biggest lesson Enzo taught me—the most important thing I brought back with me from Italy—was about mentorship. Even though I was a foreigner with a plan to profit eventually from his 20 years of pizza-making knowledge, he saw and honored my genuine enthusiasm. He saw that I loved pizza just as much as he did. He forced me, as the student, to earn his trust and respect, and he rewarded that in kind.

Had I not drunk liters of grappa with Enzo, chatting with him until late in the night, he probably would have still been calling me Alex and telling me to slice the mushrooms. Instead, years later, when Emily and I got married, he came to our wedding and spent a week in the kitchen at my new Italian restaurant in New Orleans, telling us how much we were screwing things up.

Before I left Italy, he led me downstairs to his garage, where he kept his Ferrari. He let me watch as he turned it on and revved the engine a couple of times.

"Can we go for a ride in it?" I asked.

"No," he said, with a smile. "Aspetta."

DOUGH FOR PIZZA AND PITA

YIELD: ENOUGH FOR
4 PIZZAS OR 8 PITAS

1½ cups warm water
1 teaspoon instant yeast
4½ cups (540 grams) bread flour, divided, plus more as needed
2 tablespoons canola oil, plus more for your bowl
3½ teaspoons Morton kosher salt

I learned so much about dough from Enzo. He taught me to look beyond the finished dough and into its elemental parts: flour, yeast, starter, salt, and water. I found out how to bring together a dough that would not only have a lot of flavor but would also brown well, get crispy, and have a slight, pleasant chew. The very same dough becomes pizza and pita, both brought to life with a little time and a hot oven.

It's important to allow plenty of time—nearly 4 hours at room temperature, when you'll check it intermittently, and then at least one night in the fridge—for the dough to develop fully in both flavor and texture. Don't be discouraged if, at first, you have trouble handling and shaping it. I've gotten it down through plenty of practice; over the last several years, I've also trained dozens of cooks to handle dough, and it takes them time, too. Keep at it. The beauty of a dough is how simple it is—make it often and you'll soon become adept.

1. Combine the water and yeast in a large mixing bowl (if you have a stand mixer, use that bowl) and let sit for 5 minutes.

2. Reserve ½ cup (60 grams) bread flour and add the remaining 4 cups to the mixing bowl along with the canola oil.

3. If you have a stand mixer, fit it with the dough hook and knead the mixture on low speed for about 3 minutes, until a sticky but cohesive dough starts to form. Pause occasionally to scrape down the bowl if the flour is clinging to the sides and bottom or climbing up the hook. If you're making the dough without a stand mixer, mix it with a wooden spoon. In either case, loosely cover the bowl with plastic wrap or a dish towel and let rest for 30 minutes.

4. With your stand mixer on low or while stirring by hand in the mixing bowl, add the salt and, over the course of 2 or 3 minutes, add the remaining ½ cup flour, 2 tablespoons at a time. The dough should be more tense; it will feel soft but tacky, although it will pull from the sides of the bowl.

5. Flour your hands generously and use them to pull the dough onto a clean, unfloured work surface. Cup your hands around the dough, rolling it in short, circular strokes and

(recipe continues)

using the sides of your hands to nudge it into a relatively smooth ball.

6. Lightly wipe the inside of a large bowl with canola oil and place the dough inside, flipping it once or twice to coat. Loosely cover the bowl and let the dough rise at a warm room temperature for 1 hour.

7. After 1 hour, the dough will be stretchy but very soft. Leaving it inside the bowl, stretch opposite sides of the dough over the center. Rotate the bowl a quarter-turn and stretch the dough in the same way, then flip the whole mound of dough upside down and cover again. Let rise for 1 hour.

8. Repeat this series of folds one more time, allow it to rise at room temperature for 1 hour, then tightly cover the bowl and refrigerate overnight or up to 2 days. The longer the dough is refrigerated, the more flavor it will have. After this rise, it's ready to be shaped either for pizza (recipe follows) or pita (page 302); bear in mind that, once it's shaped, it will need more time for a final rise, so plan ahead.

PIZZA ENZO

This is Enzo's signature recipe, so good that he served it only to family and close friends. The combination of flavors—tomato, basil, and mozzarella, accented with candylike fresh cherry tomatoes, salty anchovies, and perfect mortadella—was, in his estimation, too special to serve to customers. Being an incorrigible capitalist, I knew back then that people would fall in love with it if I could only include it at a restaurant of my own. Sure enough, it's been on the Domenica menu since day one. When Enzo came to New Orleans for my wedding, he wanted to make pizzas. We spent a few hours tossing pies on the line at Domenica, and the first time our sous-chef called out an order for "Pizza Enzo," he gave me a look of delight and a giant smile that I'll never forget.

Note that a baking stone is an absolute must. They're easy to find, affordable, and indispensable for creating a crust that's nearly on par with what you'd get in a scorchingly hot wood-fired oven. You might, of course, veer off-recipe for the toppings, and because it makes four pies, you can use different toppings for each one. But you'll want to make a mental note of the tomato sauce, so simple that the term "sauce" belies the effort required—good canned tomatoes are such an excellent ingredient that you don't need to do anything more than crush and season them.

Canola oil for the pan
1 recipe dough for pizza and pita (page 297)
All-purpose or bread flour for dusting
One 15-ounce can peeled whole tomatoes
2 tablespoons extra-virgin olive oil
½ teaspoon Morton kosher salt
1 pound low-moisture mozzarella cheese, grated
¼ cup finely grated Parmesan cheese
1½ cups cherry tomatoes, halved
16 anchovies
16 to 20 fresh basil leaves
2 teaspoons dried oregano, preferably Sicilian
1 teaspoon red-pepper flakes
4 thin slices mortadella

1. Wipe a thin coat of canola oil on a baking sheet and set it aside. Dump the dough onto your work surface and, with a bench scraper or sharp knife, cut it into four evenly sized pieces.

2. Lightly flour your hands and cup your palm around a piece of dough, with your fingertips resting around it to make a sort of "cage." Roll it in brisk, small circles until it forms a smooth ball. Repeat with the rest of the dough.

3. Flip the rounds of dough once or twice on the baking sheet so they're lightly coated with oil, then space them apart with the seam side down. Tightly cover the whole sheet with plastic wrap to keep the dough from drying out and let rise at room temperature for at least 2 hours and up to 4 hours, until the rounds are pillowy and have doubled in size. Meanwhile, heat your broiler with a baking stone set

(recipe continues)

about 6 inches beneath the heating element, giving it at least 1 hour to build plenty of heat.

4. To make the sauce: Fish 5 whole tomatoes out of the can (save the rest for another use). Chop them, or mash them between your fingers, and season with the olive oil and salt. Separately, combine the mozzarella and Parmesan. Set the sauce and cheese aside, along with the cherry tomatoes, anchovies, and basil.

5. Dust some flour on a pizza peel or a flat baking sheet. Dust a little more flour over one piece of dough and use the pads of your fingers, with even pressure, to pat it down and outward; flip and repeat on the opposite side until you have an approximately 8-inch circle.

6. Now you're ready to start shaping a pizza pie the way you've always seen in the movies. Flour your hands and drape the dough over your knuckles. With your hands staying near the outer edges rather than the center, gently stretch the dough by rotating your wrists wider and wider apart. Keep moving until you have an 11-to-12-inch circle; take extra care not to let the dough rip or become too thin at the center.

7. Place the dough on the floured pizza peel for assembly. Top it first with some of the cheese mixture; about ½ cup per pizza is plenty. Follow it with a small handful of cherry tomatoes, then roughly tear about four anchovies and four basil leaves and scatter them over the pie. Dollop a scant ¼ cup tomato sauce all over, ensuring that the peel stays dry. Finally, sprinkle each pie with ½ teaspoon dried oregano and ¼ teaspoon red-pepper flakes.

8. Loosen the pizza on the peel by flicking your wrist in short, brisk motions, then partially pull the rack out of the oven and shimmy the pizza onto the center of the stone. Bake for 2 to 3 minutes, until the crust is pale golden all over with some light charring.

9. Using a spatula or tongs, rotate the pizza on the stone a half-turn; with the oven door cracked open, keep baking 2 to 4 minutes, until there are some beautifully charred pockets and a nice brown underside on the crust.

10. Use your tongs to grab the pizza gently by the crust and pull it onto the pizza peel. Lay a slice of mortadella over the pizza, slice, and serve right away. Repeat with the rest of the dough and toppings.

PITA

When I first started sneaking Israeli flavors into my food at Domenica, I dreamed of leaving the toppings off the pizza and baking it naked—presto, I'd have pita. Now, at Shaya, that's exactly what we do. If you've only ever had dry supermarket pita, this is a different animal entirely, puffed up like a pillow, savory on its own, and ready to scoop up anything you like.

Canola oil, for the pan
1 recipe dough for pizza and pita (page 297)
All-purpose flour, for dusting

1. Wipe a bit of canola oil on a large baking sheet. Dump the dough onto a clean, dry counter, and use a bench scraper or sharp knife to cut it into eight equal pieces; make clean, decisive cuts rather than use a sawing motion, so you don't deflate all the air inside.

2. Lightly flour your hands and place one palm directly over the dough ball, with all your fingertips touching the counter to make a sort of "cage" around the dough. Roll it in brisk, small circles on the countertop so it tightens itself into a smoother, more taut ball.

3. Space the rounds of dough a few inches apart, seam side down, on the sheet, and roll to coat them lightly in oil. Tightly cover the sheet with plastic wrap so the dough doesn't dry out, and let them rise at room temperature for 2 to 4 more hours, until they're pillowy.

4. Meanwhile, set a baking stone on the center rack of your oven and turn on the broiler. You're emulating a 700°F wood-burning oven, so you need to give the stone a good long while to preheat before you bake.

5. When the dough is ready, lightly flour a work surface, and use a bench scraper or thin metal spatula to coax one piece into your palm; be sure you don't manhandle it or you'll force out the pockets of air that formed while it rose. Dust a little more flour on the top of the dough and onto your rolling pin.

6. With firm, even pressure, briskly roll the dough a few times along its length. Flip it upside down, rotate it a quarter-turn, and roll it the same way, keeping it as round as possible. Repeat, dusting a little extra flour as needed, until it's about 6 inches across.

7. This next part happens fast and furiously, so make sure you have no distractions—screaming children and natural disasters will have to wait. Use tongs or a good oven mitt to pull the oven rack with the baking stone partially out. Carefully pick up the pita, drape it over your palm, and slap it down onto the stone as if you're giving it a high-five (just be careful not to touch the hot stone!). Set a timer for 1 minute, and close the oven. Broilers vary in strength but all are quite hot, so don't turn your back on the oven or the pita may burn. Check on it—it should puff up and build in color, with some beautiful blistered spots. If it's still pale, close the oven and let it keep baking for 30-second intervals.

8. Use tongs to flip the pita, and let it finish baking with the oven door cracked so you can watch it finish. Pull it out when the second side is as pretty as the first; this can take anywhere from 30 seconds to 2 minutes, depending on your broiler.

9. Bake off the rest of the dough this way; as you get the hang of it, feel free to bake two pitas at a time. Serve these hot or at room temperature.

23

✦✦✦

From Sunday to Domenica

So many months of travel, study, and planning culminated in a single evening when I stood before a stove in New Orleans, tossing olive oil into a pan full of tagliatelle with rabbit-and-porcini ragù. Chef Marc Vetri, who'd helped me start my journey to Italy what seemed like a lifetime ago, was standing beside me in the kitchen. But this was *my* kitchen, the kitchen of my new Italian restaurant, Domenica, which is the word for "Sunday" in Italian. Our pastry chef, Lisa White, handed Marc a piece of biscotti she'd just pulled from the oven, a simple recipe studded with almonds and darkened with brown sugar. "It's amazing," Marc said. When I heard those words as I looked out over the gleaming kitchen, it felt almost as if I was living in a dream—the very dream I'd had two years earlier. *Almost* that dream.

I'd returned from Italy with my notebooks full and my energy high, ready to dive into the project of opening my restaurant. While I looked for a space, I started curing meat in my office, hanging culatelli, coppe, and pancette on racks that *occasionally* dripped meat juices onto the office's wall-to-wall carpet. It took me a while to figure out how far I needed to turn down the office air conditioner to get the temperature and humidity just right for curing the meat. Then I carted in humidifiers. Thanks to my time at Podere Cadassa, I knew the precise conditions I was looking for, the ones that would produce salumi with just the right earthy, mushroomy funk. At home, I was testing pizza dough constantly. I'd reunited with Emily as soon as I returned from Italy, and she and her friends were my test subjects. They'd come over, and I'd have five different doughs ready to make into pizzas for them to try.

We'd found a space for Domenica in the grand historic Roosevelt Hotel in New Orleans's Central Business District. It had been empty since the flooding after Hurricane Katrina but had been beautifully restored. I spent tens of thousands of dollars of our opening budget on a wood-and-stainless-steel case for curing salumi and cheese, a big red Berkel slicer like Enzo had, and a Carrara marble counter at the bar. I had a wood-fired pizza oven built with a rotating stone deck. The neighborhood was still spookily quiet at night, but I was confident we could draw diners in. The evening before we opened, I stood in the darkened dining room, admiring the large chandeliers we'd hung there. Someone turned on the air-conditioning for the first time, and, as cool air blew through the dining room, the crystals of the chandeliers trembled slightly. It felt like the restaurant coming alive, getting animated. This was it: I was going to re-create all my favorite food experiences from Italy for New Orleanians. People would come, I was sure of it.

And they did. From the day we opened our doors, Domenica was popular. But that didn't mean I had it all figured out. In fact, the restaurant's first months were humbling for me, starting with our opening night. I'd decided that, instead of serving bread, we should serve grissini, traditional Piemontese bread sticks, long, slender, and crunchy. We put a bouquet of grissini in a glass on each table. They looked gorgeous—some plain, some coated with sesame seeds. Yet, for that whole long evening, the dining room was filled with the sound of breaking glass. It kept happening: someone would reach across the table for wine, or move a menu the wrong way, and would hit the grissini, knocking the whole thing onto the floor. My brilliant idea resulted in explosions of breadcrumbs and broken glass everywhere. We kept it up with the grissini for 2 months, to the point where we were struggling to keep the floor clean of sesame seeds. That's when I decided it might be a good idea for us to serve ciabatta instead.

Then there were the meatballs. The ones on my menu were tiny, served on top of polenta, the way I'd seen at a restaurant in a Tuscan town called Pietrasanta. I'd snuck into the kitchen to watch a little old woman making them, one by one. In New Orleans, customers kept asking if they could have them on top of spaghetti, and then they'd complain.

"Were they too dry? Were they poorly seasoned?" we'd ask.

"No," they'd say, "they're too small. My mama made big meatballs."

Ah, I thought. It was starting to add up. In New Orleans, Italian food had been cooked by Sicilian immigrants for a century. Our customers were used to that style of Italian cooking. It was one I liked, too—who doesn't enjoy a plate of hot sausage and red "gravy," a local term for marinara? I wasn't trying to replace those New Orleanian favorites—just to add to them. We were curing our own meats, wood-firing our pizzas, and making squid-ink pasta by hand at a time when few others were doing so in this city. The learning curve went both ways: I figured out what my customers wanted, and they discovered that this Italian food from other regions *was* different but also good.

The bottom line was that I wanted to cook for people and

make them happy. Every time there was a dissatisfied guest, I thought back to feeding people after Katrina and knew I was ready to do whatever it took to help people enjoy their meals. No more temper tantrums from me if they didn't like my gnocchi or ordered fettuccine Alfredo (which wasn't on the menu).

One of my triumphs was torta fritta. It's a fried dough, typical in Parma or Emilia-Romagna, made with a little milk, vinegar, flour—and pork fat. The dough is layered several times, rolled out, cut into squares, and fried in more pork fat. You use it instead of a cracker or bread to eat with prosciutto, coppa, or some kind of cheese. Customers didn't understand it at first. But then I told the staff just to describe them like savory beignets, the doughnuts beloved throughout New Orleans. Everyone loved them then, these savory beignets. *I want to give people the chance to experience these foods,* I thought, *but I also have to remember where I am.* And where I was, fortunately, was Louisiana. The more I read our customers correctly, the more I provided them with dishes that satisfied both their desires and my interests, the more they trusted us.

BAGNA CAUDA

L iterally translating to "hot dip" or "hot bath," this is a classic Piemontese dish that I fell in love with while eating my way through Italy, and which we've served at Domenica. Garlic and anchovies are essentially poached in a mixture of olive oil and butter until they've melted into the sauce itself, making a superb partner to crudités and crusty bread, and an unconventional topping for pasta. You'd be hard-pressed to find something that matches its elegant, well-rounded flavors with the minimal effort it requires.

5 large cloves garlic, unpeeled
½ cup extra-virgin olive oil
6 tablespoons unsalted butter
5 anchovies
1 sprig fresh oregano
½ teaspoon Morton kosher salt
2 pounds raw vegetables, such as carrots, sugar snap peas, radishes, fennel, broccoli, and summer squash

1. Heat the oven to 250°F with a rack in the center of the oven.
2. Leaving the skin on the garlic, lightly crush the cloves. Combine them with the rest of the ingredients except the raw vegetables in an ovenproof saucepan or a deep, not-too-wide casserole dish. Bake, uncovered, for 1½ to 2 hours, until all the garlic is golden and your whole kitchen smells incredible.
3. Prepare the vegetables, peeling if necessary and breaking them down into bite-sized pieces. Serve the sauce straight from the pan (wait a few minutes, so it's cool enough to touch), or pour it into a bowl, with vegetables scattered alongside.

BRESAOLA SALAD WITH ARUGULA AND PARMESAN

T his salad was inspired by the bresaola I tried at the Bolzano restaurant whose speck (in combination with Céline Dion) inspired tears of joy. It made me realize that cured beef can achieve the same silky texture as cured pork. I put this on Domenica's opening menu, and it was among our most loved dishes. Because it's so simple, there's no point in making it unless you have the best cured meat you can get your hands on—if you can't find good bresaola, of course, you can also use prosciutto di Parma. This salad is best with arugula, or any greens with a really peppery bite. The dressing is the only thing that requires active time in the kitchen (and it's worth it, not only here but also on any other vegetables you could find), but you could take a shortcut and dress it with only lemon juice and olive oil and it would still shine.

¼ pound bresaola, thinly sliced

6 tablespoons preserved lemon vinaigrette (page 393), divided

6 cups lightly packed fresh arugula

1½ teaspoons Aleppo pepper

⅓ cup finely grated Parmesan cheese

1. Shingle the slices of bresaola in an overlapping layer on a large plate or serving platter, and drizzle 2 tablespoons dressing all over.

2. Toss the arugula with the last ¼ cup dressing and the Aleppo pepper, then pile the greens in a big tuft over the bresaola. Shower the whole thing with the cheese.

RICOTTA CAVATELLI WITH WHITE BOLOGNESE

If you were to sit me down for a game of word association, I'd say "pizza" when you said "Enzo." But the non-pizza dishes that I learned at his restaurant, Il Gabbiano, were also excellent, and this is one that I still make (and love) regularly, both at home and at Domenica. Back in Italy, we would make such big batches that I remember Enzo's sister unceremoniously dropping the leftovers into her dog's bowl. That's one of many moments that encapsulate why I fell in love with Italy and brought it home with me.

Cavatelli is a great gateway pasta, because you get the tangible experience of kneading dough and making noodles without needing a roller to shape it. The ricotta makes it a little softer and more forgiving to work with, while giving the cooked pasta some pleasant heft. Because you roll each noodle individually, it's good to allow a little extra time and maybe enlist a kitchen helper. No matter what you add, it's a smash hit, but I recommend going all out and adding the richest white pork bolognese (recipe follows).

3½ cups all-purpose flour, plus more for dusting
1 cup ricotta
2 eggs
1 gallon water
2 tablespoons Morton kosher salt
1 recipe white bolognese (recipe follows)
Parmesan, for serving

1. Combine the flour, ricotta, and eggs in a large bowl. Use your fingers to rake them together, gradually and slowly incorporating the flour. As the dough starts to come together, you can use your knuckles and the heels of your hands to punch it down; don't worry about overworking it. Once the flour is almost completely incorporated, empty the dough onto a clean work surface, and continue to knead for about 8 minutes, until it's smooth and stiff, like clay. Wrap it in plastic, and let it rest for at least 30 minutes.

2. On a lightly floured surface, roll the cavatelli dough into a large rectangle, flipping it as you work to prevent sticking; it should be about ⅛ inch thick, so put some muscle into it. Square the dough off, and knead together the scraps. Use a sharp knife or pizza wheel to cut the dough into ¾-inch strips, then cut each strip into 1-inch pieces.

3. To shape the cavatelli: Press two fingers into the top edge of each piece of dough. With firm, even pressure, pull your fingers toward you so the dough curls around itself. Pull

(recipe continues)

until your fingers roll off the bottom of the strip, leaving a thinner, jagged-looking edge. No need to be delicate; you want it thin with a distinct "cave" in the middle. Once all the noodles are shaped, you can cook them right away or spread them in a single layer on a baking sheet, freeze until firm, then move to an airtight bag and freeze for up to 1 month; no need to defrost them before cooking.

4. Combine the water and salt, and bring the pot to a boil. Cook the pasta for about 2 minutes, until it's cooked through but not mushy. Drain into a colander, then toss with the bolognese. Generously shave some Parmesan over each bowl (a vegetable peeler will give you nice wide swaths that stay distinct as they melt).

WHITE BOLOGNESE

YIELD: 4 TO 6 SERVINGS

People have a romanticized notion of Italian food, including an idea that sauces like bolognese must be cooked for the better half of a day, preferably with a nonna hunched over the pot. This version—so called because it doesn't contain tomatoes—is done in less than 2 hours, and has a concentrated richness that helps it go a long way wherever you put it. It's perfect for chilly weather, since eating it feels like a warm, soft blanket. Of course, you don't need to put it on homemade cavatelli: orecchiette and pasta shells are both excellent alternatives to trap the sauce, delivering some in each bite.

1. Trim the core and stalks from the fennel, and chop the bulb into small pieces, along with the celery and onion. Mince the garlic, and set all the vegetables aside.

2. Heat ¼ cup olive oil in a heavy pot over medium-high heat. When it's just starting to smoke, carefully add the pork in a single, even layer—be careful here, since all that moisture will create steam, and the hot oil will want to spatter. Leave it alone for 5 to 7 minutes; as it starts to brown, the smoke will dissipate, and the sizzle you heard at first will turn into more of a crackling, the sound of the pork frying in its own rendered fat. Let it build a deep, burnished crust before you stir.

3. Now give the pork a good stir, breaking apart any large chunks so they cook evenly, and scraping any brown bits from the bottom of the pot. Tamp it back down into a single layer, and cook for another 3 minutes or so. It will be tempting to linger over your stove and keep idly stirring, but it's essential to be patient and not touch the pork while it builds up this flavorful crust. As soon as it's evenly golden, use a slotted spoon to remove the pork, and reserve.

4. Add the remaining ¼ cup oil to the pot, along with all the vegetables. Cook over medium heat, stirring occasionally, until they're soft and becoming lightly golden along their edges, 5 minutes or so. Again, patience is key—every minute you wait is another minute of developing flavor.

5. Add the pork back to the pot, along with the chicken stock, orange juice, bay leaf, salt, and spices. Decrease the heat to low, and let the pot burble away, uncovered, for 40 to 50 minutes. There shouldn't be too much movement in the pot, just a gentle simmer along the edges.

6. When nearly all the liquid has reduced and you're left with a thick, chunky ragù, add the cream and orange zest, and simmer for another 5 minutes. Take the pot off the heat; as it cools, it will thicken and settle into itself. Remove and discard the bay leaf before serving.

1 fennel bulb
2 stalks celery
1 small yellow onion
1 clove garlic
½ cup extra-virgin olive oil, divided
1½ pounds ground pork shoulder
3 cups chicken stock
⅓ cup orange juice
1 dried bay leaf
1 teaspoon Morton kosher salt
¼ teaspoon ground allspice
⅛ teaspoon ground cloves
⅛ teaspoon finely grated nutmeg
1 cup heavy cream
Grated zest of ½ orange

CHERRY AND PISTACHIO COOKIES

Grated zest of ½ orange
½ cup granulated sugar
12 tablespoons (1½ sticks) unsalted butter, softened
1 cup packed light-brown sugar
2 eggs
1 teaspoon vanilla extract
1½ cups all-purpose flour
1¼ cups almond flour
2 teaspoons ground cinnamon
1 teaspoon baking powder
½ teaspoon Morton kosher salt
⅛ teaspoon baking soda
1 cup pistachios, toasted, roughly chopped
1 cup dried cherries

Most people who dislike biscotti just haven't had a good version; made well, they have a crunch that doesn't break your teeth, soften when dipped into a foamy cappuccino, and make you want to keep eating. Inspired by the very similar biscotti that we serve at Domenica as an accompaniment to espresso, these capture all the same qualities but take the form of drop cookies, which are faster and friendlier; they have biscotti's distinct crisp edges but a soft, chewy center. Lightly spiced and brightened with citrus, they're the perfect way to end a meal.

1. In a large bowl, rub the orange zest into the granulated sugar with your fingers. Add the butter and brown sugar, and cream the mixture with an electric or stand mixer, starting on medium speed and gradually increasing to high, until light and fluffy. Add the eggs and vanilla; beat until combined.

2. In a separate bowl, whisk together the flours, cinnamon, baking powder, salt, and baking soda. Mix this into the rest of the dough until just incorporated, then fold in the pistachios and cherries. Tightly wrap the bowl, and chill for at least 1 hour, preferably overnight.

3. Heat the oven to 350°F, and line two baking sheets with parchment. Drop the dough onto the sheets in mounds about the size of golf balls, spaced 2 to 3 inches apart. Bake for about 20 minutes, rotating the sheets after 10 minutes, until the cookies are soft and golden, especially around the edges. Cool for a few minutes on the baking sheets, then move them to a rack to finish cooling.

CHOCOLATE-ESPRESSO COOKIES

Our first pastry chef at Domenica, Lisa White, created this cookie by brewing fresh espresso and whipping it into a chocolaty confection with an ethereal, meringue-like crust and a melty, fudgy center. Simply put, it was one of the best cookies I'd ever had. We served them at a party once, and someone said, "These are so good, every guest at Domenica should try one before leaving." We took that advice to heart, and now a plate of them arrives with the bill as our way of saying thanks. We've served more than a million since then.

5 ounces dark chocolate, chopped
2 tablespoons unsalted butter
1 teaspoon Morton kosher salt
1½ tablespoons espresso or freshly brewed strong coffee
1 teaspoon vanilla extract
2 eggs, separated
2 tablespoons all-purpose flour
2 tablespoons cocoa powder
¼ teaspoon baking powder
½ cup granulated sugar
½ cup best-quality dark-chocolate chips
   Confectioners' sugar, for rolling

1. Combine the chocolate, butter, and salt in a double boiler or a large heatproof bowl set over a pan of boiling water, and stir until it's completely melted. Remove from the heat, stir in the espresso and vanilla, and let cool.

2. Use a mixer to beat the egg whites until they hold stiff peaks. Separately, combine the flour, cocoa powder, and baking powder. Set both bowls aside.

3. In a separate large bowl, use the mixer to beat the egg yolks with the granulated sugar on high speed until they're pale and fluffy, then fold in the melted chocolate mixture, followed by the dry ingredients—it will be very thick and almost like cement. Add half the egg whites to loosen it up, then fold in the rest until just incorporated. Add the chocolate chips, cover, and refrigerate for at least 2 hours or overnight so the dough has a chance to firm up.

4. Heat the oven to 375°F, and line a baking sheet with parchment paper. Place the confectioners' sugar in a wide, shallow bowl. Scoop the dough into golf-ball-sized mounds (it might still be a little tacky), flatten them slightly, and toss them in the confectioners' sugar until they are very generously coated.

5. Space the cookies a couple of inches apart on the sheet, and bake for 9 to 10 minutes, until the edges are set and the tops are dry. They'll still be quite soft. Let them cool on the sheet, and use a thin metal spatula to peel them away.

V

HOMECOMING

24

✦✦✦

Family Meal

Emily woke me up to tell me. I couldn't believe it. Gideon had just been here, visiting us in New Orleans, a few days earlier. It wasn't possible that he was gone.

As children, Gideon and I were good friends despite our ten-year age difference. After my parents split up, the house my aunt Debbie had bought for my mom in Philadelphia was just a 10-minute walk from where she and my uncle lived with my cousins Gideon, Ariel, and Tali. I went to their house as often as I could, whenever I wanted to avoid being home alone after school. It was the only place where I could truly be a kid. We'd swim in their pool, play video games, read stories, and build forts in the living room together, using couches, chairs, and blankets. On the weekends, Debbie would take me along with her own children to the zoo or the aquarium. If they went camping, I went, too. In return, I helped out however I could, babysitting and entertaining the younger kids. An inquisitive child, Gideon radiated positive energy. Whenever he got into a subject—be it something scientific, a video game, or, say, trains—he'd throw himself into learning about it with such excitement that you couldn't help getting excited, too. Also, I felt he looked up to me, and I liked that.

As I got older and started getting into more and more trouble, my aunt and uncle didn't want me to spend time around their kids anymore. I saw them less and less. My after-school jobs at the bakery and, later, at Sonoma, gave me other places to go. I started feeling distant from my family then. Going away to culinary school a few years later felt like a chance at a new life, a blank canvas on which I could draw an entirely new picture of myself, unencumbered by the past. My family became lumped in with the darkness of my struggles as a teenager. I wanted to put all of that behind me and focus solely on cooking.

The next time I saw Gideon was when we were all visiting my safta in Israel. I was struck by how much he'd grown up; he was more reserved, no longer the bright-eyed, spunky kid. He was a senior in high school, almost as tall as I was, with scruffy facial hair. In our group of cousins, he was the quietest, almost at a remove. I had no idea, at the time, what he was going through internally. Within a few years, his problems became more obvious: a heroin addiction that gradually alienated him from his family.

That was a dark time for everyone, but I wasn't present for it. Months would pass without my calling my mother. I went several years without seeing any of my family. I told myself that I couldn't afford to travel back to Philadelphia, but the reality was that I didn't even really think about it. There were banquets to prepare for, a new menu to launch, a new cook to train.

The next time I heard from Gideon, he was in better shape. He'd hit bottom with his drug addiction, moved to Florida, and gone to rehab. He was living with some other recovering addicts, going to meetings twice a day. It seemed as if he'd found a community of people who were dedicated to helping each other stay clean. When he first called me, I didn't know what to say—I felt awkward. But then he told me that he'd gotten a job cooking in a restaurant to pay the bills, and food was something we could connect over. He'd tell me about working the sauté or the garde-manger station, and I'd offer him little tips, things he should do in the kitchen that would impress his chef.

Gideon texted me a few weeks before Emily and I got married, asking if I'd like a food mill as a wedding gift. "Would you ever use one?" he asked. I was touched that he was thinking so deeply about what kitchen gadgets I might take pleasure in. "Sure!" I texted back. "I can make gnocchi with it!" A few nights before the wedding ceremony, I held a dinner in Domenica's private dining room for my whole family. It felt like a small miracle. There were my dad and my aunt Debbie at the same table. They hadn't spoken to each other in decades. There was Gideon, well dressed, his new girlfriend beside him. Happy. *I got Gideon back,* I thought.

After the wedding, we continued to text about food. I was glad to be clicking with him again, but I also felt that he needed to do something more with himself. He was so smart and capable, and though cooking was a vocation for me, I knew that for him it was a stopgap measure, something to help him get by. I was thrilled when he told me that he wanted to be a doctor. He was acing the pre-med classes he was taking. A few months later, in October 2012, he came to New Orleans to interview at Tulane Medical School. We spent 3 days together, sightseeing around New Orleans, smoking meat for goat tacos in my backyard, watching *Dexter* on Showtime, and daydreaming about the future. If Gideon moved here to go to med school, I could give him a job in the kitchen at Domenica so he could make extra money; we could cook together at my house; I could watch out for him, as I should have done more when he was younger. We could really become friends again.

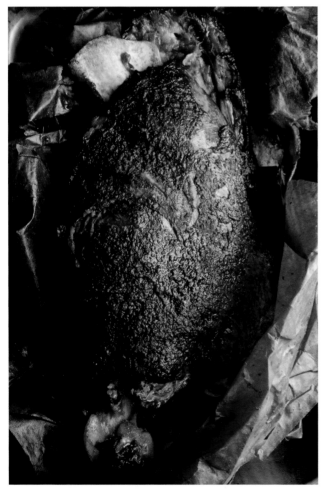

SMOKED GOAT SHOULDER

Four days later, he was gone. He'd flown back to Philadelphia, gotten some heroin, and overdosed.

For the first time since I'd immersed myself in the restaurant world, I dropped all my plans. Emily and I headed to Philadelphia to sit shiva with my aunt Debbie. When we got there, I didn't know what to say. So I came up with an idea. I told Debbie that I'd be back in a month to cook Thanksgiving dinner. Usually, she was responsible for the holiday meal. Food was something I could offer my family in the wake of Gideon's death, I thought. "You don't have to worry about a thing," I told her. "I'll take care of all of the cooking."

Thanksgiving is one of the busiest days of the year at Domenica; we have a full dining room all day long. We do a special menu, which means all of our line cooks are dealing with new dishes, and our servers are juggling lots of customers and needing to make everyone feel special for the holiday. It's one of the hardest days of service of the year. I didn't think twice about leaving, though. It was clear to me that I needed to show up for my family—a profoundly unfamiliar feeling.

Once my family and I were in Debbie's kitchen, we all distracted ourselves from the overwhelming sadness of Gideon's absence by focusing on the tasks we had to accomplish. Everyone was intent on being involved. Ariel helped brine the turkey, and Debbie pulled out a bag of hawaij, a Yemenite yellow curry spice she'd brought back from Israel, for us to season it with. I'd brought a second turkey from Domenica, an Italian version of it, a roulade with a Parmesan-and-nutmeg stuffing. I'd already cooked it sous vide, so it was ready to go. My mom and I baked cheddar biscuits together and stewed down cranberries with orange and rosemary. My Home Ec teacher, Donna, came; she'd taught Gideon, too, and had grown close with the family. Tali and I were making sweet-potato pie, and, ever my teacher, Donna gave me instructions as we rolled out the dough. She suggested a little chilled vodka instead of water in the pie dough, explaining that the alcohol evaporates faster and makes for a flakier crust. "And you need to clean off your rolling pin!" she nagged at me. It felt good to have us all there together, doing something in concert.

All these years I'd been burying myself in work, I'd missed out on this kind of experience with my family. *Damn,* I thought, *we could've done this dozens of times together.* I thought about all the moments I could have been there—when I'd found out

OUR THANKSGIVING SPREAD

about Gideon's drug addiction, at certain moments in my sister's life when she needed support, when my grandparents died. So much missed time. In the kitchen that Thanksgiving, I began to nurse my *own* wounds through my cutting board and knife. I had meant the cooking of this meal to be a comfort to my family—and perhaps it was—but the true gift it offered was to me, a soothing of much older hurts.

Several years later, I was walking through the dining room at the restaurant when a stranger called out to me. He introduced himself as the doctor at Tulane Medical School who'd interviewed Gideon. "We were so happy with his application and offered him a spot here," he told me. "Where did he end up going?" I could barely keep myself together to tell him that Gideon had passed away. But, in the midst of that renewed wave of sadness, I realized something: The hardship of Hurricane Katrina had taught me I could cook to serve my city, to help strangers. Losing Gideon had helped me see how important being connected to my family was, with or without food.

W hen my cousin Gideon visited me in New Orleans before he died, we made this together at my house. It took hours to cook, which was a blessing, because it provided the perfect excuse for us to hang out together all day long, idly chatting, as we waited for the meat to fall off the bone. When it was ready, we sat around the kitchen table with Emily, passing bowls of toppings as we built tacos and ate. Goat, which is mildly gamey, tastes so good with a little smoke, especially when it's set off by tons of fresh herbs both in its pre-seasoning and as a garnish. It might seem like a specialty meat, but it's actually the most widely eaten meat in the world, sure to keep growing in popularity here in the United States. Most halal butchers have it, but if you have difficulty tracking it down, feel free to substitute pork or lamb shoulder of roughly comparable weight.

Save this special recipe for a day when you've got nowhere to be and want to keep things casual. Invite people you love and embrace the full day (up to 12 hours, start to finish) of low-key cooking as a chance for quality time. If you don't have a smoker of your own, borrow one from a friend who's happy to accept quality time and tacos as payment. You can also jury-rig a standard charcoal grill for smoking, but unless you've got the time and patience for frequent tinkering, I wouldn't advise it; in order to keep the temperature consistent, you have to keep lighting new coals in a chimney, topping off the fire just a few coals at a time, and constantly monitor the vents.

⅓ cup herb salt (page 391)
One 5-pound goat shoulder
2 tablespoons Aleppo pepper
1 quart wood chips, such as applewood or pecan
Water, for the wood chips
Charcoal, for the smoker
2 cups lightly packed fresh cilantro leaves, chopped
1 cup lightly packed fresh mint leaves, chopped
2 avocados, sliced
2 jalapeños, seeds and pith removed, thinly sliced
2 limes, cut into wedges
12 small corn tortillas
¼ cup Honduran crema or sour cream
Maldon or other flaky sea salt, to finish
Green Tabasco sauce, to finish

1. Rub the herb salt all over the top, bottom, and sides of the goat shoulder. Tightly wrap it in plastic and refrigerate it overnight.
2. Unwrap the goat and pat it dry all over. Rub it to coat with the Aleppo pepper, then let it come to room temperature while you get the smoker ready. Meanwhile, soak the wood chips in plenty of water for at least 1 hour.
3. Close your smoker's dampers halfway, fill it one-third to halfway with charcoals, and light them. Once the charcoals' edges are white-hot, give them a stir to disperse the heat. Add the soaked wood chips, a heat deflector (if you have one), and the grill rack.

(recipe continues)

4. Close the lid and let the smoker start to warm up. This means playing with the dampers and being patient: cracking them open a bit more will have a warming effect, whereas closing them slightly will limit airflow and decrease the temperature. Keep in mind, though, that all these changes are slow and gradual, and smokers will escalate beyond your control if you try to make any changes too quickly, so give it time, have a beer, and open or close the dampers only ⅛ inch at a time.

5. Once the smoker is hovering between 250°F and 270°F, add the goat. Close the lid and close the top vent and bottom damper so both are barely cracked. Within that first hour of cooking, check the smoker's temperature every 15 minutes or so and play with the dampers if you need to so the temperature hovers between 225°F and 235°F (it may dip when you first add the goat). Once the temperature reaches equilibrium, you can basically kick back.

6. Every hour or so, make a note of the goat's internal temperature. Don't be alarmed when it stays the same—likely around 150°F or 160°F—for hours on end. This is called stalling; as the meat cooks from the outside in, it gives off enough moisture to seem like it's cooking at a standstill. This is where most people start to freak out and jack up the heat. Don't. Have another beer. As long as your smoker's temperature is correct, you're spot-on.

7. Once the goat comes out of its stall—when the moisture has evaporated and its internal temperature begins to creep up around 175°F—use tongs or a large meat fork to transfer it to a large piece of parchment or butcher paper. Wrap it up like a present (it is!), secure it with masking tape, and place it back in the smoker. Every 30 minutes or so, check the temperature by sticking the meat thermometer through the paper and into the thickest part of the shoulder (but, again, don't agonize; this cooking happens so slowly that you have a little wiggle room). Remove the whole package when the meat reaches 195°F—expect that it could take 8 to 10 hours. Let it rest in the parchment until you're ready to serve.

8. When the goat is cool enough to handle, use tongs or your fingers to pull the meat off the bone; it will yield easily. Give it a rough chop and move it to a serving bowl. Set out the cilantro, mint, avocados, jalapeños, and limes in their own bowls, or in separate piles on a big platter.

9. I like to warm my tortillas directly on the stovetop, which keeps them tender and adds a little char. Place one tortilla directly on the burner—you can do this over a low flame or an electric burner on the lowest setting—and let it sit until it's blistered. Transfer to a plate and cover with a clean dish towel to keep warm until all the tortillas are ready.

10. The beauty of tacos is that the assembly is anything-goes, but here's how I assemble mine: Slather about a teaspoon of Honduran crema on a warm tortilla. Fill the taco with goat, then pile in tufts of herbs and a couple slices each of avocado and jalapeño. Squeeze lime over everything, and sprinkle with flaky sea salt and Tabasco.

BRUSSELS SPROUT SALAD WITH MUSTARD AND TOASTED ALMONDS

This salad was a big hit at the Thanksgiving meal I cooked for my family—and for good reason. So much is happening here—two mustards, cilantro, dill, rosemary, thyme—but it all settles down in the company of shredded raw sprouts. Next to all the bold, bright flavors, the golden raisins add little puckers of sweetness, while the almonds are crisp and warm. You rarely see all these flavors together, but they combine well here, becoming an entirely different thing together from what they'd be on their own.

- 3 tablespoons Dijon mustard
- 3 tablespoons whole-grain mustard
- 3 tablespoons apple-cider vinegar
- 2 teaspoons honey
- 1 teaspoon Morton kosher salt
- ½ teaspoon red-pepper flakes
- ½ cup lightly packed fresh cilantro leaves
- 2 tablespoons lightly packed fresh dill fronds
- 1 sprig fresh rosemary
- 1 sprig fresh thyme
- 1 small shallot
- 1 small clove garlic
- ¾ cup extra-virgin olive oil
- 2 pounds Brussels sprouts
- ¾ cup golden raisins
- 1 cup sliced almonds, toasted

1. At the bottom of your salad bowl, whisk together the mustards, vinegar, honey, salt, and red-pepper flakes. Chop the cilantro and dill; strip the leaves from the rosemary and thyme, and mince them along with the shallot and garlic. Add all these ingredients to the bowl, then stream in the olive oil, and whisk until combined.
2. Peel away any tough outer leaves from the Brussels sprouts. Shred the sprouts until they look similar to slaw. Toss with the dressing and raisins, and sprinkle with the almonds just before serving.

PARMESAN AND NUTMEG STUFFING

Forget the mushy stuffing of Thanksgivings past. This one is nearly as decadent as bread pudding. It's baked in a big skillet—the wider the better, since that gives you plenty of crispy crust and just enough of the soft, cheesy middle. The Parmesan and nutmeg, a commonplace pairing in Parma, are what make it so distinct and special. It may seem as if a crazy amount of each is called for, but they somehow mellow each other out. One bite and you'll become a believer. At Thanksgiving, it's clutch to top it with cranberry sauce (recipe follows), although its flavors get along with so much more—try fast tomato sauce (page 155) or pesto (page 237) in the summer.

1. Heat the oven to 450°F with a rack set in the upper-middle position.
2. Separate three of the eggs; whip the egg whites to soft peaks and set aside. In a separate, large bowl, beat the yolks with the remaining three whole eggs and the stock.
3. Stir half of the breadcrumbs into the bowl with the eggs and stock, along with all the Parmesan, salt, and nutmeg. Gently fold in the egg whites to lighten up the loose batter, followed by the remaining breadcrumbs.
4. Set a large cast-iron skillet or ovenproof pan over medium-high heat, and melt the butter in it. With the butter sizzling, but before it gets any color, pour in the batter, and spread it in an even layer. Immediately transfer the skillet to the oven, and bake for 20 to 25 minutes, rotating halfway through, until the stuffing is set all the way through and a knife comes out clean.
5. If you're serving the stuffing right away, crank up the broiler and cook the stuffing for 1 to 2 more minutes, so it becomes

6 eggs
2½ cups chicken stock or turkey stock (page 344)
4 cups fresh breadcrumbs, divided
½ pound Parmesan cheese, finely grated
1 teaspoon Morton kosher salt
½ nutmeg seed, grated
4 tablespoons (½ stick) unsalted butter

deeply golden on top. If you're making it ahead, keep it in the skillet, then rewarm it in a 175°F oven, and wait to do the broiling step until shortly before dinnertime.

6. After you've broiled the stuffing, set the skillet on a rack to cool. When it's cool enough to handle, invert it onto a serving platter or cutting board. Eat this while it's warm.

CRANBERRY SAUCE WITH ROSEMARY AND ORANGE

Of all the recipes I've created in my lifetime, this may be the most consistent; it hasn't changed since culinary school. Hey, if it ain't broke, don't fix it. Left to their own devices, cranberries can be so shrill, too often overlooked or tipped directly out of a can. This version has enough nuance to give people pause; it lingers on their palates. Rosemary, bay, and vanilla work with the orange to balance the sour berries and transform them into something downright luxurious, *just* this side of savory, whether you're passing the sauce as a relish for turkey, piling it atop Parmesan stuffing (preceding recipe), or eating it with dessert. I make a huge batch and squirrel away the leftovers for breakfast; they're amazing on toast or in yogurt. Thawed frozen cranberries will work if you can't find fresh.

3 pounds cranberries
Grated zest of 1 orange
2½ cups orange juice
1½ cups sugar
½ cup honey
1 teaspoon Morton kosher salt
¼ teaspoon minced fresh rosemary
¼ teaspoon freshly ground black pepper
2 dried bay leaves
½ vanilla bean pod

1. Give all the ingredients a good stir in a pot or Dutch oven over medium-high heat (scrape the seeds from the vanilla bean, and drop them in along with the pod). Bring to a boil, then decrease the heat to medium-low, so that the berries are gently but steadily simmering. Keep cooking, stirring occasionally, to coax them into a jammy, puddinglike sauce, about 1 hour or a little longer; reduce the heat to low if you're worried they'll scorch, or bump the heat up slightly if the juice won't cook down.

2. When the sauce is quite thick, not runny but still shiny— when you scrape your spatula across the bottom of the pot, it should stay clean for a moment before the sauce comes rushing back in—take it off the heat and cool it to room temperature. Fish out the bay leaves and vanilla bean pod before serving.

CURRIED SWEET POTATO AND LEEK PIE

YIELD: 6 TO 8 SERVINGS

The yogurt in this savory pie keeps it light and delicate and does an even better job of making a thick custard than cream—try adopting that trick in your favorite quiche recipe and you'll have an excellent centerpiece that makes a complete, satisfying meal if you add a crunchy salad. Hawaij elevates the sweet potatoes and leeks into something that keeps people coming back, but if you don't have it, and don't have the time to make it, substitute a good-quality yellow curry powder, one that smells good to you and piques your interest on its own. This recipe makes enough to fill a deep-dish pie crust; if that's not what you've got, you'll just have a little extra filling, which you can scramble or bake.

- 1 medium sweet potato
- 2 tablespoons unsalted butter
- 1 leek, white and light-green parts only, thinly sliced
- 1-inch knob fresh ginger, peeled and minced
- 1½ teaspoons Morton kosher salt, divided
- 6 eggs
- 1 cup Greek yogurt
- ⅓ cup heavy cream
- ½ teaspoon hawaij (page 390)
- 1 recipe flaky pie crust (recipe follows), pre-baked and cooled
- ½ cup finely grated Pecorino Romano cheese

1. Heat the oven to 400°F with a rack in the center of the oven. Peel the sweet potato, and chop it into ½-inch pieces.

2. Melt the butter in a lidded skillet (preferably nonstick) over medium heat. Add the sweet potato, leek, ginger, and 1 teaspoon salt; give everything a good stir so it's coated in the fat, then cover the pan and reduce the heat to low. Let the vegetables sweat and soften until the sweet potato is tender but holding its shape and the leek has a soft, melting texture, 15 to 20 minutes. (If your skillet isn't nonstick, you'll need to come back and give it a stir every few minutes.) Set aside to cool.

3. Crack the eggs into a large bowl, and beat them together with the yogurt, cream, remaining ½ teaspoon salt, and hawaij. When the vegetables have cooled enough so they won't scramble the eggs, fold them into the custard, and pour into the pre-baked shell.

4. Bake the pie for 40 to 45 minutes, rotating the plate halfway through; it's done when the top is golden brown all over, just barely set in the center. Scatter the Pecorino in tufts all over the top of the pie, and serve warm or at room temperature.

Donna's presence at my family's Thanksgiving table inspired an impromptu pie-making lesson. Years after I took her Home Ec class and became a professional chef, I was still learning things from Donna. I still am today.

Here are some tricks I've picked up over the years: Grating and freezing your butter first (as in buttermilk biscuits, page 214) allows you to bring a crust together before the fat can melt. Vodka adds the moisture you need to form a dough without adding any of its own flavor, and with its high alcohol content, it evaporates faster than water, to create light layers in the oven. And a step as simple as keeping your rolling pin clean and floured goes a long way toward keeping you in control and producing a perfectly flaky crust for any pie, savory or sweet. This crust makes enough to fill a deep-dish pie plate, which is my preference for the curried sweet-potato-and-leek pie (preceding recipe), but don't sweat it if your pie plate isn't deep—you'll just have more scraps of dough that you can bake for a snack.

2 cups (240 grams) all-purpose flour, plus more for working the dough
½ teaspoon Morton kosher salt
12 tablespoons (1½ sticks) unsalted butter, very cold or frozen
¼ cup vodka, ice-cold
¼ cup ice water, plus more as needed

1. Whisk the flour and salt together in a large bowl. Using the largest-size holes on your box grater, coarsely grate the butter directly on top of the flour; use your spatula to scrape away any pieces that are clinging to the grater. Freeze the whole bowl until the butter is thoroughly chilled.

2. Use a spatula or fork to quickly fold in the butter until all the pieces are coated in flour. Add the vodka and water, and continue to stir just until all the flour is moistened (the dough should still be a bit crumbly); if you need to, add more ice water, 1 tablespoon at a time.

3. Lightly flour a work surface, and dump out the dough. Gently push it into a mound with the sides and heels of your hands until the flour is completely incorporated but you can still see streaks of butter. Shape it into a roughly 6-inch disc, and wrap it in plastic or a ziplock bag. Refrigerate for at least 2 hours, until it's firm and cold to the touch, or freeze it as long as you'd like and thaw it completely in the fridge when you're ready for it.

4. Flour your work surface and rolling pin before unwrapping the crust; flour the top of that, too. With firm, broad strokes, roll it from the center outward, flipping it upside down and rotating it every so often to keep your rolls even

and the dough round. As you work, make sure your rolling pin stays clean and well floured, and use a bench scraper or the side of your hand to push in and reinforce the dough along the edges as it thins and cracks. Sprinkle flour as needed so that the dough never sticks, and move it to the refrigerator if you notice the butter starting to soften. You're aiming for a 14-inch circle about ⅛ inch thick.

5. Fold the dough in half (a bench scraper makes it easy to manipulate), then fold it in half again. Gently lift it into a 9-to-10-inch pie plate (preferably deep-dish), and unfold it, nudging it into the corners and up the sides. Leaving a 1-inch border at the top, trim away any extra, then flute the edges by gently pinching them around your fingertips. Freeze for 30 minutes, or cover and refrigerate for at least 2 hours.

6. Heat the oven to 425°F, and place a baking sheet on the oven's bottom rack; the sheet's heat will promote even browning on the bottom of the crust as it bakes. Prick the bottom of the crust all over with a fork, and cover it completely with parchment paper or foil, weighed down with dry beans or pie weights. Place it directly on the preheated sheet to bake for 15 to 20 minutes, until the bottom looks set, still pale but no longer translucent. Remove the foil, and bake for another 10 or 15 minutes, until it's pale golden all over. Cool completely before adding the filling. You can make this up to 1 day in advance and keep it covered at room temperature until you're ready to fill it.

SOUS VIDE TURKEY

There are a million theories on the best way to prepare a turkey, but it always takes a certain amount of planning, and someone's bound to disagree with your method. Why not make it as tasty and moist as you can get it? This method does just that, without holding you to a constraining timeline. Amid the chaos that's happening in most kitchens around the holidays, the last thing you want to do is search for the perfect window of time when you can roast a big bird for hours and have it carved, perfectly cooked, and still warm at the moment when everyone sits down. With this method, you can cook it ahead—follow the recipe through step 9, plunge the vacuum-sealed bags into an ice bath to stop the cooking, and make the stock whenever's convenient—then pick up where you left off at least 30 minutes before dinner. It also travels well; that's why I brought it with me from New Orleans to Philadelphia for Thanksgiving with my family.

Immersion circulators, once massive (and massively expensive) contraptions limited to five-star restaurant kitchens, are growing increasingly accessible and affordable. As long as you've got the gear—including vacuum-sealable bags and a large vessel for cooking—my method asks you for no added effort at serving time, since you're just "carving" the turkey before you cook it, rather than after.

- 2 cups water, plus plenty more for cooking
- ¼ cup plus 2 teaspoons Morton kosher salt, divided
- ¼ cup sugar
- 2½ cups ice water, plus more if needed
- 1 small turkey (about 12 pounds), thawed
- 1 teaspoon red-pepper flakes
- Grated zest of 1 lemon
- ½ cup extra-virgin olive oil, divided
- 8 tablespoons (1 stick) unsalted butter, divided
- 2 cloves garlic, crushed, divided
- 2 small sprigs fresh rosemary, divided

1. Combine 2 cups water with ¼ cup salt and the sugar; bring to a boil until everything's dissolved. Remove from the heat, and add the ice water.

2. If the turkey came with a neck and/or giblets (usually, you'll find them stuffed inside the cavity), remove them and set them aside; no big deal if they weren't included. With the breast side down, use a sharp knife to cut through the "elbows" (leaving the first joint attached to the body) and remove the turkey's wings. You can wiggle the wing to find the ball joint and make short cuts until you reach it. Save the wings for another use—you can add them and the neck to turkey stock (recipe follows).

3. Turn the turkey so the breast faces up, and pull the legs away from the carcass. Cut the legs away at the hip joint,

(recipe continues)

using your hand to pop them out of the socket if you're having trouble, and keeping your knife as close to the spine as you can until you've completely separated them both.

4. Run your knife down either side of the breastbone, staying close to the bone and angling your knife in so you don't waste any meat, and separate the breast meat from the ribs. Leave all the skin on the meat; set aside the carcass with the wings and neck for stock. Put the legs and breast halves in a container where they'll fit snugly, and pour the brine over them. Cover, and refrigerate overnight.

5. Find a very large stockpot or other heatproof container (even a heavy-duty bucket will do the trick, since it won't be on the stove) that's big enough to hold all the turkey parts with plenty of room for water to move around it. Clip your immersion circulator to the side, fill the vessel with hot tap water, just enough to reach the circulator's neck, and set its temperature to 145°F.

6. While the water comes to temperature, prepare the turkey. Pull it out of the brine; no need to pat it dry. Sprinkle the red-pepper flakes, lemon zest, and remaining 2 teaspoons salt evenly over the tops of all the pieces, and pat it in.

7. Get two vacuum-sealer bags (each one about 14 inches long) and seal each on one end; place the breasts in one bag and the legs in the other. To each bag, add ¼ cup olive oil, 4 tablespoons butter, 1 clove crushed garlic, and 1 sprig rosemary. The bags shouldn't be too big or they won't hold a vacuum seal, so trim them if necessary to leave about 3 inches of space above the meat.

8. Press out as much excess air as you can, then vacuum-seal the open ends and add them to the water as soon as it reaches 145°F. The water's temperature will decrease with this addition; if you're impatient, you can boil some water and pour it in to speed things along. Keep an eye out for the temperature to work its way back up to 145°F, and when it does, leave it be for 2½ hours.

9. After 2½ hours, the white meat should be opaque and firm to the touch (although, of course, it won't yet be crackly or golden, like your textbook roast turkey). Take it out of the water and, with the bag still sealed, let it rest (or, if you're making this in advance, plunge it into a big bowl or pot full of ice water). Allow the dark meat to cook for another

30 minutes; to check for doneness, pinch along the bone of the drumstick—the meat should yield enough so your fingers meet. The juices around the meat will still be red, which is the norm when you cook meat sous vide, but don't worry—it's fully cooked and will have some extra time in the oven later. Fish this bag out of the water and let it rest for another 10 minutes (or add it to the ice bath).

10. If you refrigerated the turkey after cooking, let it come completely to room temperature before proceeding. Heat the oven to 400°F with a rack in the center of the oven. Set the bags upright, and carefully cut into the top, so you can reserve the juices and let them cool.

11. Pat the turkey dry all over, and arrange the pieces, skin side up, on a rimmed baking sheet (make sure you don't take along the garlic or rosemary, which will scorch). Once the juices in the bags have cooled, the fat will have risen to the top; brush or drizzle that all over the turkey's skin, then discard the rest. If you refrigerated the turkey after cooking it, the fat will already have separated and solidified, so you can easily scrape away and discard the broth (which will be pink) and baste the turkey with the fat (which will be a pale yellow).

12. Bake the turkey for about 20 minutes, rotating the pan after 10 minutes. This step is meant to give you the good coloration and crisped-up exterior that you're used to seeing (and scarfing down) at the holidays while also taking the turkey through its final cooking stage. Once it looks good enough for a feast, pull it out of the oven and let it rest for at least 10 minutes.

13. To serve the turkey: Cut the joint between the thigh and drumstick. Lay the drumsticks on your serving platter, and thinly slice the thigh meat, leaving the bone behind; thinly slice the breast meat on a bias as well. Serve with gravy (page 345).

W hen you break down a turkey for cooking sous vide, you're left with a raw carcass and wings (and, typically, a neck) that are full of flavor and perfect for stock. Of course, you could throw these pieces into a pot with some water and call it a day; the stock would still be far richer than what you get in a cardboard box at the store. But roasting gives them a big head start in terms of flavor, and using a little restraint with the water level—the bones won't even be fully submerged inside the pot—fortifies your finished product. As an added perk, the whole thing won't set you back much longer than 2 hours.

1 yellow onion
2 stalks celery
1 medium carrot, peeled
2 tablespoons extra-virgin olive oil
1 tablespoon Morton kosher salt
  Carcass, wings, and neck from 1 small turkey (see page 341)
½ cup white wine
2 quarts water
1 small sprig fresh rosemary
10 whole allspice berries

1. Heat the oven to 500°F, and set a rack in the center of the oven.

2. Peel and quarter the onion; roughly chop the celery and carrot. Place all the vegetables in the bottom of a roasting pan, and toss to combine with the olive oil and salt. Nestle the turkey carcass, wings, and neck over the top.

3. Roast for 50 to 60 minutes, flipping the turkey pieces upside down about halfway through roasting so they can get nice and dark on both sides.

4. Once they're ready, move the bones to a stockpot. Pour the wine into the roasting pan and scrape up as many browned bits as you can—the more the merrier—and pour those juices along with the vegetables into the stockpot.

5. Top the pot off with the water (the turkey may not be completely submerged, which is okay), and add the rosemary and allspice. Bring it to a simmer over medium heat, and let it bubble away, uncovered, for 1 hour or so. Flip the carcass after about 30 minutes so it cooks evenly.

6. When the meat that's been clinging to the carcass is easily pulled away (and delicious), the stock is ready. Strain it into a heatproof bowl, and cool to room temperature. Pull the meat off the bones to add to the gravy or have a top-notch cook's snack. Don't be tempted to skim off the fat that rises to the top as it cools—you'll want to save that for your gravy.

GRAVY

YIELD: ABOUT 2 CUPS,
PLENTY FOR 1 SMALL
TURKEY

Since living in Louisiana, I've learned a thing or two about good gravy. For one, there's a lot of power in making a good roux. Be patient with it, letting it slowly get deeper and darker. That makes all the difference in its depth of flavor, and it creates a full-bodied sauce that really coats the inside of your mouth. Pomegranate molasses is a surprise twist, a subdued burst of acidity that brings the whole thing into focus.

6 tablespoons unsalted butter, divided
¼ cup all-purpose flour
2¼ cups turkey stock (preceding recipe) or chicken stock
1 teaspoon pomegranate molasses
¼ teaspoon Morton kosher salt
½ cup lightly packed fresh parsley leaves, chopped

1. Melt 4 tablespoons butter in a skillet over low heat. Whisk in the flour, and cook, whisking constantly, until the roux is the color of milk chocolate. This can take 15 to 20 minutes, depending on your stove, but keep at it and don't jack up the heat—roux has a tendency to burn the second you look away, which makes it so bitter that you'll have to start over.

2. Whisk the stock and pomegranate molasses into the roux, and increase the heat to medium-low. Continue to cook at a gentle simmer for about 20 minutes, until the roux is as thick as heavy cream and tastes rich and complex. Remove from the heat, and stir in the last 2 tablespoons butter with the salt. Just before serving, add the parsley.

25

The Reluctant Israeli Chef

For some reason, I felt as though there was something missing. And I was having trouble pinpointing just what it was. As I walked through the Carmel Market in Tel Aviv, the sounds, sights, and smells felt familiar to me. In one stall, sesame was being ground into tahini. In another, a guy was squeezing fresh pomegranate and mixing juices. There were stalls with a whole rainbow of eighty different spices, others with halvah and syrupy pastries. I heard Hebrew and flashed back to a time when I could still speak it with my grandparents. *What would have happened if my family and I had stayed here? Would I still be a chef? Would I have had a more stable childhood? This is*

my land, I thought. *This is where I'm from. Why am I not cooking these foods?*

I was in Israel for a trip that had been organized by the Jewish Federation of Greater New Orleans with our sister city, Rosh Ha'ayin—a kind of culinary culture swap. This was the first time I'd traveled through Israel with a group of fellow chefs. I realized that I'd already made a mental checklist of everywhere we needed to eat, which places had the best falafel and the best hummus. One side of me was excited to show everybody all of these spots, and the other side was transported back to being young, recognizing how deep in me all these smells and tastes were. Now I felt I was discovering the food of Israel with the mouth of a chef, not that of a child, as if something that had been in black and white was suddenly, vibrantly, coming into full color. And then I realized that I had left all this behind to pursue things Italian.

After my time in Italy, I'd wanted to be the next Mario Batali. I bought a Vespa. Emily gave me an Italian leather man-purse for Hanukkah. I remembered the pushback I'd gotten from customers when we opened Domenica. If I'd had to work hard to convince New Orleanians that this kind of Italian food was worthwhile, how could I possibly do it with Israeli food?

But since Domenica was open already, maybe I could just . . . sneak it in. Hummus could be called "ceci purée." I could put a dollop of tahini on an oven-roasted eggplant and combine some roasted peppers with onions and rosemary. With a little camouflage, no one would know it was Israeli food masquerading as Italian food. I was worried, though. Would I be disrupting the delicate balance of Domenica's identity and existence? One bad dish, one month of doing less business is all it can take to threaten a restaurant's future. I was taking a risk, and knew it.

Then came the roasted cauliflower. When I was in Israel, I'd eaten in a modern restaurant called North Abraxas that specialized in cooking whole vegetables. They'd put whole onions and heads of cauliflower in their wood-burning oven, which immediately made me think of Domenica's wood-burning pizza oven. *We could totally do a dish like this,* I thought. I wanted to add labneh as the dipping sauce for it, which would approximate the classic Israeli dish of fried cauliflower with yogurt. I could use goat cheese instead, though, to make it seem a bit more Italian. Then I talked with a local goat farmer in Louisiana and realized he made a goat feta cheese. It felt like worlds colliding. A whole roasted head of cauliflower—browned in the oven and served regally, with a knife rising from it like a flag, a small pool of whipped feta by its side—went on the menu at Domenica. Immediately, it took off. Everybody loved it—which thrilled me. Soon, though, a silent resentment started building in me. I'd walk through the dining room and ask people if they were enjoying what they were eating. Our pizza dough had taken years to figure out. Each night, we were hand-rolling our pastas. Our salami cured for months, and our culatelli for years. But what would everybody say to me? "The cauliflower! It's so amazing! What's the recipe?"

The cauliflower was the gateway drug. It led to harder stuff. Soon lamb bolognese landed on a bed of tahini with za'atar crostini. Charoset, a sweet paste of fruit and nuts traditionally associated with Passover, was being served like a mostarda with duck-liver pâté. I started getting bolder. The charoset went with cured lardo, silky pork fat wrapped around grissini. Shakshouka, the classic Israeli breakfast dish of eggs cooked in tomato sauce, was topped with slow-roasted capretto, chanterelle mushrooms, roasted peppers, and olives. Our customers ordered all of these with gusto. Soon I stopped feeling I might indirectly burn the place down with this identity crisis. But I certainly didn't imagine that I'd be opening an Israeli restaurant in New Orleans with over a hundred seats, a filled reservation book, and accolades coming in from around the country.

PREPARATION OF
WHOLE ROASTED
CAULIFLOWER

WHOLE ROASTED CAULIFLOWER WITH WHIPPED FETA

YIELD: 4 TO 6 SERVINGS

This is the dish I count as the turning point in my attempt to sneak Israeli food onto an Italian menu in the American South. It was inspired, in part, by the popular Israeli snack of fried cauliflower with labneh (page 38), a thick yogurt. When I decided to serve this at Domenica, I was trying to find the most Italian incarnation of the dish I could, so it wouldn't come out of left field. It turned out to be wildly popular, which totally surprised me. We serve seven hundred heads a week at Domenica; nearly every table orders it. I never intended to become known for my cauliflower, of all things!

It looks really impressive, and there's something nicely communal about a whole group tucking into this burnished centerpiece. It's equally good as a vegetarian main dish. The whipped feta, like labneh, is creamy with some tang; the whole is greater than the sum of its parts, and it's such a huge batch that you'll likely be able to enjoy it leftover. I've seen people drag their pizza crusts or pita through it so they don't miss a drop.

- 2 quarts water
- 2½ cups white wine
- ⅓ cup plus 2 tablespoons olive oil, divided, plus more for serving
- 1 tablespoon plus ½ teaspoon Morton kosher salt, divided
- 3 tablespoons lemon juice
- 2 tablespoons unsalted butter
- 1 tablespoon red-pepper flakes
- 1 tablespoon sugar
- 1 dried bay leaf
- 1 large head cauliflower
- ½ cup goat cheese (4 ounces)
- 3 ounces cream cheese
- ½ cup crumbled sheep's-milk feta, preferably Bulgarian
- ⅓ cup heavy cream
  Maldon or other flaky sea salt, to finish
- ½ teaspoon Aleppo pepper

1. Heat the oven to 475°F. Fill a large pot with the water, wine, ⅓ cup olive oil, 1 tablespoon salt, lemon juice, butter, red-pepper flakes, sugar, and bay leaf. Bring this broth to a boil over high heat.

2. Trim the cauliflower's stem, and add the head to the pot. Turn the heat down to medium, and cook, stirring occasionally, for 7 to 10 minutes, until the bottom is approaching tenderness. Gently flip it in the pot, and cook for another 5 to 8 minutes, until the center is easily pierced with a knife.

3. Gently pull the cauliflower from the pot—you can do this by fishing it out with two slotted spoons or draining it over a bowl—and discard the broth. Move the cauliflower to a rimmed baking sheet or roasting pan, and roast for 30 to 40 minutes, rotating the pan after 20 minutes, until the top is burnished deeply brown but it's still got nooks of white and isn't slouching in the pan.

4. While that's in the oven, pulse the goat cheese, cream cheese, and feta with heavy cream, remaining 2 tablespoons olive oil, and last ½ teaspoon salt in a food processor until the

mixture is smooth and light (or let all the ingredients come to room temperature, and use a whisk and plenty of upper-body strength). Transfer to a bowl for serving.

5. Move the cauliflower to your serving platter; drizzle more olive oil over it, as well as the whipped feta. Serve with a sprinkle of flaky sea salt and Aleppo pepper. Give people some steak knives so they can serve themselves, dragging each bite through a big puddle of the cheese.

CHAROSET

A traditional food at Passover, this bittersweet fruit-and-nut relish is little known outside the Jewish community. It's got such a range and depth of flavors: savory and sweet, bright and warm. This soft, spiced version is my go-to throughout the fall and winter as an accompaniment to any cheese board or turkey sandwich. If you want to impress your friends—whether they're Jewish or not—make some gribenes (page 394), or crispy chicken skins, and use them to scoop the charoset, chip-and-dip style, next time you're entertaining.

1. Roughly chop the dates, figs, and apricots, removing any woody stems or ends. Add them to a food processor along with the hazelnuts and pistachios, and pulse to chop coarsely, taking care not to pulverize the mixture into a paste. It's okay if some of the nuts remain whole. Set aside.

2. Add the apples and onion to a large saucepan with the vinegar, wine, and sugar. Bring to a simmer over medium heat, then turn the heat down to low and cover the pot. Cook until the onions are translucent but the apples still hold their shape, 6 to 8 minutes.

3. Scoop everything from the food processor into the saucepan with the onions and apples; add the honey, apricot preserves, salt, spices, and zests. Cook over medium-low heat, stirring occasionally, until all the dried fruit has softened and absorbed the juices from the pan and the liquid has reduced to a point where it's no longer bubbling. When you give it a taste, the flavor should be warm with fruit, alive with spice, with just a savory note in the background. The apples should still have some body to them.

4. Remove from the heat, and cool to room temperature before stirring in the orange and lemon juice. Leftovers keep well in the fridge for several days.

10 Medjool dates, pitted and chopped

7 or 8 dried figs (6 ounces), chopped

6 ounces (about 1 cup) dried apricots, pitted and chopped

½ cup hazelnuts, toasted

½ cup pistachios, toasted

3 Granny Smith apples, peeled, cored, and chopped

1 small yellow onion, chopped

⅓ cup rice wine vinegar, preferably seasoned

⅓ cup sweet sparkling white wine, preferably Moscato d'Asti

⅓ cup sugar

3 tablespoons honey

3 tablespoons apricot preserves

¼ teaspoon Morton kosher salt

½ teaspoon ground cinnamon

¼ teaspoon ground cardamom pods

¼ teaspoon ground allspice

Grated zest from ½ orange

Grated zest from ½ lemon

1½ tablespoons lemon juice

1½ tablespoons orange juice

TAHINI CHICKEN SALAD

Poaching chicken in herbs and aromatics makes the meat so tender and evenly cooked, especially ideal for a salad as simple as this one. Anytime I make schmaltz and gribenes (page 392), I'm left with two whole chickens, and there's no better way to put them to use than here, where the skin isn't necessary. With the tahini mayo, the salad tastes familiar but new; duqqa and scallions provide lots of great texture. I love to eat it on a toasted potato roll, on a bed of greens, or simply with a fork.

1. If you haven't already removed the skins from the chickens, follow the directions in the recipe for schmaltz and gribenes.

2. In a large stockpot, combine the chicken, ¼ cup salt, herbs, and garlic. Add the water, topping it off with more if necessary, until the chicken is completely submerged. (If two whole chickens won't fit in your pot, break them down following the directions on page 220.) Squeeze in the lemon and drop it in.

3. With the heat on medium-low, bring the pot just up to a mellow simmer, then turn the heat down to low, and let the chicken gently cook with the broth bubbling around it. When you glance into the pot, bubbles should be slowly floating to the top, less than an active simmer—this will keep the meat moist.

4. Check the chicken by cutting into the thickest part of the leg; it's ready when it's no longer pink at the center. This can take up to 2 hours, depending on the size of the chicken and the power of your stovetop, but check it after 1 hour, and then every 10 or 15 minutes after that. When it's ready, pull the chicken out to cool; strain the broth, and save it for another use (you can cool it completely and freeze it).

5. Once the chicken is cool enough to handle, pull all the meat off the bones, being mindful not to bring along the tendons or excess fat. Give it an even chop, then combine it in a bowl with the tahini mayo, scallions, remaining ½ teaspoon salt, and lemon zest. Stir in the duqqa shortly before serving. This is a great thing to have in the fridge all week, but it's equally good the same day it's made.

2 whole chickens (4 to 5 pounds each), skins removed
¼ cup plus ½ teaspoon Morton kosher salt, divided
2 sprigs fresh oregano
2 sprigs fresh thyme
4 fresh sage leaves
2 cloves garlic, crushed
1 gallon water, plus more as needed
1 lemon, halved
½ cup tahini mayo (page 395)
1 bunch scallions, thinly sliced
Grated zest of ½ lemon
¼ cup duqqa (page 388)

This merging of an Italian American and a Jewish classic—matzo-ball soup and Italian wedding soup—feels almost second nature to me, given my culinary upbringing. We started making this dish at Domenica for Jewish holiday meals, so you could say the Italian-Jewish marriage was inevitable. Every Rosh Hashanah and Passover, I'd work on showcasing what the Jews would eat in the Italian ghettos. That's how this soup came about.

The foundation of deep, savory flavors is in the stock, and this recipe has two of them. The duck and chicken stock is the soup itself, full-bodied, rich, and deeply soothing; the second stock, in which you cook the matzo balls, uses the first stock's spent solids, a thrifty French technique called *remouillage* that makes the most of every ingredient. These take time but little effort, and there are a couple of ways you can make this recipe fit your timeline and keep it super-manageable: knock it all out in a long, lazy day at home; make both stocks (and the duck meat)

in advance and refrigerate them all separately or add the duck back to its stock and freeze; or prepare the matzo balls first, cook them in water or any other broth, and make only the duck stock.

Some people have a weird reaction to chicken feet. They do look sort of like dinosaurs' hands, but they're totally safe to eat. They're available in many grocery stores' poultry sections (or you can ask the person at the butcher counter), but wings also make a really great substitute.

1. Lay the duck on a cutting board, breast side up, with the legs facing you. Discard the giblets and neck, or save them for another use. With your knife angled toward the body, cut through the seam between the thigh and the breast. Once you hit the hip joint, pop it loose with your hands, and slice through it to separate the legs.

2. Keeping your knife very close to the bone so you don't waste any meat, carve along either side of the breastplate and the ribs to remove the meat. Pull the wings taut, away from the body, and cut through the ball joint that attaches each of them to the breast (pop it with your hands, as you did the hip joint, if you have trouble getting through). Set the legs and wings aside to come to room temperature (you'll be cooking them in about 1 hour) and refrigerate the breasts.

3. In a large stockpot, combine the duck's carcass with the chicken feet and 1 gallon water over high heat. Once the water is simmering, reduce the heat to medium and skim away any foam. Continue to simmer, skimming frequently, for about 10 minutes, until you've removed as much of the foam as you can.

4. Add the onion, carrot, celery, thyme, 1 tablespoon salt, and all the spices. Gently simmer, uncovered, for about 1½ hours, until the chicken feet have softened but are not falling apart and all the aromas in the broth are coming together. Decrease the heat a bit if the stock is bubbling too rapidly.

5. Submerge the duck legs and wings in the stock, and cook for another 75 to 90 minutes, until the meat is pulling away from the bone (the wings may be falling apart). Pull them out and reserve, then add the duck breasts to the stock and cook for just another 15 minutes or so, until they're firm to the touch and no longer pink in the center. Reserve with the rest of the meat, and remove the pot from the heat.

(recipe continues)

1 duck (5 to 6 pounds)
3 pounds chicken feet
1 gallon plus 3 quarts water, divided
1 yellow onion, quartered
1 carrot, peeled and chopped
2 stalks celery, chopped
2 sprigs fresh thyme
3 tablespoons plus 2 teaspoons Morton kosher salt, divided
1 cinnamon stick
8 whole allspice berries
2 star anise pods
2 dried bay leaves
1 teaspoon whole coriander seeds
1 teaspoon whole black peppercorns
1⅓ cups matzo meal
¾ teaspoon onion powder
¾ teaspoon garlic powder
½ cup schmaltz (page 392) or ghee, melted
4 eggs
2 cups cherry tomatoes, quartered
1 quart lightly packed fresh arugula
1 tablespoon lemon juice
   Best-quality extra-virgin olive oil, for serving

6. Once the duck meat is cool enough to handle, trim away and discard all the skin and any remaining fat. Slice the breast against the grain, and then cut it into bite-sized pieces; pull the meat off the legs and wings, and roughly chop it. Store all the duck meat in the refrigerator until the soup is ready.

7. Strain the duck stock, reserving the solids, and allow the stock to cool. You'll see some fat rise to the top, which adds flavor and body, but you can skim away some or all of it. While it's cooling, make the second stock: Add all the solids to a separate wide pot or Dutch oven, which you'll later use to cook the matzo balls, and cover them with 3 quarts water and 2 tablespoons salt. Bring to a boil over high heat, then reduce the heat to medium, and continue to simmer for about 30 minutes, until it's fragrant and tastes well seasoned.

8. While the second stock simmers, make the matzo balls: In a large bowl, combine the matzo meal, onion powder, garlic powder, and remaining 2 teaspoons salt. Separately, beat the schmaltz and eggs together, then add them to the dry ingredients and stir until well combined, with no dry pockets of matzo meal. Press a sheet of plastic wrap directly onto the surface of the dough, and refrigerate for at least 1 hour and up to 4 hours.

9. Strain the second stock (discard the exhausted-looking solids), and either store it for later use or, if you are finishing the recipe now, return it to the same wide pot and bring it up to a simmer over medium heat.

10. Roll the chilled matzo-ball dough in tablespoon-sized balls, and as soon as you shape them, drop them into the second stock; they should float in a single layer with a bit of room between them (they will expand as they cook). Leaving the heat on medium, partially cover the pot to cook for about 1 hour. The matzo balls are done when they're the same color throughout; if you cut one open, it should have the same texture as pound cake. Cover, and remove the pot from the heat while you assemble the soup.

11. Put the duck stock back in your large pot, and bring it to a simmer over medium heat. Reduce the heat to low, and immediately add the duck meat, tomatoes, arugula, and lemon juice. To serve: Place a couple of matzo balls at the bottom of each bowl, then ladle the soup over it. (The broth you used to cook the matzo balls can be discarded.) Finish with a drizzle of olive oil.

26

✦ ✦ ✦

An Israeli Restaurant
in New Orleans

It was a gorgeous autumn day in City Park, just down the street from my house in New Orleans. I sat on a decaying picnic table that was damp from the thick humidity and looked out over the bayou, shaded by a two-hundred-year-old live oak tree that was hung with Spanish moss. Here—away from my office at Domenica, where I'd have to listen to the ice machine drop 5-pound loads of ice every 10 minutes; away from the servers gossiping about who was dating whom; away, even,

from the kitchen—here I could think freely. I could breathe. This was the heart of Louisiana, but what I was there to think about was the food of Israel. I needed to write the menu for the Israeli restaurant I was about to open.

With little prompting, the ideas poured out of me. Falafel: of course! Hummus: there should be an entire section for that! We could top it with spicy lamb ragù and a bright dash of harissa. We could do another hummus topped with warm garbanzo beans, prepared tahini, and garlic. Kebabs: Safta's recipe. Lutenitsa, her roasted-pepper-and-eggplant spread, should be front and center on the menu, and it could be surrounded by everything else I might want to dip pita bread into. Pita: wouldn't it be great if there was a wood-burning oven in the dining room and we made it to order? And since we're here in Louisiana, maybe we should add *shrimp* to our shakshouka! Why not use the satsuma oranges, also abundant in this region, in our tabbouleh recipe? I'd written many menus in my career, but none as personal as this. I thought back to my family's roots in Bulgaria and Romania but kept on going, pondering other contributors to Israeli cooking, the foods of Morocco, Greece, Turkey, and Syria. I thought about what Arabs had been cooking on that land for over a century before Israel became a state. *That's the biggest influence on Israeli cuisine today,* I thought, and I wanted to showcase it, along with the many immigrant foods that had melded together in this place. My menu quickly took shape.

Only a couple of weeks earlier, Octavio had called and asked me to meet him in a shuttered restaurant on Magazine Street. A real-estate agent walked us through the large two-story building, with its white-painted brick walls and wooden floors, its courtyard garden. It had enough seating, potentially, for two hundred people. At first, I was taken aback. "Octavio, we'd talked about a small place in a residential neighborhood! One where only twenty people could fit in at once and order their hummus. We can't get hundreds of people to show up here every day, looking for hummus!"

The plan had evolved in my mind gradually as I realized I needed some expression for the Israeli food I was longing to cook before it overtook the menu at Domenica. I couldn't keep adding tahini to my lamb bolognese forever. But this space took my idea for a restaurant into new terrain. I loved it—it reminded me of Tel Aviv. There were small ferns growing from the cracking brick façade, but it also had a concrete bar and modern light fixtures; it mixed the old and the new. Immediately, I shifted from thinking about it as a little hummus shack, perfect for a quick snack, to imagining a full-blown Israeli restaurant.

After my day of menu writing in the park, it was time for me to build a team. Shannon White, my general manager at Domenica, was the first person I approached. A master of organization and hospitality, she'd started out as a server at Domenica and worked her way up through the ranks. "Will you help me create this restaurant?" I asked. She didn't hesitate: "What else would I do?" My next recruit was Mike Wilson, who'd just helped me open Pizza Domenica and had been curing meats and working all the stations at Domenica for years. "Would you be willing to come cook Israeli food with me?" I asked him. "Hell, yes," he said. Then there was Zach Engel, who reminded me of myself, a food nerd through and through. His dad was a rabbi in Orlando, and after he'd helped me open Domenica, he got some experience working in restaurants in Israel; he wanted nothing more than to cook Israeli food himself. I also brought in Liz Mervosh, one of the cooks at Domenica, and Peggy Keplinger and Sean Courtney, who were front-of-house managers.

We all gathered around a table and began to design the inner workings of the new restaurant. I wanted them all to be involved in the decisions, big and small; I didn't want to sit around saying yes and no to everyone. For the next few months, we tested recipes, cooking each dish together, tasting them together, deciding together what should be paired with what. "The Jerusalem mixed grill needs something bright," Liz said. That was a combination of sweetbreads, chicken livers, and chicken hearts, tossed in the spicy green chili sauce called zhoug. "How about a few rasps of orange zest?" someone else offered. Perfect. "Hey, I have a great recipe for matbucha," Zach said, referring to a stew of tomato, onion, and roasted pepper, spiced with paprika. "This *has* to go on the menu," I exclaimed as soon as I tasted it.

Even though the menu had begun from an intensely personal place for me, through this collaboration it grew into something bigger and more inclusive, the most fulfilling work I'd ever done. Instead of being the director, giving orders and delegating tasks, I was combining my energy and passion with those of the people I'd brought together. We all put some of ourselves into the restaurant, and that was transferred to other staff members. Liz, with her Polish heritage, added a pierogi recipe from her family's collection. Danny, another sous-chef, was wild about barbecue and came up with a way to make goat-shoulder pastrami. It was superb.

As we neared our opening date, though, I kept having to defend the concept for the restaurant. "Are you sure it's a good idea to open an *Israeli* restaurant in New Orleans?" people close to me were asking. "Lots of folks don't even know what Israeli food is." "Can't we call it Middle Eastern?" I had to convince them of my vision.

It was the fastest I'd ever opened a restaurant: three months from when we acquired the space to when our doors opened. We didn't overthink things; we couldn't. There wasn't enough time. It didn't really hit me what we'd accomplished until my mom flew down from Philadelphia to eat at Shaya. She tasted the lutenitsa we'd put on the menu and began to cry. "Your safta would be so proud to know that this restaurant exists," she told me. A short time later, my father came to visit, and Zach took a photo of us sitting together in Shaya's dining room and eating paprikash, a dish I was excited for him to try, because it was a homage to his Romanian and Hungarian background. Looking at that photograph, I was struck by the realization that I'd come full-circle: From my family's roots, and back again. From Israel, and back again.

Much of the first few weeks Shaya was open were surprisingly emotional for me. I'd hear people compliment the food—"This is the best pita I've ever had," or "the best hummus"—and I'd get a little wash of feeling. The restaurant reviews were overwhelmingly positive. It was about more than the praise the restaurant was receiving, though. Before dinner, I'd be telling the servers about a special and I'd get a little choked up. For the first time since I was a small boy, arriving in America from Israel, I felt I could really be myself again.

There is something so powerful about showing your true self to the world and having it be embraced, received so glowingly. It was as if, finally, the boreka-cooking demonstration I'd attempted in second grade had gone the right way. Each time I walked through the kitchen and saw peppers and eggplants roasting on the stovetops, I thought: *My safta* would *be proud.*

TABBOULEH WITH PRESERVED LEMON AND ALMONDS

his simplest of salads always surprises people at Shaya. "How can parsley salad be so complex?" they ask. The answer is twofold: preserved lemon and baharat. Taking the time to find (or make) these ingredients will pay off with flavor, although ¼ teaspoon of pumpkin-pie spice is a pretty good replica of the baharat, and freshly grated lemon zest can stand in for preserved lemon. Bear in mind, tabbouleh is a parsley salad—even the bulgur plays a supporting role—so it is only as good and fresh as the parsley you get. Find bunches with crisp, bright-green leaves at the grocery store or farmers' market.

¼ cup water
⅛ teaspoon plus 1 teaspoon Morton kosher salt, divided
2 tablespoons bulgur wheat
5 tablespoons lemon juice
1 teaspoon minced preserved lemon
½ teaspoon baharat (page 387)
¼ teaspoon ground allspice
¼ cup extra-virgin olive oil
2 quarts lightly packed fresh flat-leaf parsley leaves (from about 4 bunches)
1 cup sliced almonds, toasted
¼ red onion, finely chopped

1. Bring the water to a boil with ⅛ teaspoon salt (this won't take long, since there's so little of it). Put the bulgur in a small heatproof bowl, cover it with the boiling water, cover with plastic wrap or foil, and let it rest until all the water is absorbed, 15 minutes or so. Fluff it with a fork, and let it cool.

2. Whisk together the lemon juice, remaining 1 teaspoon salt, preserved lemon, baharat, and allspice. Stream in the olive oil while you whisk to finish the dressing.

3. Finely chop all the parsley, and toss it in a large bowl with the bulgur, almonds, and onion. Drizzle in the dressing, and mix by hand. Serve right away.

MOROCCAN CARROT SALAD

Every hummus joint in Israel has a carrot salad on the table along with other salatim (or mezze), such as baba ganoush (page 368) and labneh dip (page 38). We knew we needed a carrot dish like that at Shaya, a way to highlight the heirloom carrots of all shapes and colors that are grown throughout Louisiana's winter and spring. This salad, as effortless as the ones that inspired it, is spiked with harissa and perky with spices and fresh mint, and its flavors get even better as they sit with each other.

It's really important here to use thin, young carrots with a great snap and tons of natural sweetness; they're roasted so quickly—almost akin to searing a steak hard and fast—and won't have anything to hide behind if you use the bland supermarket carrots the size of a baseball bat. Scrawny ones, thin enough that you could use them whole without even peeling, usually have the sweetest flavor, but if yours are bigger, peel them first and cut them into smaller chunks, about 3 inches long.

- 2 pounds carrots, no tops
- 1 tablespoon plus ¼ cup extra-virgin olive oil, divided
- 1½ teaspoons Morton kosher salt, divided
- 2 tablespoons apple-cider vinegar
- 1½ tablespoons harissa (page 389)
- 1½ teaspoons sugar
- ½ teaspoon sweet paprika
- ¼ teaspoon ground caraway seeds
- ¼ teaspoon ground cumin
- Grated zest of ½ orange
- ½ yellow onion, thinly sliced
- 2 tablespoons lightly packed fresh mint leaves

1. Heat the oven to 400°F.
2. Toss the carrots with 1 tablespoon olive oil and 1 teaspoon salt, and spread them over a rimmed baking sheet. Roast for 12 to 15 minutes, until they're sweet and tender on the outside but still have that raw crunch in the center. Let cool to room temperature.
3. In a large salad bowl, combine the remaining ¼ cup olive oil with the vinegar, harissa, sugar, spices, orange zest, and remaining ½ teaspoon salt. No need to worry about emulsifying. Thinly slice the onion, toss it in the dressing, then pile in the carrots. Tear the mint leaves over the salad just before serving.

BABA GANOUSH

YIELD: ABOUT 2 CUPS

Eggplant that's been charred to the point of no return—in so many ways, that's the aroma I associate with first falling in love with food, when Safta roasted vegetables for lutenitsa (page 8) directly on the stovetop. It makes a repeat performance here, but this time, eggplant gets to be the headliner. It spends lots of time on the flames, and the only remotely challenging part of this recipe is actually having the patience to let its charring skin become white. By that point, the smokiness is imbued throughout, and its flesh has melted into something so creamy it's almost unbelievable that this was once a humble vegetable that someone grew from dirt.

2 large (1-pound) eggplants
1 large clove garlic, crushed
3 tablespoons lemon juice
3 tablespoons raw tahini
1 tablespoon ice water
¼ cup sour cream
½ teaspoon Morton kosher salt

1. Prick the eggplants all over with a fork before you roast them. To cook these on a gas stovetop, you may want to line your burners with foil if you're worried about a mess. Lay each eggplant on its side directly on the burners of a gas stovetop, and cook over a medium flame for 25 to 30 minutes, until the bottoms are haggard and blistered with bits of papery white char—just when you think they're ready to rotate, you can probably cook that side for another 5 minutes.

368 · SHAYA

2. Flip the eggplants, and cook until the other side is equally charred; rotate them slightly if you notice that any parts aren't coloring. They're ready when they're uniformly charred and you can pierce them at the neck with no resistance, 40 to 50 minutes total. The uglier they are, the more flavor there is inside. Take them off the heat, and let cool.

3. Steep the garlic in the lemon juice for at least 30 minutes, then remove and discard the garlic. Whisk the lemon juice with the tahini and ice water, and don't worry if at first it looks curdled—keep whisking and, like magic, it will become light and smooth.

4. Cut the tops off the eggplants, halve them lengthwise, and gently open them up. Scoop out the flesh, taking care not to bring along too much of the papery char, which is bitter. It's not the end of the world if you have a few stowaways— they'll just add a little extra smokiness.

5. Scoop all the creamy flesh into a fine-mesh sieve to drain away any excess liquid, then give it a few chops to make it spreadable. Fold it together with the prepared tahini mixture, sour cream, and salt, and serve at room temperature.

PROPERLY CHARRED EGGPLANT

AVOCADO TOAST WITH SMOKED WHITEFISH

YIELD: 4 TO 8 SERVINGS

Say what you want about avocado toast—I say it's a classic for a reason. It's not often you see the avocado schmeared on pumpernickel, though, and even less common to see it paired with smoked fish. To me, this is a tribute to bagels with lox and cream cheese, a treat I inhale whenever I'm back in the Northeast. I can't get enough of that collision of textures: crisp, chewy, creamy, and tender. Don't be shy with the pink peppercorns, which add a note of mild, fruity brightness to the toast, and if you can't get your hands on pumpernickel, rye or a dark, seedy wheat is a good stand-in.

Four ½-inch-thick slices pumpernickel, sliced on a bias
¼ cup extra-virgin olive oil
4 ounces smoked whitefish
1 large avocado
½ lime
2 teaspoons whole pink peppercorns
2 to 3 radishes, thinly sliced
Maldon or other flaky sea salt, to finish

1. Heat the oven to 450°F with a rack in the center. Smear 1 tablespoon olive oil over each slice of bread, and toast them on a baking sheet for 2 to 3 minutes, until they're bronze with dark, crunchy edges. Flip the bread, and toast for another 1 to 2 minutes, keeping an eye on them to make sure they don't scorch. Don't be shy of deep browning—it complements the avocado perfectly.

2. Remove the skin and any large bones from the whitefish, then use your fingers to flake the flesh off the pin bones as you would lump crabmeat; be gentle, to keep the chunks as big and intact as you can. The pin bones are tiny, so it's worth paying a little extra attention here. Set the fish aside.

3. Thinly slice the avocado, and tile the slices evenly over the bread; use the back of a fork to gently mash them, then squeeze the lime all over it. Divide the fish among the toasts.

4. Crush the peppercorns roughly between your fingers as you sprinkle them over the toasts, followed by the radishes and flaky sea salt. Slice the toasts diagonally to serve.

CHARRED CABBAGE WITH OLIVE OIL

YIELD: 4 TO 6 SERVINGS

Cabbage is an underrated ingredient, with a mellow sweetness that I'm crazy about. One day, I figured that if cauliflower could take Domenica by storm, I should be able to use the same technique to find some cabbage converts. We now serve it at Shaya paired with nutty and spicy muhammara (page 376), which melts along the leaves' blackened edges and sinks into the tender center, a winning combination of textures. Call me a purist, but, because it's cooked in such a deeply aromatic broth, I almost prefer it with nothing more than good olive oil by way of seasoning. People always say, "I had no idea cabbage could be that good," which I take as the highest praise.

1. Get a pot that's deep and not too wide, something to hold your head of cabbage as snugly as possible. Fill it with the water, ½ cup olive oil, 2 tablespoons salt, and all the other ingredients except the cabbage. Bring to a boil, then reduce the heat to medium, and simmer for 10 to 15 minutes, allowing the flavor to build.

2. Meanwhile, trim any tough outer leaves from the cabbage, and halve it lengthwise. Taste the broth—when it's been infused with the jalapeño and garlic, carefully lower the cabbage halves into the pot (a couple of large spoons can help you manipulate it if you're worried about splashing), and reduce the heat to low. Cover, and cook for 30 minutes; then give it a quick stir to rotate any parts that have not been submerged. Cover, and cook for another 30 minutes.

3. Check the cabbage; it's ready when it's easily pierced with a knife but still resists slightly. If, after an hour, it's still a bit too firm, rotate it again, cover, and continue to cook, checking every 5 to 10 minutes, until it's ready. Depending on the size of your cabbage, cooking can take up to 1½ hours—the perfect amount of time to make matbucha (recipe follows), if you plan on serving this with muhammara.

4. With a slotted spoon or a strainer (tongs will rough it up too much), move the cabbage to a rimmed baking sheet, and set it aside to cool slightly. You can strain and reserve the broth for any other use; it makes a great soup base. Meanwhile,

2	quarts water
½	cup plus 3 tablespoons extra-virgin olive oil, divided, plus more for serving
2	tablespoons plus 1 teaspoon Morton kosher salt, divided
½	cup orange juice
½	cup rice wine vinegar, preferably seasoned
2	tablespoons sugar
2	cloves garlic
1	jalapeño, seeds and pith removed, sliced
1	star anise pod
	Grated zest of 1 lemon
1	medium head green cabbage

heat the broiler with a rack in the upper-middle position of your oven.

5. Leaving the stem ends intact, cut each half of cabbage lengthwise into halves or thirds; drain away the excess liquid, and remove any leaves that are so soft they're falling off. Place each wedge on the baking sheet with the curved side down, so both flat sides are exposed, then brush or drizzle them with the last 3 tablespoons olive oil, and sprinkle the last 1 teaspoon salt all over.

6. Broil for 10 to 12 minutes, rotating the sheet halfway through, until there's plenty of charring all along the edges—this is what adds a *ton* of flavor and interest to an otherwise overlooked vegetable. Serve the cabbage warm, dressed simply with olive oil or with a big scoop of muhammara (page 376).

CHARRED CABBAGE WITH HAZELNUT AND POMEGRANATE MUHAMMARA

MATBUCHA

Think of this humble dish as a cousin to lutenitsa (page 8), with a rustic, coarse texture from tomatoes, peppers, and onions that are cooked together with generous spices until they thicken into something greater. Like lutenitsa, it requires a bit of patience, though most of the time it takes is inactive, and the complexity of flavor that builds in that long, slow cooking is well worth the wait. It can be eaten proudly with a spoon, rubbed on crostini, or spooned over your roasted fish. At Shaya, we serve it with kebabs (page 16), and it's also the base for one of my favorite Syrian condiments, muhammara (recipe follows). You can take a short cut if you like by buying pre-roasted red peppers. Spanish piquillo peppers are my favorite.

1. Set the peppers on their sides directly on a gas stovetop's burners or on a grill. Roast over a high flame until they completely blacken, with bits of papery white char; it should take 10 to 15 minutes on a stove. Flip and keep cooking for another 10 minutes or so, until they're equally charred all over, then pull them off the heat and set aside to cool.

2. When the peppers are cool enough to handle, peel away all the charred skin (it can be helpful to keep your fingers wet as you do this, but don't run the peppers directly under the tap or you'll lose some smoky flavor), then remove the stem, seeds, and any remaining white pith. Roughly chop the peppers, and set them aside.

3. Heat the canola oil in a wide, high-sided pan or Dutch oven over medium-low heat. Add the onion and garlic, and cook, stirring occasionally, until they're translucent but haven't browned too much, 5 to 6 minutes.

4. Add the salt and spices. Let them toast for a minute while you stir; once they're fragrant, add the vinegar, and cook, stirring occasionally, just until the liquid thickens up a bit in the pan.

5. Reduce the heat to low, and add the tomatoes, sugar, and reserved red peppers. Use your spoon to break the tomatoes apart roughly in the pan. Let everything simmer gently, with the heat low enough that there's barely any movement in the pan, and stir every so often to break up the vegetables as they keep softening. After 1 to 1½ hours, when the matbucha is thick and dry with super-concentrated flavors, remove it from the heat and stir in the olive oil. Cool completely before serving on its own or blending into muhammara (recipe follows).

3 red bell peppers
2 tablespoons canola oil
½ yellow onion, thinly sliced
1 clove garlic, thinly sliced
½ teaspoon Morton kosher salt
1½ teaspoons Aleppo pepper
½ teaspoon smoked paprika
½ teaspoon ground coriander seeds
¼ teaspoon ground cumin
3 tablespoons white-wine vinegar
One 15-ounce can peeled whole tomatoes
1½ teaspoons sugar
3 tablespoons extra-virgin olive oil

HAZELNUT AND POMEGRANATE
MUHAMMARA

YIELD: ABOUT 3 CUPS

I t's hard to think of a single savory dish that couldn't be improved by this muhammara, a paradoxically thick yet airy purée of caramelized tomatoes and peppers, toasty hazelnuts, and concentrated pomegranate bittersweetness.

1 recipe matbucha (preceding recipe)
1¼ cups hazelnuts, toasted
3 tablespoons Aleppo pepper
1 teaspoon pomegranate molasses
¾ cup extra-virgin olive oil

1. Combine the matbucha, hazelnuts, Aleppo pepper, and pomegranate molasses in a food processor, and run the machine until the nuts are finely chopped (you may need to pause and stir once or twice to keep everything moving).
2. With the machine still going, stream in the olive oil, and process until you have a smooth purée. You can refrigerate this for a few days, but let it come to room temperature before serving.

MALABI WITH STRAWBERRIES,
ROSE, AND PISTACHIO

YIELD: 4 SERVINGS

Y ou'll see this dessert, a kind of milk pudding, eaten from plastic cups on the streets of Israel. It's typically topped with a rose-water-infused syrup. I jumped on board with that idea but made it less sweet; strawberries puréed into the sauce give it some dimension, too. (Feel free to substitute any berries you'd like.) The milk pudding is like an ultra-light panna cotta, spiced so well that it tastes like the milk left at the bottom of your cereal bowl, in the best possible way.

1½ teaspoons unflavored gelatin powder
2 cups milk, divided
½ cup heavy cream
¼ cup plus 4 teaspoons sugar, divided
⅛ teaspoon ground cinnamon
Seeds from ½ vanilla bean pod
1⅛ teaspoons rose water, divided
8 large strawberries, hulled
4 teaspoons water
¼ cup pistachios, toasted

1. Sprinkle the gelatin in an even layer over 1 cup milk so it can hydrate.
2. Combine the remaining 1 cup milk with the cream, ¼ cup sugar, cinnamon, and vanilla in a saucepan over low heat. Whisk frequently until the mixture comes to a simmer, then pour in the milk and gelatin, whisk to combine, and cook for another 5 minutes.
3. Pour everything in the pan through a fine-mesh sieve into a heatproof bowl. Add 1 teaspoon rose water, then divide the

mixture evenly among four 6-ounce ramekins or teacups. Chill until set, at least 4 hours and ideally overnight.

4. To make the strawberry syrup: combine the strawberries, water, remaining 4 teaspoons sugar, and remaining ⅛ teaspoon rose water in a blender, and let it whir for a minute or two so that it warms up enough for the sugar to dissolve completely. Chop the pistachios well.

5. Right before serving, spoon 2 tablespoons of syrup and sprinkle 1 tablespoon of nuts over each ramekin.

HALVAH ICED LATTE

T he flavor combination of sesame and coffee was a huge breakthrough for us at Shaya. A friend of the restaurant (and the gentleman who sells us our coffee beans) brought us a gift of halvah syrup that he had whipped up on a whim. I tasted the syrup, then looked at him, and put two and two together: *Syrup. Coffee guy. Let's try that all together.* It was mind-blowing in that inaugural cappuccino and has been on the menu ever since.

A good cappuccino is only as good as its espresso and steamed milk, and it's hard for most of us to nail those components at home. This iced latte version, the cappuccino's counterpart, is more manageable, a better use of that halvah syrup. Of course, if you *really* want to get your way, do as our coffee guy did and bring some as a gift to your favorite barista.

1 tablespoon sugar
1 tablespoon baharat (page 387) or pumpkin-pie spice
1 shot espresso
1 cup milk
¼ cup halvah syrup (recipe follows)
Ice, to fill your glass

1. Combine the sugar and baharat in a small plate or bowl. Wet the rim of your glass, then dip it in the spice mixture to coat the rim.
2. Pour the espresso into the same glass, and stir in the milk and syrup. Top with ice to serve.

It's very important to use the best halvah you can find here—its rich, nutty flavor is intense, so you'll notice if it's not great. Go to a Middle Eastern grocery store, talk to the store owner, and ask them for their favorite brand. Keep this on hand for easy lattes (preceding recipe), mix it into a bourbon milk punch or eggnog, or give it as a gift.

1 cup water
½ pound halvah
¼ cup sugar

1. Bring the water to a boil, then remove from the heat and let cool for a minute or two.
2. Add the halvah and sugar to a blender, and pour the hot water over it. Blend until very smooth. Transfer to a lidded jar or bottle, and store in the fridge for up to 1 month.

MOROCCAN MINT TEA

T he ritual of sweetened mint tea is such a beautiful and thoughtful note on which to end a meal, and you'll see it all over Israel, and beyond that, into the Middle East. The smell alone is intoxicating—piles of fresh mint layered with fresh lemon and sugar. The French press is the perfect way to capture it all without overinfusing. If you have a ton of fresh mint, pile it into each glass—the more, the better, and it makes a really impressive presentation.

1 quart water
¼ cup sugar
3 tablespoons loose gunpowder green tea
2 tablespoons lemon juice
4 to 5 fresh mint leaves, plus more for serving
2-inch strip of lemon peel, yellow part only

1. Bring the water to a boil, and dissolve the sugar in it.
2. Add the tea and lemon juice to a French press, then pour the sweetened hot water over it. Cover and steep for 4 minutes.
3. Press down the French press's plunger before topping it off with the mint leaves and lemon peel. Serve immediately, with more fresh mint floated in each glass.

VI

ESSENTIALS

BAHARAT

Baharat" simply means "spice" in Arabic. Think of it almost like a fancy pumpkin-pie spice—it has the same warmth, dimension, and soulful richness—though that would imply it has boundaries, limited to desserts or to the autumn, whereas really it's got a home in everything from tabbouleh to halvah lattes. Use a good grinder—something that can work through the papery skins on the cardamom, which I keep intentionally, because they balance the otherwise domineering cardamom scent. If your spice grinder isn't up to the challenge, use only the seeds from twelve pods.

6 heaping tablespoons whole allspice berries
1 teaspoon whole black peppercorns
¼ teaspoon whole cumin seeds
48 cardamom pods
28 whole cloves
2 small dried rosebuds
2 tablespoons ground cinnamon
2 teaspoons Aleppo pepper
1½ teaspoons finely grated nutmeg

Grind the whole spices and rosebuds together (in batches, if need be) until they're a powder. Stir to combine with the cinnamon, Aleppo pepper, and nutmeg. Stored in an airtight container, this will keep for 1 month at room temperature or for 6 months in the freezer.

DUQQA

Use any spices and any nuts you'd like; if you pound them together, you can technically call them "duqqa," which translates in Arabic to "to pound." That's exactly what happens with all the ingredients. The very slow frying of the garlic and shallot makes for something special—it mellows and enhances their sweetness, crisping them up with zero bitterness—so do be patient. Put it anywhere you want a burst of flavor and great crunch. Save the oil you cook the shallots and garlic in; it's lovely drizzled on salads or anything else you like.

1 head garlic
1 large shallot
¾ cup extra-virgin olive oil
1 cup raw pistachios
2 tablespoons whole coriander seeds
2 tablespoons black sesame seeds
2 tablespoons white sesame seeds, toasted
1½ tablespoons whole pink peppercorns
1 tablespoon Maldon or other flaky sea salt
2 teaspoons ground sumac
2 teaspoons Aleppo pepper

1. Heat the oven to 325°F. Leaving the cloves intact, peel the garlic, trim the ends of each clove, and slice them as thinly and evenly as you can. Trim both ends of the shallot, halve it lengthwise, and thinly slice it, too. Place both in a cold pan with the olive oil, and set it over low heat until they're a deep, even golden, 30 to 40 minutes; stir occasionally, to make sure the heat circulates evenly. This is how they build flavor without any bitterness, so don't try to speed it up with a higher flame.

2. Roast the pistachios on a rimmed baking sheet while the garlic and shallots cook. Remove them from the oven when they're fragrant, after 7 minutes or so.

3. Line a plate with paper towels. Strain the garlic and shallots over a clean bowl, and spread them on the plate in an even layer to drain. Wipe out the pan, and fill it with the oil from the bowl along with the coriander seeds, black sesame seeds, and white sesame seeds. Toast, still over low heat, until they're crunchy and aromatic, another 8 minutes or so. Drain on the same plate as the shallots and garlic.

4. Add the shallots, garlic, and seeds to a large ziplock bag with the nuts, pink peppercorns, salt, sumac, and Aleppo pepper. Pound the mixture with a rolling pin or mallet, just until everything is roughly crushed. (If you prefer a more homogeneous texture, chop the nuts by hand before you add them to the bag.)

HARISSA

Harissa is a thick, tangy, deep-red chili paste, a familiar condiment across North Africa that came to Israel via the Tunisians, Libyans, Algerians, and Moroccans. You can buy harissa at the store, and if there's a brand that you already know you like, feel free to use it. Making it yourself, though, gives you the chance to use the best spices and peppers.

At Shaya, we stir in some of the olive oil by hand so that it doesn't perfectly emulsify. That gives you versatility: you can use the whole sauce, or skim off some of the hot oil from the top. If you can't find guajillo peppers, use four additional ancho peppers.

Water, for the peppers
15 dried árbol chili peppers
2 dried guajillo chili peppers
1 dried ancho chili pepper
1 tablespoon whole cumin seeds
1½ teaspoons whole coriander seeds
2 large cloves garlic, crushed
2 tablespoons lemon juice
1 tablespoon white-wine vinegar
1 teaspoon Morton kosher salt
1½ teaspoons smoked paprika
1 tablespoon tomato paste
¾ cup olive oil, divided

1. Fill a small saucepan with water, and bring it to a boil. Add all the dried peppers, and remove from the heat. Cover, and steep for at least 1 hour, or until the water has completely cooled.

2. Strain the peppers and, with a paring knife, trim away the stems and split them lengthwise. Scrape away their seeds

(recipe continues)

and any of the stringy pith inside; wearing latex gloves will keep your fingertips from burning. Be sure to get rid of all the seeds and pith, or else the harissa will be crazy spicy. Add to the bowl of a food processor, and set aside.

3. Toast the cumin and coriander in a small skillet over low heat, stirring occasionally, for about 3 minutes, until you start to smell them. Crush them with a mortar and pestle, or in a ziplock bag with a meat mallet, to release all their aromas.

4. Add the garlic, lemon juice, vinegar, salt, paprika, and tomato paste to the peppers in the food processor, and combine. Once everything is blitzed together, stream in ½ cup olive oil.

5. Scrape the sauce into a container, and stir in the remaining ¼ cup olive oil by hand. This last addition lingers on the surface and absorbs all the flavors around it. Harissa keeps for months in the fridge, and once you start using it, you'll find it has a home on just about everything. With its smoky heat, it's one of the best "hot sauces" around.

HAWAIJ

Sometimes called "soup spice," this hits all the same notes: it's savory, hearty, warm, just bright enough to keep you coming back for more. As with baharat, it's important to start with whole spices to achieve the most balanced flavor.

Grind the cumin, black pepper, cardamom, and cloves (in batches if need be), and then combine them with the turmeric and Persian lime. Stored in an airtight container, this will keep for 1 month at room temperature or for 6 months in the freezer.

2½ tablespoons whole cumin seeds
2 teaspoons whole black peppercorns
24 whole cardamom pods
14 whole cloves
¼ cup ground turmeric
2 teaspoons grated Persian lime

HERB SALT

I t feels like money in the bank when you've got this in your freezer. It's a great way to put stray herbs to use—adapt the quantities of each to whatever's available in your fridge or garden—and you can use it to deliver fresh herb flavor to everything from salad and roasted vegetables to chicken, duck, pork, or fish.

½ cup Morton kosher salt
1 cup lightly packed fresh parsley leaves
¼ cup lightly packed fresh thyme leaves
¼ cup lightly packed fresh rosemary leaves
¼ cup lightly packed fresh sage leaves

Run everything in a food processor until it's all finely and evenly chopped. To keep the salt bright green, with that same fresh, lively flavor, store it in a ziplock bag in the freezer; it will last for months.

With its earthy sesame depth, brightened up by lemon and garlic, this is like an Israeli version of mayonnaise (not to be confused with tahini mayo, page 395) or good butter. It adds a mild yet savory dimension anywhere you put it. When we hit a creative roadblock while developing a new menu item at Shaya, we often daydream about drizzling it with prepared tahini. It's a natural fit with classic hummus (page 114).

¼ cup lemon juice
2 cloves garlic, crushed
1½ cups raw tahini
1 teaspoon Morton kosher salt
1¼ cups ice water, plus more as needed

1. Combine the lemon juice and garlic in a nonreactive bowl; set it aside for 30 minutes to steep.
2. Meanwhile, whip the tahini with a stand mixer or an electric mixer on high speed for about 10 minutes, until it's glossy and light, like cake batter. It's nearly impossible to overwhip it, so feel free to spend a little time here.
3. Strain the lemon juice. Decrease the mixer's speed to medium, and add the juice and salt; the tahini will seize up at first, but don't freak out! Keep whipping it at medium speed and it will be incorporated.
4. When the tahini has a uniformly tacky, almost fudgy consistency, add the ice water, about ¼ cup at a time, and increase the speed to high. At first, the sauce may seize up again and look almost curdled, but keep adding the ice water, whipping well after each addition. It will smooth itself out and should look like a thick mousse. Every tahini is different; if, after you've added all the water, it's still too thick, keep adding water by the tablespoon until it lightens up.
5. Prepared tahini will stay good for about 2 days in the fridge. If you're making it in advance, let it warm up just slightly on the counter, and whip in 1 to 2 tablespoons ice water to restore some of its lightness.

PRESERVED LEMON VINAIGRETTE

O f all salad dressings, this one could be my staple. Preserved lemon gives funk, brightness, and salty depth all at once; it's surprisingly versatile, and its brash flavors mellow out when you combine it with others. (Make sure you get rid of the seeds; then you can chop up the whole fruit.) It's gotten pretty common in supermarkets, but if you can't find it, and don't have time to make it, you can substitute the grated zest of 1 lemon.

⅓ cup white-wine vinegar
¼ cup lemon juice
1½ tablespoons minced preserved lemon
4 teaspoons za'atar
½ teaspoon Morton kosher salt
½ cup extra-virgin olive oil

Stir together the vinegar, lemon juice, preserved lemon, za'atar, and salt. Stream in the olive oil, and whisk it to incorporate.

ROSE TAHINI

I love the pairing of rose and tahini. There's a beauty to the floral and nutty notes coming together, and the sauce really shows this off, complemented by the bright yet warm spices. Spoon it over pancakes, French toast, ice cream, or yogurt and granola. If you can't find dried Persian lime, an equal amount of freshly grated lime zest works nearly as well.

6 dried rosebuds (about 1 heaping tablespoon)
6 whole allspice berries
3 whole cardamom pods
1 teaspoon whole pink peppercorns
1 teaspoon whole coriander seeds
¼ teaspoon grated Persian lime
⅛ teaspoon whole caraway seeds
1 cup water
¾ cup sugar
½ teaspoon Morton kosher salt
½ teaspoon rose water
¾ cup raw tahini

1. Combine the rosebuds, allspice, cardamom, pink peppercorns, coriander, lime, and caraway seeds; lightly crush them all together with a mortar and pestle, or in a ziplock bag with a meat mallet, to release all the scents.
2. In a small saucepan, combine the spices with the water, sugar, salt, and rose water over high heat. Bring to a boil, then cook over high heat for another 2 minutes, until it thickens just slightly. Remove from the heat and cool completely before straining.
3. Whisk the strained syrup with the tahini until it's smooth. Use right away, or store in the refrigerator for up to 1 week.

SCHMALTZ AND GRIBENES

In some international markets, you can buy chicken skins on their own; if you've got a good butcher, you may be able to ask him to set some aside for you. But even if you can't, it's worth buying whole chickens—you'll need two chickens' worth, and you can use the remaining chickens for tahini chicken salad (page 354)—because this is such an extra-special treat.

For minimal hands-on work, this recipe gives you two distinct and equally awesome products: schmaltz, a rich fat that's ideal for cornbread (page 243), kale jambalaya (page 222), and roasted potatoes (page 34), and gribenes, like cracklings crossed with potato chips. I love to crumble them over a salad or scrambled eggs or use them to scoop up charoset (page 353).

Skins and fat from 2 whole chickens (about 1 pound total; see procedure)
1 teaspoon Morton kosher salt

1. Heat the oven to 350°F, and line a large rimmed baking sheet with parchment paper.
2. If you're cutting the skin directly from the chickens, use your knife to make shallow incisions and, keeping the blade nearly flush with the chicken's body, cut through all the connective tissues to loosen the skin without cutting into the meat. Work your way around the chicken to remove all the skin piece by piece, and set it aside. Trim away any visible white fat on the outside of the chicken, and save that, too.
3. Lay the chicken skins flat on a cutting board, and thoroughly pat them dry, then cut them into 1-to-2-inch pieces. (They're slippery, so kitchen shears can make an easier job of this, or you can lay them flat and freeze them until they've solidified a bit before cutting.) Spread them and the reserved fat on the baking sheet, and sprinkle with the salt. Bake for about 1 hour, until the skins are very crisp and evenly golden.
4. Line a plate with paper towels. With a slotted spatula or spoon, move the skins to the plate to drain until they've completely cooled. They're your gribenes.
5. When the baking sheet is cool enough to handle, carefully pour the rendered fat into a clean jar for safekeeping. That's your schmaltz.

TAHINI MAYO

Tahini and mayo make a lot of sense together, even more so when you combine them with your favorite sandwich or good raw spring vegetables. Best-quality olive oil will add a lot of peppery flavor.

2 egg yolks
¼ cup raw tahini
3 tablespoons lemon juice
1 tablespoon water
1 teaspoon Morton kosher salt
½ cup extra-virgin olive oil

1. Combine the egg yolks, tahini, lemon juice, water, and salt—preferably in a food processor, otherwise with a good whisk.

2. Slowly drizzle in the olive oil with the processor still going—or while you whisk vigorously—and continue to blend until the mixture is extremely thick and velvety. Be thorough in this step: a tight emulsion is the difference between having all those flavors hit you in equal measure or having them fall flat. Once the mayonnaise is nice and smooth, you can use it right away or refrigerate it for a couple of days.

ZHOUG

Zhoug is a Yemenite green chili sauce; it's like pesto, Middle Eastern style. I put it on *everything*. It's got a great thrum of heat behind its bright-green freshness. The cloves are key; they set off the flavors. You can use only one or two serrano chili peppers if you want a milder version.

2 heaping cups lightly packed fresh cilantro leaves
1 cup lightly packed fresh parsley leaves
3 serrano chili peppers, halved, seeds and pith removed
1 clove garlic
Grated zest of ½ orange
1 teaspoon Morton kosher salt
½ teaspoon ground cumin
¼ teaspoon ground cloves
¼ teaspoon ground cardamom pods
¼ teaspoon sugar
⅓ cup distilled white vinegar
2 tablespoons extra-virgin olive oil
Water, as needed

Make sure the herbs are thoroughly patted dry if you've just washed them. Combine them in a food processor with the rest of the dry ingredients, the vinegar, and the olive oil. Blitz until saucy. If it's not quite coming together, add 1 tablespoon water at a time.

ACKNOWLEDGMENTS

First and foremost, I want to acknowledge Tina Antolini. When I began working on this book, I questioned how the stories and recipes would flow seamlessly in a way that would feel natural and make people hungry as they read. I didn't want the recipes to overpower the history behind them. Tina Antolini, who I knew from her work as the producer of the podcast *Gravy,* is a master of creating that seamless connection. I showed her some of the stories I wrote, and she urged me to go read one of her favorite cookbooks, *Home Cooking* by Laurie Colwin. She said my writing reminded her of the narrative form that Laurie became known for. I read it and felt a sense of clarity on how to move forward with the book. Little did I know I'd be working with Vicky Wilson, who told me when I first sat down in her office that the only cookbook she had ever published was *Home Cooking* by Laurie Colwin. It was moments of fate, like this, that made working on this book with Tina such a joy. Tina has a way about her, the way she approaches conversations, the way she remembers details I never see, that got me to the heart of my story.

Thank you to . . .

My beautiful wife, Emily, for being by my side, for teaching me what love is, and for your sense of style in all that you do. You have brought me to a place that I never could have dreamed of getting to on my own. You have always believed in my dreams and have allowed me to chase them even when they took me far away from you. None of this journey would be worth it if I wasn't happy. With you and our doggies, Henry and Ceci, I am happiest.

My Saba and Safta, for teaching me the lessons that I live by today.

My father, Alex, for walking down the long hard road so that I could fly.

My sister, Anit, for never doubting my future and for understanding me like no one else could.

My aunt Debbie, my uncle Ivan, and my cousins Tali, Ariel, and Gideon, for being rays of sunshine throughout my childhood and for gifting me with so many beautiful memories.

Rémy Robert, for being so damn meticulous, passionate, and hardworking in helping to create and test every single recipe in this book. We cooked and ate our hearts out and every second of it was a pleasure.

Vicky Wilson, for allowing me to fulfill my vision, while never letting me fall. Your wisdom and guidance have taught me that looking into my own heart for inspiration is worth doing.

Shannon White, you have been the keystone to all the success our teams have had. We all depended on you to help us climb the mountains of the restaurant business, and you never let us down. None of what we've accomplished as a team would have been possible without you.

Zach Engel: you inspire me every day to be better at what I do. You are one of the most talented, intelligent, and genuine people I know. I couldn't imagine cooking Israeli food without you.

Meredith Dunbar: you've helped keep our lives organized and our minds clear to be creative, take risks, and follow our passions without interruption. You are the architect, the cheerleader, and the sounding board for so many of the great things we do as a team. We'd be lost without you.

The entire team at Knopf, for all of your expertise in creating such a beautiful cookbook.

Stephen Jeffcoat, Sean Courtney, Morgan Angell, and Michael Wilson, for being true leaders and friends to everyone we work with. You challenge me to do better every day. No words can communicate my gratitude to all of you.

Gia Vecchio, for being Shaya's biggest fan, and paving the road that allows us to reach for the stars.

Rush Jagoe, for taking the most beautiful photographs and for making it look so easy. You have incredible vision, and are creating something timeless with your art.

Frances Rodriguez, for bringing my most cherished memories back to life with your gorgeous illustrations.

Donna Barnett, for taking my hand and showing me what I had to offer the world.

The people who opened doors for me to walk through; chefs, friends, and bosses through the years who took a chance on me: Seth Schram, Alan Nesonsohn, Michael Zitin, Derek Davis, Watch Chumphol, the late William Chumphol, Kenney Bayless, Jeff Michoud, Marc Vetri, Keven Lee and the entire Lee family, David and Bonnie Brody, Alan and Diane Franco, and so many more.

David Vigliano, for your mentorship, friendship, and believing that my life story was worthy of a book.

The entire Ostuw, Davis, and Taylor families for letting me test out my new recipes on you during family gatherings. All of your support for Emily and me means so much.

My Italian mentors, Edgarda Meldi, Enzo Desantis, Alex and Massimo Dassena: you along with your families took me into your homes and taught me lessons of life and food I will never forget. You entrusted your most sacred dishes to a stranger, when you didn't have to. I learned from you that tradition and culture make food taste best.

Ai miei mentori italiani Edgarda Meldi, Enzo Desantis, Alex e Massimo Dassena. Tu insieme alle tue famiglie mi ha portato nelle tue case e mi ha insegnato lezioni di vita e cibo che non dimenticherò mai. Hai fiducia nei posti più sacri con uno sconosciuto quando non dovevi. Ho imparato da voi che la tradizione e la cultura rendono il cibo migliore.

This book wouldn't exist without the teams at Shaya, Domenica, and Pizza Domenica. I owe all the servers, stewards, cooks, food runners, bartenders, bussers, managers, and hostesses so much gratitude. I count on all of you every day to meet our goals, but you have exceeded my wildest dreams. You have shown me how to take pride in my work in ways no one else could have ever done. I vow to help all of you achieve your goals the way you have facilitated mine.

To the community of friends that Emily and I gathered around us: so many of you helped to test recipes, listened to my ideas (even when they were bad), and supported us with your love through the years. Having you in our lives makes them worth living.

To the city of New Orleans and the state of Louisiana, for taking me in as one of your own. I now say "y'all" with the best of them. You've provided me a community to love and support.

To all of the guests who have dined with us at the restaurants, past, present, and future. You have given us a platform to serve you. We don't take that for granted and we never will.

RECIPES BY CATEGORY

SALADS

VEGETABLE DISHES

INDEX

Page references in *italics* refer to illustrations.

A NOTE ON THE TYPE

This book was set in Adobe Garamond. Designed for the Adobe Corporation by Robert Slimbach, the fonts are based on types first cut by Claude Garamond (c. 1480–1561). Garamond was a pupil of Geoffroy Tory and is believed to have followed the Venetian models, although he introduced a number of important differences, and it is to him that we owe the letter we now know as "old style." He gave to his letters a certain elegance and feeling of movement that won their creator an immediate reputation and the patronage of Francis I of France.

Composed by North Market Street Graphics, Lancaster, Pennsylvania
Printed and bound by C & C Offset Printing Co., Ltd., China
Designed by Iris Weinstein